c|net Do-It-Yourself Digital Home Office PROJECTS

24 cool things you didn't know you could do!

About the Author

S. E. Slack is a lifestyle and technology writer and author with more than 17 years of experience in business and technical writing. She specializes in simplifying complex topics. Slack has written seven books and numerous articles that have appeared internationally in business magazines and online business sites.

Working from her home office, Slack has also been an executive and business transformation communications consultant to IBM, Lenovo International, and State Farm Insurance. In addition, she writes for Microsoft, IBM, CDW, Sony, and other companies. As a corporate consultant, she has written general, strategic, marketing, and technical internal communications and education.

Slack is married and has a toddler at home, who routinely helps mommy learn new and more inventive ways to keep the home office humming.

c|net Do-It-Yourself Digital Home Office PROJECTS

24 cool things you didn't know you could do!

S. E. Slack

Mc Graw Hill

New York   Chicago   San Francisco
Lisbon   London   Madrid   Mexico City
Milan   New Delhi   San Juan
Seoul   Singapore   Sydney   Toronto

The **McGraw·Hill** Companies

Cataloging-in-Publication Data is on file with the Library of Congress

McGraw-Hill books are available at special quantity discounts to use as premiums and sales promotions, or for use in corporate training programs. For more information, please write to the Director of Special Sales, Professional Publishing, McGraw-Hill, Two Penn Plaza, New York, NY 10121-2298. Or contact your local bookstore.

CNET Do-It-Yourself Digital Home Office Projects:
24 Cool Things You Didn't Know You Could Do!

1234567890 QPD QPD 01987

ISBN-13: 978-0-07-148983-6
ISBN-10:   0-07-148983-5

Sponsoring Editor Roger Stewart	**Proofreader** Megha Ghai	**Illustration** International Typesetting and Composition
Editorial Supervisor Janet Walden	**Indexer** Broccoli Information Management	**Art Director, Cover** Jeff Weeks
Project Manager Vasundhara Sawhney, International Typesetting and Composition	**Production Supervisor** Jean Bodeaux	**Cover Designer** Jeff Weeks
Acquisitions Coordinator Carly Stapleton	**Composition** International Typesetting and Composition	**Cover Illustration** Sarah Howell
Copy Editor Bill McManus		

For Greg and Alia, who keep me in smiles when the days get long and the deadlines are tight.

Contents

Part I   Organize Your Workspace

Part II   Take It on the Road

Part III   Communicate with Clients and Employers

Foreword

The home office combines industriousness and organization with our personal style. It's not a new idea, but it has taken a quantum leap forward in this age of digital, Internet-connected everything.

For some, a home office is an alternate company office, allowing us to multitask family responsibilities while getting our work done—in our pajamas! Telecommuting's stigma as a goof-off is fading fast as companies and employees realize a lot more gets done when commute time and in-office interruptions are taken out of the equation. And working at home no longer means being less present: digital phone technology, web conferencing, e-mail, VPN, and instant messaging are the tools that make the at-home employee almost as present as if they were sitting in a cube.

For others, a home office means a place to run a home-based business, whether it's an eBay storefront or a consulting service. Thanks to the Web, a home-based sole proprietorship may, to the customer, look indistinguishable from a brick & mortar company with many employees.

But for most of us, a home office is where we take care of the business of life. Managing finances, writing and e-mailing, doing our taxes, editing a home movie, or printing party invitations; the home office is where life gets organized, creating more time to enjoy it.

These and many other scenarios are what we teach you in this book. Some projects enable your gear, like setting up a webcam or a second monitor on your PC. Others save you money, like using VoIP for calling and conferencing. And still other projects extend the home office to wherever you want to be, through mobile and wireless technologies.

Whatever "home office" means to you, we're about to show you how to make it amazing with the clear, concise projects in the pages to follow. Enjoy wearing your pajamas!

Brian Cooley
CNET Editor-at-Large

Acknowledgments

There are many people behind the scenes who bring a book from concept to the bookshelf. First and foremost, I'd like to thank Roger Stewart at McGraw-Hill for giving me the opportunity to share my experiences with other home office workers through this book. Without his vision and guidance, this book would never have been written. Thanks, Obi-wan! I'd also like to thank the editors at CNET for working with McGraw-Hill to provide a terrific series of informative books for consumers.

Carly Stapleton at McGraw-Hill was immensely helpful and invaluable as I was writing this book. Carly, you are a joy to work with! From a production standpoint, kudos go to Vasundhara Sawhney and Bill McManus for all the work they did to make me look and sound good in print. And a big thank you to everyone behind the scenes who helped with graphics and overall editing. Your expertise is greatly appreciated.

I cannot write these acknowledgments without mentioning Neil Salkind and Studio B. Neil, you are a continued inspiration to me and I thank you from the bottom of my heart for all you do for me. You are head and shoulders above all other agents; you have my undying trust and loyalty. Studio B, too, is forever in my heart. From Linda and Jamie, to Renee, Julie, and Lisa; it's a pleasure working with an agency that understands writers and works so hard to keep me happy. I couldn't do what I do without each and every one of you.

Finally, I must thank Greg and Alia. The two of you keep me sane, and remind me that every moment of life should be savored.

Introduction

This book is designed to help you create a tech-savvy home office environment so you can do what you do best: your work. Each of the 24 projects in this book was carefully planned to meet your needs as a home office worker.

The book is organized into parts, with projects in each section ranging in difficulty from easy to advanced. Every project is designed as a stand-alone project; you don't need to complete a particular project before you can begin the next. As you consider a project, don't be afraid to try it even if it is challenging or advanced. You just might be surprised at how quickly you can complete a project, regardless of your technology skill level.

Part I, "Organize Your Workspace," offers projects that can help you organize your office. Whether you have a simple desk to work from or an elaborate office space, each project brings unique organizational aspects to any home office.

In Part II, "Take It on the Road," you'll discover how to use the Internet and other technologies to your advantage. Each project was developed after careful research into the mobile reality of today's home office environment. Just because you work from home doesn't mean you have to be stuck there!

Part III of the book, "Communicate with Clients and Employers," addresses projects that can help you stay in touch with others outside your home office. You can stay visible and accessible, no matter what your home office environment.

Part IV, "Enhance Your Sales and Marketing," shows you a variety of ways you can generate additional income and take advantage of the latest technologies to locate customers and clients. Regardless of your occupation, these projects will spark ideas for you.

Finally, in Part V "Work Securely from Home," you'll discover different methods to make your computer work with you instead of against you.

As you work through the projects in this book, you'll notice that the beginning of each project offers information about what you'll need for the project and the difficulty level involved. Each project is divided into manageable steps with helpful hints and tips to guide you along the way.

Don't be shy! Jump right into any project in the book—you can start wherever you like. As you complete each one, give yourself a pat on the back and then jump into another project. You'll be your own IT department before you know it!

Part I

Organize Your Workspace

Project 1

Set Up a PC Messaging Center

What You'll Need:

- **Operating system: Windows 98, 2000, ME, XP, or Vista**
- **Software: Message center software**
- **Hardware: Voice-enabled analog modem, sound card, microphone, speakers, phone line**
- **Cost: $30–$199**
- **Difficulty: Easy**

Few people who work from home have the luxury of a large office space, let alone the desk space to hold a computer, telephone, answering machine, and fax machine. Yet all of those things are required in today's 24/7 world, especially for home office users who travel and must check in often for voicemail and fax messages. The solution is to turn your PC into a message center: one that can let you read, listen to, and manage daily information.

There is software on the market that lets you do exactly that. To get your PC to work smarter for you and become a virtual assistant, you need to choose a message center software program, get it installed, and start using it. Once you do, you'll discover what others have learned: your computer can do more for you than just house documents. It can keep you organized, in touch with others, and one step ahead of the constantly moving world around you.

These programs are great because they turn your computer system into a true office assistant. As long as you have Internet access, you can take the assistant with you wherever you may go.

Step 1: Install the Hardware

To complete this project, you need a voice-enabled data/fax modem, a sound card, a microphone, speakers, and a phone line that can connect to your modem. The modem receives and sends phone calls through your computer, the sound card transfers sound to your computer, and the microphone and speakers allow you to leave and receive voice messages.

Newer computers typically have these items built-in, but if you have an older system, you need to determine whether or not your computer needs one or all of them. Instructions for determining whether you have a sound card or a modem on a Windows XP or Vista system are listed here. Older systems will follow similar steps; check Microsoft.com for specific instructions for an older operating system.

To get on the Internet, you are probably using a DSL or cable modem. Both are great modems, but they don't connect to a phone line in the way an analog modem does. In fact, with cable modems, the entire concept is to use cable lines to receive and send signals—not phone lines. DSL modems use phone lines as a transport medium only; they don't dial out or accept phone calls. Faxing and, of course, answering phone calls require an analog modem and a telephone line along with the ability to dial a telephone number.

To use messaging center software, your modem must be a data/fax modem that connects to a standard, analog phone line. The phone line plugs directly into the modem through a phone plug in the back of your computer if your modem is internal; otherwise it just plugs into an external modem sitting on your desk. Using an analog modem should not disrupt the use of other modems on your system.

tip *The phone line connected to your computer should be one that you use for business—you don't need a new phone number. You can bypass the modem by picking up the telephone handset on your desk before the modem answers.*

note *When the modem is in use, other calls are blocked. If you typically make and receive a lot of phone calls, you might want to invest in a second phone line so that calls and faxes can be received on the modem while you're on the telephone.*

As for headphones, microphones, and speakers, well, you probably already know if you have those. The headphones are external and plug into the front or back of your computer. Some headphones include a microphone although you can purchase one separately too.

tip *Microphones may also be included in a webcam, but your sound quality might not be as high as when using a microphone with a headset.*

How do you know if you have speakers? Simple—if you hear more than a "beep" on your computer, you have speakers. If you don't, you need to purchase some external speakers from your local computer store. You plug them into the back of your computer and place them on your desk wherever you want.

Windows XP

To check for hardware and sound on a Windows XP system:

1. Right-click My Computer.

2. Click Properties.

3. In the System Properties dialog box, click the Hardware tab.

4. In the Device Manager section, click Device Manager.

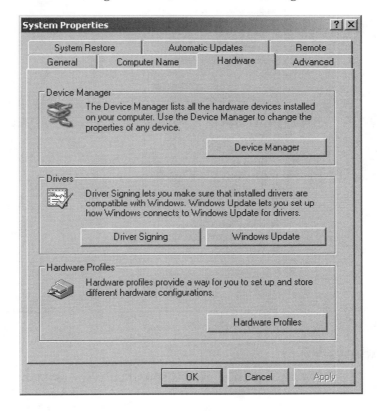

When the Device Manager window opens, you will see a list of all the hardware installed on your computer.

5. Click the plus sign next to Modems to expand the information about modems. If you do not see "Modem" or any items listed under Modems, you do not have a modem installed.

6. Click the plus sign next to Sound, Video And Game Controllers to see information about sound cards. If you do not see any sound cards listed, you do not have one installed.

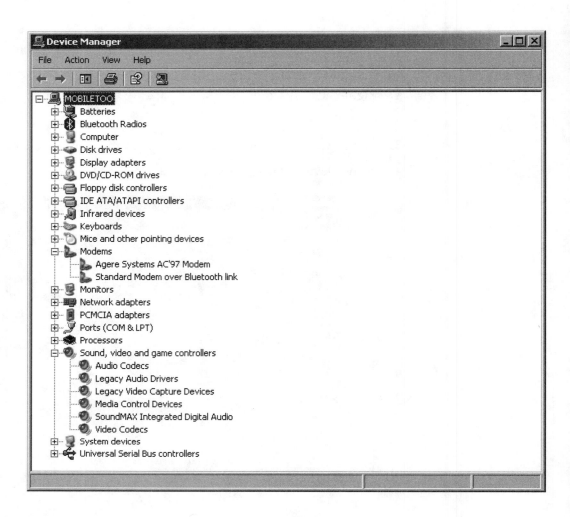

Windows Vista

To check for hardware and sound on a Vista system:

1. Click the Start button and type Device Manager in the Instant Search box.

2. Click Device Manager when it appears under Programs. When the Device Manager window opens, you will see a list of all the hardware installed on your computer.

3. Click the plus sign next to Modems to expand the information about modems. If you do not see "Modem" or any items listed under Modems, you do not have a modem installed.

4. Click the plus sign next to Sound, Video And Game Controllers to see information about sound cards. If you do not see any sound cards listed, you do not have one installed.

Step 2: Choose Your Software

Message center software can receive and send faxes, answer the phone for you and take voicemail messages, and reassign e-mails to voicemail. Beyond the hardware mentioned here, you do not need to set up any additional equipment. The software translates all the incoming information to your computer for you.

tip   *Many messaging software programs will answer fax calls but not voice calls if your telephone service offers distinctive ring services. Otherwise, your computer will answer all calls.*

There are several programs on the market that work well with most Windows operating systems; some have simple approaches to handling faxes and voicemail, while others have more comprehensive messaging center approaches. A few offer services to manage the system for you on a subscription basis, while others allow you to download a program once and manage your own system. If you don't want to deal with installing regular updates, a subscription service is a good choice. On the other hand, you're paying for that convenience every month—and some of these programs can be downloaded free if you're willing to take on some of the long-term upkeep.

A few fax modems supply message center software along with the modem. There are literally dozens of programs to choose from; some are shareware, others are proprietary. Home versions of this type of software are typically the least expensive, but also do not have all the capabilities business versions have. However, check out the home versions anyway—if you don't send or receive faxed documents and don't need an answering service often, the home version might be perfect for you.

No matter which program you choose, it must have at least these three items in order to make it a true message center:

- Ability to compose, edit, send, and receive faxes
- Voicemail system that can handle an unlimited number of messages (depending on the size of your hard drive, of course)
- Compatibility with your voice-enabled modem and your e-mail program

A fourth item is becoming available on a limited basis: the ability to retrieve e-mail messages by phone, either the entire message or notification of new messages. It's not standard in most of these programs yet, but if you find one with this option that suits your budget and needs, it's worth taking a good look at. This feature means you don't need to drag a laptop with you or find an Internet connection; you can simply use any telephone to dial in for your messages.

tip   *If you're using Windows Vista, check carefully to be certain the software you choose will work with Vista. Sometimes the software will partially work—you might be able to use the program for messaging purposes but Help files created in earlier versions of Windows by the software provider might not work in Vista.*

It does take some time, by the way, to get used to working with this kind of software. That's because it takes traditional office concepts and takes them to a different level—you're used to checking a phone for voicemail messages, for example, or grabbing a piece of paper from a fax machine. Moving to an electronic messaging system means your computer becomes your source of information—you need to build in some time in your learning curve to get used to doing all these types of things on your computer.

note *Many message center software programs offer trial versions. Take advantage of this—you sometimes can test the software for up to 30 days to determine how well it will work for you. If you don't like it, try another program until you find what you like.*

Step 3: Install Your Software

Once you choose the message center software that meets your needs, you need to install it on your computer. If you purchased it in a store, use the installation CD provided. If you downloaded it online, like the example in Figure 1-1, follow the prompts provided by the software. Before you install it, be sure your modem and sound card have been installed and are working.

Figure 1-1

Venta Fax and Voice 5.71 downloading off the Web.

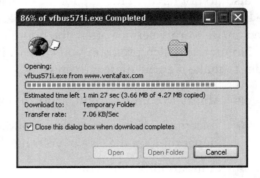

As you step through the installation prompts, keep these things in mind:

● If you will use the program often, accept prompts that ask whether you want the program icon placed on your Start menu or toolbar.

● Carefully note the installation folder destination for your software. Some programs do not automatically install to the Program Files folder, and if you need to uninstall and reinstall it later for some reason, you'll save yourself some time!

Your software should have a Program Settings or Properties area where you can view pretty much everything involved with your program, such as Modem, Fax, Voice, Transmission, and Print settings. When the installation is complete, if you experience trouble with any of these during testing, you should check this area first to determine the current settings. In the example shown in Figure 1-2, the Caller ID program setting clearly indicates that the modem being used does not support Caller ID settings. Most programs have similar easily identifiable information. You may find a new modem is required rather than a reinstallation of your software.

Figure 1-2

In this Program Settings dialog box, the right pane states in red that this feature is not supported by the currently installed modem.

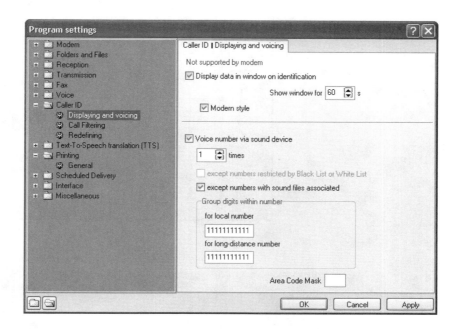

> **note** If you have a voice modem but your message center software doesn't seem to recognize it as a voice modem, it could be that your modem is what's sometimes referred to as a "soft modem"—a modem with capabilities defined by the driver rather than the modem itself. To some software, this type of modem appears to be nonvoice. Check with your modem manufacturer to see if an additional driver will add the recognition your software needs.

Step 4: Test and Use Your Message Center

Once you have installed the program, you need to walk through it to be sure all aspects of it work the way you expect. This is critical because if, for example, the program does not recognize your modem or has some other issue, you can do some troubleshooting now instead of waiting until you have an urgent message to send and finding out then. In Figures 1-3 and 1-4, you can see how testing determined a communication error between the modem and the software.

Figure 1-3

The demo screen
allowed input for a test
fax and did not show
any potential problems.

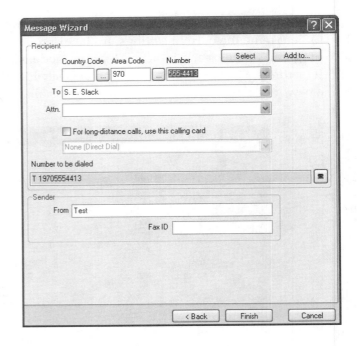

Figure 1-4

Upon dialing, a notice
appeared advising that
the selected modem
had not been found.

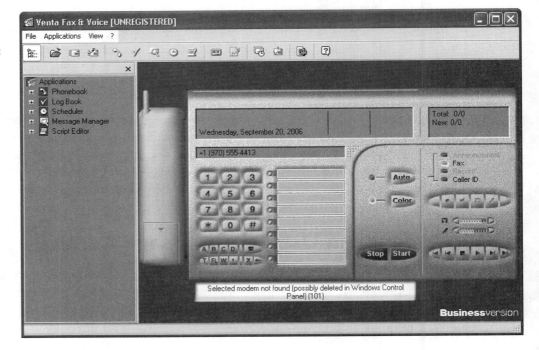

This notice prompted checks to the system to determine the cause of the modem error. As you walk through each section to test it, wait to set up personal preferences until you have confirmed that the entire software package is working as it should.

Setting Up Phone and Address Books

You can typically import contact information from your e-mail program by accepting prompts from your message center software. The information will automatically flow into your message center's phone and address books as long as you have selected software that is compatible with your e-mail program.

It's a good idea to import contact information on a regular basis if you add new contacts often—that can save you time when you're in a hurry and just need to send a quick fax, for example. If your contact list hasn't been updated recently, take the time now to do it. Message center software won't be able to determine whether a contact's fax number is current or not; you'll save yourself time and aggravation in the long run by cleaning up any problems with your contacts now.

When you set up preferences for your phone and address books, you may see the warning shown in Figure 1-5 when using Microsoft Outlook as your e-mail program. This is designed to protect you from malicious programs accessing your contact list. Go ahead and select a time limit for your message center software to access Outlook and click OK.

Figure 1-5

Microsoft Outlook is cautious when new programs want to access its contact lists for information.

Sending and Receiving Faxes

Many message center programs require that a source document be converted to a facsimile format. This is typically handled in Windows applications by opening the document you want to fax and selecting the option of printing to the message center program. During the installation process, your software should have installed this feature. If you can't find the program as your printer, check Help for your program. You may need to uninstall and reinstall the program.

When the fax document is created, your message center software will offer you options for creating a cover page, information header, stamps, and other design features.

Choose the options you want, and follow your program's prompts (such as saving the fax, the number it should be sent to, etc.) to send the fax.

Incoming faxes are typically saved in a graphic format such as TIF. This makes them easy to view and open with any image viewer. Some programs, however, do automatically convert incoming faxes to PDF files—you'll need the Adobe PDF reader to view those.

note   *Some message center software is compatible with distinctive ring services from the phone company as long as the fax modem is Distinctive Ring Capable. This compatibility feature stops the program from answering voice calls, for example, when you only want it to accept faxes. Without this feature and accompanying modem, the program can't tell the difference in the calls until the handset is lifted and it can analyze the fax sounds.*

Accessing Voicemail

Voicemails are saved in an audio format file such as WAV so that your computer can save and play them from designated areas. In VentaFax, for example, incoming voicemails are saved in the Inbox folder under the Message Manager. Simply open the folder and open the individual audio files to hear your messages. If you have remote access to your computer (see Project 10), you can access these voicemails while on the road, too.

If you want your incoming messages automatically forwarded to you via e-mail, you need to set that feature up in the software you're using. Most programs send e-mail messages by their own built-in SMTP protocol rather than the e-mail system you typically use. If you need to, you can find the SMTP server settings in your e-mail account properties. Ask your IP provider for help if you aren't sure where to find them.

note *You'll want to follow your software's setup instructions for the announcement that callers will hear; do that during this test phase. Recording is easy—most message center programs even let you do it in any recording program. Always play back the recording before finalizing it to be sure the sound quality is crisp and clear. You may want to dial in to see what the announcement sounds like over an actual phone line—sometimes computer recordings sound great on a computer but not so great on a phone. Keep at it until you get it just the way you want it.*

Your message center software may have additional features or steps to follow; just take your time and walk through each item carefully. These programs are designed for simplicity and ease of use, so there shouldn't be any steps that you can't follow easily or for which you can't quickly obtain help. Once you're set up, there is one more question: What are you going to do with all that new-found room on your desk now?

Project 2

Expand Your Desktop with Multiple Monitors

What You'll Need:

- Operating system: Windows XP, Windows Vista
- Software: None
- Hardware: Two monitors; one video card with two or more monitor connections or an additional Peripheral Component Interconnect (PCI) video card to add to your already installed video card
- One open PCI slot
- Tools: Phillips screwdriver
- Cost: $100 and up
- Difficulty: Easy

If you are the type of person who is constantly switching between applications and Internet windows on your computer screen, you might need to add another monitor to your computer. Adding a second monitor to your system essentially broadens the number of items you can see on your system at once—it's sort of like having a huge monitor that's split in half, with different programs displayed on each half of the screen.

For example, you can have your e-mail program and instant messaging program displayed on one monitor while you are working diligently on your Excel spreadsheet on the other monitor. Instead of wondering whether you have a new e-mail or message, you can simply glance occasionally at the other monitor and check. If you do receive a message you want to respond to, just move your mouse across monitors and respond, then move your mouse back and keep working in Excel. Or, let's say that Excel spreadsheet has lots of columns that can't be viewed on a single screen. No problem—just stretch Excel across both monitors to facilitate viewing of more columns at once. You can also drag programs from one monitor to another to help you with organization or tasks.

With Windows XP and Vista operating systems, support is already there for additional monitors—up to ten, in fact. In this project, we'll focus on adding just one additional monitor. You can repeat the steps if you decide to add more in the future.

note *Additional monitors can be added to some laptop computers but not all. Check your owner's manual or with your manufacturer to see whether your laptop computer video card can support multiple monitors.*

Step 1: Obtain a Second Monitor

Before you can install a second monitor on your PC, you need to obtain one. Costs can vary widely depending upon the kind of monitor you add. A good rule of thumb to follow is to use a second monitor that has the same size or larger image area as your current monitor and use the same type of monitor. The entire reason to add multiple monitors is to broaden your screen, so there's no point in going smaller—you might as well not bother, unless your first screen is a fabulously expensive type and you simply can't afford to buy that kind again. Monitor size is measured diagonally, by the way, just like your television set.

There are two types of monitors used with desktop PCs: LCD and CRT monitors. LCD technology—the use of a liquid crystal display—was initially used on laptop computers and other portable devices because it offered low power requirements and was lightweight, portable, and compact. CRT technology—officially known as cathode ray tube—has been used in televisions for decades and was the first choice as a monitor for desktop PCs as they became popular. CRT monitors (see Figure 2-1) are much larger in size than LCD monitors (see Figure 2-2). LCD monitors are thinner and take up much less desk space than CRT monitors. For example, an LCD monitor might have a depth of 4 inches while a CRT monitor might have a depth of 12 inches or more.

Figure 2-1

A CRT monitor

Figure 2-2

An LCD monitor

Personal preferences and budget can often make the decision for you when comparing monitors. To optimize desk space and minimize screen glare, go with LCD monitors. They are also much easier to lift due to the smaller size. Other bonuses for LCD monitors? Less radiation and heat are emitted from an LCD monitor than from a CRT monitor.

Using LCD and CRT monitors together means you will have differences in screen quality and sharpness—you can do it, but it's not the optimum working environment. It's particularly helpful if all monitors have the same adjustability features as well. When you work with multiple monitors all day long, it's a little disconcerting to have one screen darker than another. You won't go blind or anything, but when working for long stretches, similar views on both screens will make your life more comfortable.

Due to a lack of electromagnetic shielding, some CRT monitors become distorted when placed next to another CRT monitor. If you start seeing purple or green along the edges of the screen when you place monitors next to each other, try moving them a little farther apart. If the monitors are too far apart to use comfortably, or the distortion doesn't disappear, then try using a different monitor or make the switch to LCD screens. LCD monitors produce pictures differently and don't require the electromagnetic shielding. Leaving distorted CRT monitors together for long periods of time can cause permanent and irreversible damage to the monitors.

Here are some things to consider when shopping for your new monitor.

If You Have LCD Screens

If you are using LCD screens, keep the following in mind:

- Corners of the screens should not change in color or brightness.

- Both monitors should be the same from a brightness perspective when viewing light and dark images alike.

- Both monitors should automatically adjust to the timing of the analog (VGA) signal.

If You Have CRT Screens

If you are using CRT screens, the following items should be considered:

- Both monitors should show images that do not change in dimension or have any distortions when the images change.

- Both monitors should have adjustable screen geometry (representation of lines and shapes). Lines should not have curves near the edge of the display and circles should not be oval or egg-shaped.

- Check for differences in convergence—both screens should be clear and crisp with no colors on the edges.

If you are a digital photographer or graphic artist, it might be wiser for you to stick with one large monitor rather than add multiple monitors. The addition of multiple monitors can sometimes make the colors you see on the screens differ from the printouts. A single, CRT monitor is probably the best choice for you.

Step 2: Verify the Number of Monitor Connections You Have

Look on the back of your computer and see how many video connections you have. They will look like one of the connectors shown in Figure 2-3. If you need to install an additional video card, follow the instructions included with your new card.

Figure 2-3

Shown here are three types of video card monitor interfaces (from top): EDI interface (digital), S-video, and composite VGA (analog).

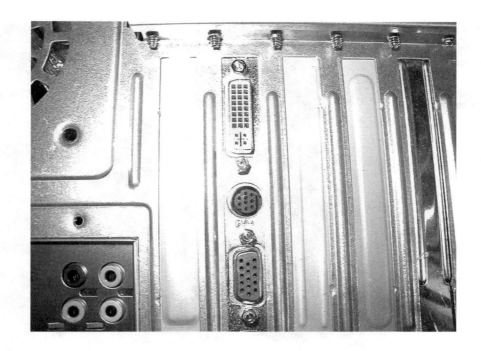

There are multiple types of video cards that can be used, including EDI interface, S-video, composite VGA, PCI, and PCI-E.

 You can't add a second AGP video card into a system. You can add a PCI video card to an AGP video card or a PCI-E video card, however. Some systems support multiple PCI-E cards but those are few and far between as of this writing.

Step 3: Install an Additional Monitor

Now that you have your second monitor, it's time to install it. The first step is to shut down your computer. Next, unplug your computer—this ensures accidentally touching something in the case won't cause your system to crash and burn. Most systems still have power running through the motherboard when Windows shuts down. If yours does, plugging a peripheral such as a video card into your system while it is still plugged in to a power source can cause damage to both the motherboard and the video card. Next, pull your tower out so you can sit somewhere comfortably and work on it.

 You need to open your computer case only if you need to add a video card.

Then follow these steps:

1. Open your computer case.

2. Plug your additional monitor into the card as shown in Figure 2-4.

Now, turn on your computer.

Figure 2-4

Once the video card is inserted, your additional monitor will be plugged into it as shown here.

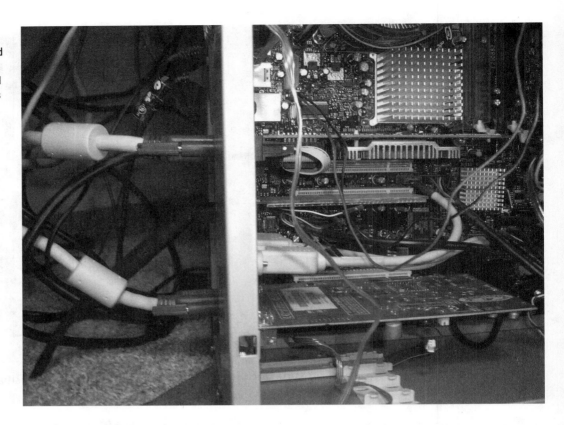

Windows XP

Follow these steps to extend your Windows XP desktop to a new monitor:

1. When Windows XP launches, click the Start button and choose Settings | Control Panel.

2. In the Control Panel, double-click Display to open the Display Properties dialog box.

3. In the Display Properties dialog box, click the Settings tab, shown in Figure 2-5.

4. Click the monitor icon representing the monitor you are adding to your system.

5. Place a check mark in the Extend My Windows Desktop Onto This Monitor check box.

6. Click OK.

Figure 2-5

The Settings tab of the Display Properties dialog box is where you tell your computer to include your additional monitor as part of your entire desktop, allowing your screen to expand to multiple monitors.

note *If the Extend My Windows Desktop Onto This Monitor check box does not display, your video adapter may not support multiple monitors. Video adapters that are part of the motherboard instead of plug-in cards must be set as VGA.*

Windows Vista

Follow these steps to extend your Windows Vista desktop to a new monitor:

1. When Windows Vista launches, click the Start button and choose Control Panel.

2. Click Personalize.

3. Click Display Settings.

4. Click the monitor icon representing the monitor you are adding to your system.

5. Place a check mark in the Extend The Desktop Onto This Monitor check box.

6. Click OK.

note *If your computer doesn't recognize your second monitor, go to the Display Properties dialog box and click the Troubleshoot button for help. You may need to install additional drivers for the video card to work properly. The correct driver should come with the video card if you purchased one, or you can obtain the driver from the video card manufacturer's web site. This is a simple download and installation process that typically has instructions provided on the web site or in the box.*

Step 4: Arrange the Monitors

Now that you have multiple monitors installed, you will see that one monitor displays the Logon dialog box when you start your computer and that most windows open on this monitor. This monitor is your primary monitor. You can also determine the primary monitor through the Display Properties dialog box, as shown in Figure 2-6.

Figure 2-6

The primary monitor is indicated in the Display Properties dialog box. It is not always the monitor marked as number one—hover your cursor over the monitor icons to see which one is primary.

If you want a different monitor as your primary monitor, go to the Settings tab in the Display Properties dialog box and follow these steps:

1. Click the monitor you want to designate as your primary monitor.

2. Place a check mark in the Use This Device As The Primary Monitor check box.

3. Click OK.

If you want to arrange your monitors differently but keep your primary monitor the same, go to the Settings tab in the Display Properties dialog box and follow these steps:

1. Click Identify. This displays a large number on every monitor so that you can see clearly which monitor corresponds to the icons in the Settings tab. Review Figure 2-5 to see how the numbers display.

Figure 2-7

Each monitor is identified by a separate number so that you can always tell where it is located and move it to a new location if necessary.

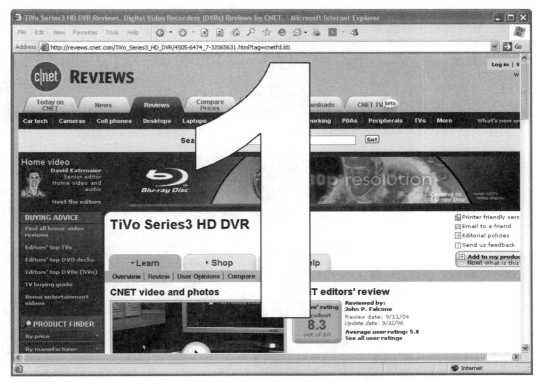

2. Click the icon for the monitor you want to move. Drag it to the new position in the Settings tab to match the physical arrangement of your monitors, as shown in Figure 2-7.

3. Click Apply.

note *Monitor icons in the Settings tab of the Display Properties dialog box do not have to correspond to the physical locations of monitors but their placement does determine the movement of items between monitors. If you like to move things from monitor to monitor by dragging them up or down, place the monitors on top of one another. Alternately, place the icons beside one another to drag items right or left.*

That's it—you now have multiple monitors to help you organize your work and expand the screen space for easier access to all your programs. Take a look at my desk in Figure 2-8 to see how your desk could look!

Figure 2-8

The author's desk, where she can't function without her three LCD monitors to track everything.

Perk Up Your Infrastructure with a Webcam

What You'll Need:

- **Operating system: Windows XP, Windows Vista**
- **Software: Included with webcam**
- **Hardware: Webcam, CD-ROM drive, computer speakers, sound card, USB port, microphone (if not provided with the webcam)**
- **Cost: $25 and up**
- **Difficulty: Easy**

If you aren't using a webcam yet, you likely will be soon. That's because so many different programs are including video capabilities in them and, as they do, more and more people are getting used to the once-futuristic idea of video-phoning and video-conferencing. Instant messaging programs are including the video option as a standard feature now, which means that instead of text chats and phone calls, you will have colleagues ringing you for a quick video chat.

This isn't a bad thing—working at home means you are often out of sight to employers or clients, and we all know "out of sight" can translate to "out of mind." Using a webcam to stay in touch often can make employers and clients feel more comfortable since they can see and talk to you as if you were right in their office.

Webcams work best with cable, satellite, or DSL Internet connections. For a webcam to work effectively, you need to lose the dial-up and upgrade to a broadband connection. Your picture will be virtually worthless on dial-up and you'll have spent your time and money on a product that will simply look cool beside your monitor.

One last thing: If you decide to install a webcam, you will need to have an Internet messaging program to use it with, such as Microsoft Live Messenger, Skype, or AOL Instant Messenger. If you currently use a messaging program, check its video capabilities before purchasing your webcam. If you don't currently use one, find out what your colleagues use and install it. After all, there is no point in having a webcam if you don't have anyone to chat with.

Step 1: Select a Webcam

Some newer laptops are offering webcams built right into the laptop case, so if you have one of these, you don't need to worry about installing a webcam at all. The rest of us, however, need to purchase a separate webcam that installs into a USB port on our desktop or laptop. Once a webcam is installed, it will *typically* work with any program that offers video capabilities.

Some webcams come with built-in microphones, while others require you to purchase a separate microphone and headset. We recommend purchasing a webcam with a built-in microphone. It's easier to use, but the main reason is that built-in microphones are designed to reduce feedback more effectively when using the webcam.

The key question to ask when shopping for a webcam is, how do you plan to use it? The answer you give will determine the type of webcam you need to shop for.

Webcam Will Be Used with a Desktop Computer

If you will be using your webcam primarily while you sit quietly at your home office desk, you'll be fine with one that stands alone beside your monitor, like the one shown in Figure 3-1, or one that sits on top of it. Some desktop webcams, like the Logitech model shown in Figure 3-1, offer face-tracking features, so if you have

Figure 3-1

A Logitech QuickCam Orbit MP desktop webcam with face-tracking features.

a tendency to walk or stand near your desk while you talk, the webcam will simply follow you. You can use a webcam designed for laptops on your desktop, but beware: these are typically designed to sit atop thin monitors and can be a bit difficult to keep stable on top of a CRT monitor.

Webcam Will Be Used with a Laptop Computer

If you travel often and want to use a webcam with your laptop computer, you want one that's lightweight and easy to set up while you're on the road. Some webcams are designed specifically for laptops—they are tiny enough to perch atop the edge of your monitor when your laptop is open, as shown in Figure 3-2. These sometimes don't allow for much adjustability, however, and can be a bit distracting when you work, so you may want to go with a slightly larger one with adjustable features that can sit beside the laptop.

Figure 3-2

Webcams for laptops are designed to perch on top of your laptop screen for easy use and portability.

When working with a laptop, it might be worthwhile to check out wireless webcams, too. If you purchase one, you won't need to follow the instructions in this project that pertain to plugging the webcam into the USB port.

note   *Digital video cameras are now being produced that double as webcams. If you want to use one of these rather than a camera designed specifically for your computer, follow the instructions included with your digital video camera to be sure you have the proper connections and drivers installed.*

Optimal Webcam Specifications

No matter which webcam you buy, there are some basic options that should not be compromised. Primary complaints about webcams involve the video—it's too pixilated or blurry. While this can sometimes be caused by broadband speed, even slower-speed connections can be improved by using a webcam that has high video capture speed and resolution. We recommend the following minimum specifications:

- 1.3 pixels gross sensor resolution
- CMOS sensor type
- 30 frames per second digital video capture speed
- 640×480 digital video capture resolution
- 1280×960 still image capture resolution
- Built-in microphone

note   *Webcams are typically USB-connected, but some newer ones are designed to work with FireWire, a connection that is faster than a USB connection. However, many computers do not have a FireWire port, so before you purchase your webcam, be sure to verify how it will connect to your computer. This illustration shows the FireWire port as a vertical port between two horizontal USB ports and two headphone ports:*

Step 2: Install the Webcam

Once you have chosen a webcam, installation will go pretty quickly. Every camera has its own setup/installation CD, and you should follow the steps it outlines for your particular camera. Before you begin, however, you need to identify where your USB port is. If you're using a laptop, the USB port is located on the side or back of the laptop case. On desktop systems, it is located at the back of the tower case, as shown in Figure 3-3, unless you have a newer system, in which case it may be located on the front of the computer case.

Figure 3-3

Most webcams use a USB connector and port like the ones shown here on the back of this computer.

Next, confirm that your computer speakers are working. If you can hear a ding on your computer as an e-mail comes in or when you do something your computer doesn't like, they work. If you can't hear a ding, follow the steps outlined next corresponding to your operating system.

Windows XP

1. Click the Start button and choose Settings | Control Panel.

2. Open the Sounds And Audio Devices Properties dialog box, shown in Figure 3-4.

3. On the Volume tab:

   - Be sure Mute is not checked.

   - Move the Device Volume slider to High.

   - Click the Advanced button under Device Volume. Check your Wave sound volume and be sure it is not muted. Close the Volume Control dialog box.

   - Click the Speaker Volume button. Move the Left and Right sliders to High. Click OK.

   - Click the Advanced button under Speaker Settings. Check to be sure your speaker setup is correct in the Speaker Setup drop-down box. Click OK.

Figure 3-4

The first place to troubleshoot sound problems is in the Sounds And Audio Devices Properties dialog box, accessed from the Control Panel.

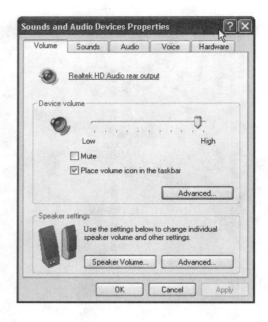

4. On the Audio tab:

    ● Click Volume under Sound Playback. Be sure nothing is muted in the Master Volume dialog box, as shown in Figure 3-5. Close the dialog box.

    ● Click OK.

Figure 3-5

Sometimes the Master Volume under the Audio tab isn't muted or turned down.

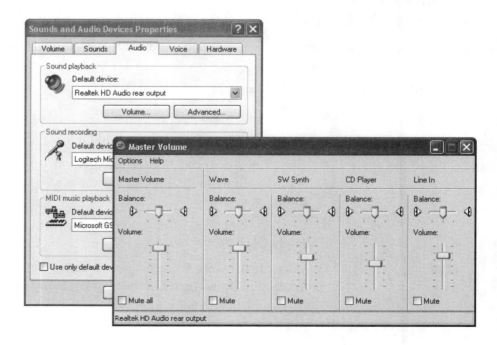

You should have sound now. If not, continue troubleshooting in the Sounds and Audio Devices Properties dialog box.

Windows Vista

1. Click the Start button and choose Control Panel.

2. Double-click Sound.

3. On the Playback tab, select Speakers. Click Properties.

4. In the Speakers Properties dialog box, click Levels.

5. Check that the speaker icon is not muted.

6. Increase the sound if necessary by clicking and dragging the sound bar to the right.

7. Click OK.

Now, go ahead and insert your webcam setup/installation CD into your CD-ROM drive. If the setup program doesn't start automatically in Windows XP or Windows Vista:

1. Click the Start button and choose Run.

2. Type **d:\setup** in the Run dialog box. If your CD-ROM drive is not on the D: drive, type in the correct drive letter with :\setup following it.

3. Follow the instructions in your camera setup program.

Plug in your camera only when prompted. Plugging in the camera at the wrong time can cause a variety of problems.

Step 3: Test Your Webcam

Now that your webcam is installed, you need to make sure others can see you. One of the easiest ways to test this is to open your instant messaging program and go to the video test section, as shown in Figure 3-6. It's usually located in the Tools or Options menu of messaging programs. In the Skype example shown here, the Video section allows you to click a button to test your webcam. When you click the button, a video window pops up. If you can see yourself, your camera is working.

Figure 3-6

Most instant messaging programs allow you to instantly test your video and see what the person you are chatting with sees.

If you can't see yourself, you need to do some troubleshooting.

Troubleshoot first within the instant messaging program to be sure you have followed the correct steps to enable video in the program. If all those steps appear fine, you need to check your webcam properties, as described next based on operating system.

Windows XP

1. Double-click My Computer on your desktop.

2. Locate and select the icon for your webcam.

3. Select Properties.

4. Many webcams have a Diagnostics section in the Properties dialog box. In Figure 3-7, Logitech's Test Camera button is shown. When the button was clicked, the Test Successful dialog box appeared. If your test is not successful, a different dialog box would appear with prompts for proceeding through troubleshooting steps.

Figure 3-7

Logitech uses a simple Test Camera button. Other manufacturers may call the diagnostics test something different.

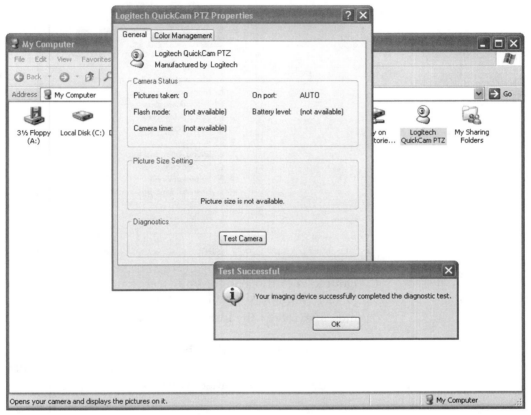

Windows Vista

1. Click the Start button and choose Control Panel.

2. Select Classic View. Double-click Device Manager.

3. Expand Imaging Devices.

4. Double-click the icon for your webcam. In the General tab, check to see that Device Status says "This device is working properly." If it has a different message, follow the instructions provided.

If absolutely everything fails (which is rare), uninstall the webcam and reinstall it. You may have missed a step in installation or something else may have gone wrong. If a reinstall does not work, contact your webcam manufacturer.

Step 4: Adjusting Your Webcam

Depending on the webcam you choose, you may be able to adjust features such as zoom, face tracking, brightness, color, contrast, flicker, image enhancement, and more. These features are often accessed through your webcam Properties dialog box or the Video section of your instant messaging program. In Figure 3-8, the Logitech Quick-Cam PTZ Properties dialog box was opened through the Skype Options menu.

It's worth taking a little time to walk through each of the features and make sure they are adjusted the way you like. Pay attention to items such as low light boost (this helps improve the picture if you are in a dimly lit room) and zoom. Use zoom if your camera is more than two feet from your face—let your colleagues see your lovely smile up close and personal. Now all you need to do is log onto your instant messaging program like the folks in Figure 3-9 and find someone to chat with—(almost) in person.

Figure 3-8

In this example, Zoom and Face Tracking features, as well as the camera's direction, are all adjustable.

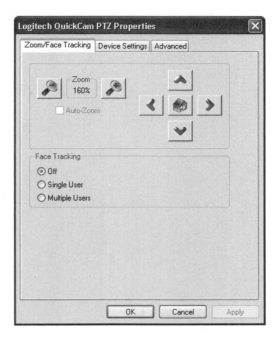

Figure 3-9

Video calls add that personal touch when talking with colleagues or clients.

Project 4

Set Up a Docking Station for Your Laptop

What You'll Need

- **Operating system: Windows XP, Windows Vista**
- **Software: None**
- **Hardware: Docking station**
- **Cost: $75 and up**
- **Difficulty: Challenging**

In today's mobile society, many people are using laptop computers as a primary computer system. Then, they return home and copy documents to their desktop or use slow-moving synchronization programs to transfer documents back and forth and update calendars. Why would you do this when you can get rid of your desktop computer altogether and turn your laptop into a networked desktop workstation when you're back at the office?

Docking stations, as shown in Figure 4-1, can help you stay organized by letting you hook up everything related to your laptop computer in one place, and allowing you to just slide your laptop computer into a single connector. Voilà! Your laptop computer has just become a networked desktop workstation through the use of a single plug that connects your laptop to a keyboard, printer, network, and other devices. Unplug your laptop from the docking station and it becomes portable again. And, docking stations are compact, so they don't take up a lot of room on your desk.

You don't *have* to get rid of that desktop computer, by the way—docking stations can be linked to both a desktop and a laptop for synchronization purposes. Once you find the docking station you want to use, it's fairly easy to set it up and get going.

 See a CNET video on setting up a docking station for your laptop at http://diyoffice.cnet.com.

Figure 4-1

A docking station can turn your laptop computer into a desktop workstation with a single click.

note Some manufacturers use terms such as "expansion base" or "base station" instead of "docking station."

Step 1: Select a Docking Station

Most laptop manufacturers create docking stations for the laptop computers they sell, but proprietary docking stations can be expensive to purchase. Manufacturers of peripheral products produce universal docking stations like the one shown in Figure 4-2—products that work with a variety of laptops instead of just one brand. No matter which brand you choose, today's docking stations are not the clunkers they were ten years ago—they

Figure 4-2

Universal docking stations work with many different laptop brands.

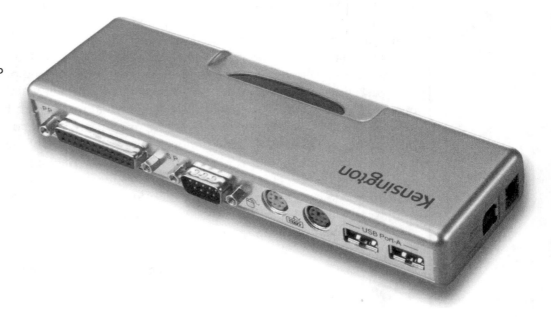

are typically slim, compact designs with plug-and-play connections and often include USB and Ethernet ports. Some also have monitor/video ports; the type and number of ports will vary by manufacturer and model.

tip *You may hear the term "port replicator" when shopping for your docking station. These are similar to docking stations but typically contain fewer connections. For example, a port replicator might not have an S-video jack or headphone jacks.*

What to Look for in a Docking Station

Many laptops use a proprietary connector to dock with a docking station or port replicator. Proprietary docking stations normally have all ports, including video, built in as pass-through devices. In addition, some docking stations have additional slots for add-on devices like video or sound cards—even hard drives. This might make it easier for you to use a docking station but can limit your options. If your laptop uses a USB port instead, it can most likely use a universal docking station and give you more options.

Look for the following when shopping for a docking station:

- **Compatibility with your laptop manufacturer**   Even when a docking station says it is universal, there are still universal docking stations that do not work with all manufacturers. Triple-check before you buy and be sure the one you choose is guaranteed to be compatible with your laptop manufacturer, as well as your model.

- **Number and type of ports**   Do you just need a keyboard and mouse setup? Do you want to play video games on a 19-inch monitor? Do you want to synchronize programs between a desktop and laptop, or will you use this docking station solely with your laptop? Determine what you want to do, then look for a docking station with the flexibility and expandability to support your needs. The best ones offer extra ports and the ability to connect to LCD or plasma screens.

- **Price**   Docking stations vary in price from $75 on up. If budget is a concern for you, determine the type and number of ports you absolutely must have and work through your decision from there. It's easy to get sidetracked by all the cool features as companies try to outperform one another.

- **Extras**   If you will be using the laptop as your primary computer, you need a docking station that offers keyboard adjustability options and the option to raise the laptop's display to eye level. Don't skimp on these two extras unless you are connecting to a desktop system that offers both.

- **Security**   If you can find it, get a docking station with electronic undocking features as well as physical ones. This will allow you to set security features with your operating system that prevent others from removing the laptop from its docking station.

Step 2: Install the Docking Station

You have done the hardest part of this project by shopping for and finding the right docking station for your needs. Some docking stations have very specific instructions but most follow these basic steps:

1. Shut down your laptop computer and unplug all peripheral attachments: power cord, mouse, cameras—anything that is attached to your laptop should be removed and you should be holding only the case.

2. On the back or side of your laptop, find the USB connector that you will use to connect to the docking station. You may need to slide a panel open—many laptops have sliding panels that protect their ports. Figure 4-3 shows an example of how a docking station and laptop work together.

3. Plug in your laptop to the docking station. The first time you do this, pay close attention to the guide pins that are typically provided with docking stations. Those will line up with your laptop's connectors. You should hear a click when the connection is made.

4. Plug in the docking station's power cord.

5. Attach the peripherals you unplugged earlier.

6. Turn on your laptop computer.

Figure 4-3

This Kensington notebook docking station sits below the laptop.

If the Add New Hardware Wizard dialog box opens, follow the prompts it provides. While your peripherals should all work automatically, there may be some laptops that need to perform an extra step or two.

Step 3: Use the Docking Station

Most docking station and laptop combinations are hot-pluggable, meaning you can have the laptop running when you plug it in. Read the instructions that came with your particular docking station to determine how your model works. It's never a bad idea to be on the safe side and shut down the laptop computer. Remove it from the docking station for a few minutes, then plug it back in and turn it on. If everything is working fine, you're ready to hit the road confidently. If you experience any trouble at all, go to the docking station instructions and be sure you have followed all the steps it recommends.

 When attached to a docking station, your laptop will be running off AC power and should begin charging the battery. When you remove the laptop, it will switch to battery power unless you plug the power cord into an AC outlet.

Step 4: Security Considerations

If you're concerned that unauthorized people might remove your laptop from its docking station, there are some security precautions you can take if your docking station has electronic undocking features:

- Check manufacturer guidelines to see whether you can assign a password to prevent anyone from undocking your laptop from its station.

- Use an antitheft device, such as a security cable. Some of these have alarms that can scare away would-be thieves.

- In Windows XP, you can enable a security policy (shown in Figure 4-4) that requires the user to log on before undocking a portable computer from its docking station. By default, a logon is *not* required, so you must disable the default.

note *You must be logged on as an administrator to change security policy options.*

Windows XP

To apply security features in Windows XP, follow these steps:

1. Click the Start button and choose Programs or All Programs.

2. Select Administrative Tools and click Local Policies | Security Options in the left task pane.

Figure 4-4

Windows XP offers
the option of requiring
users to log onto the
laptop before the
laptop can be
physically removed
from a docking station.

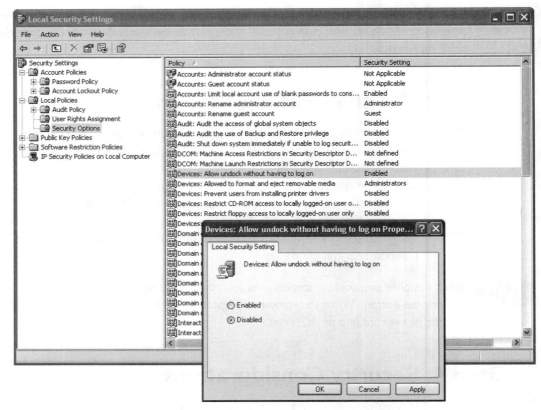

3. In the right task pane, double-click Devices: Allow Undock Without Having To Log On.

4. In the Devices: Allow Undock Without Having to Log On Properties dialog box, select Disabled, as shown in Figure 4-4.

5. Click Apply.

note *Be aware that someone could still try to physically remove your laptop from its docking station, even if passwords or logon procedures are required. If this happens, your laptop could be irreparably damaged—assuming, of course, you retrieve the laptop from the person who removed it. If you don't retrieve it, it might make you happy to know they may never be able to use the laptop!*

Windows Vista

To apply security features in Windows Vista, follow these steps:

1. Click the Start button and type **Local Security Policy in the Start Search box.**

2. Click Local Security Policy under Programs.

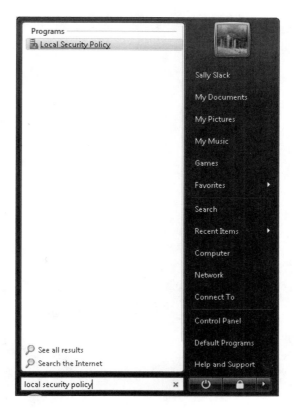

3. Expand Local Policies in the left navigation pane. Click Security Options.

4. In the right task pane, double-click Devices: Allow Undock Without Having To Log On.

5. In the Allow Undock Without Having To Log On Properties dialog box, select Disabled.

6. Click Apply.

7. Click OK.

Now that you know how to install a docking station, you'll wonder why you never used one before. The amount of time savings alone is worth the cost of these devices, and when you routinely work in and out of the home, every minute counts.

Project 5

Turn Your Monitor into a TV

What You'll Need:

- **Operating system: None**
- **Software: None**
- **Hardware: Computer monitor, video source, external TV tuner box, speakers**
- **Cost: $99 and up**
- **Difficulty: Challenging**

The price has dropped on personal computers so much that it's often cheaper now to purchase a new system with a monitor than one without since so many companies now include monitors as enticement. As a result, you may have an extra monitor lying around. It may be a perfectly good one but if you decide to store it rather than attach it to your new system for a multiple-monitor setup, you could be wasting a great opportunity. Why not turn your old monitor into a television for your office?

You can do it pretty quickly by adding a few items to your monitor and, depending upon the monitor you have, you could very well wind up with a better picture than the one on the TV in your living room. Not everyone needs all the hardware listed above, by the way. Take a read through this project before making any purchases; you might just have everything you need hiding in a closet. There is no computer attached to this—just the monitor.

note *If you prefer to add television to your computer rather than to a stand-alone monitor, those instructions are included in Step 5 of this project. Review Steps 1 to 3 to be sure you have all bases covered, then skip to Step 5.*

Step 1: Check Your Monitor

If the monitor you have has built-in speakers and standard TV inputs such as an S-video or composite input, you may not need any additional hardware. You can just plug it into an audio-visual source such as your cable box or satellite dish if it has the same connections, and start watching your favorite shows. See Figure 5-1 for an example of a monitor with these ports.

Figure 5-1

Most older monitors only have Super VGA connections. If the back of yours looks similar to this, you need to purchase an external TV tuner.

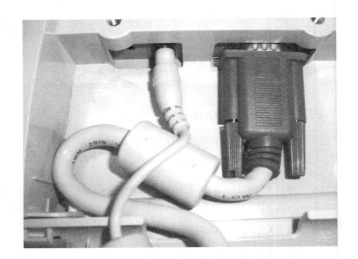

Most older monitors, however, just have SVGA connections and rely on external speakers. This means you do need to purchase an external TV tuner and connection, and may want to upgrade your speaker system. Don't worry if your monitor only has a VGA connection, by the way. Regular TV signals come through at the standard VGA resolution of 640×480 pixels, so you're not missing out on anything in the picture you receive.

tip   *If your monitor does not have built-in speakers or a connection for speakers, be sure your tuner box does. You can plug in speakers (sometimes just one) to the tuner box for sound.*

Step 2: Check and Connect Your Speakers

If your monitor has built-in speakers, you're set. If not, you'll want to obtain external speakers for the monitor like the ones shown in Figure 5-2 or hook up the monitor and tuner box into a stereo system. These don't need to be expensive; just basic speakers that make noise will work fine. After all, you're not setting up a surround-sound system here—are you? If you are, then purchase speakers accordingly and just make sure they will work with your monitor and tuner.

Connect your speakers to your monitor and move on to Step 3.

Figure 5-2

External speakers like these from Logitech should be connected to your monitor before connecting to your tuner.

Step 3: Select a TV Tuner Box

External TV tuners are just small boxes that contain the same audio-visual ports that televisions have. These boxes attach to your monitor and the television signal source—think of a tuner as sort of an intermediary between your monitor and TV signal. It converts the signal from the source to a signal that the monitor can understand. You can hook up DVD or VCR players to most tuners, as well as video game systems.

If you need to purchase an external TV tuner box, you need to decide whether to go with an analog or digital box. With any TV tuner box, you want to be able to adjust your picture for brightness, contrast, saturation, gamma, and sharpness.

If you plan on hooking up a VCR or DVD player, you want a tuner box that has at least composite and S-video inputs. External tuner boxes typically work with both LCD and CRT monitors, and newer ones are even compatible with plasma and projection displays.

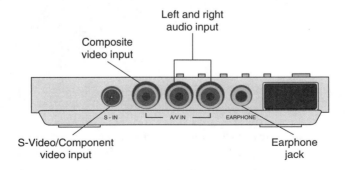

note   *Internal tuners are available as well if you prefer to have your desktop computer workstation monitor double as a television. These are PCI-card based and deliver most of the same features as the external tuner boxes. Because most home office users already have enough happening on their desktop workstations, this project focused on stand-alone monitors and external tuner boxes.*

When to Go with an Analog Tuner

Use an analog tuner when you have a standard cable or satellite box or typically only watch VHF and UHF stations. This type of tuner also works well with video game consoles and VCR or DVD players. Some VCRs also act as analog tuners—it might be worth checking out an old VCR to see if yours could double as your TV tuner. However, they don't always have S-video output, which you'll need if you want to use a DVD player.

When to Go with a Digital Tuner

Go with a digital tuner like the one shown in Figure 5-3 when you have a digital antenna, cable, or satellite connection. DTV and HDTV all come through a digital connection, for example, and many digital tuners now support those signals as well. Not all do, however, so check carefully before you put down your money.

Figure 5-3

Digital tuner boxes like this one from Aver Media receive DTV and HDTV signals.

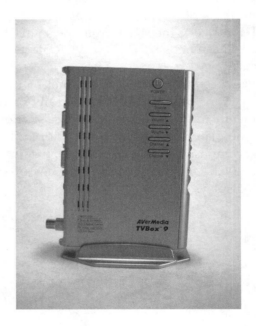

note   *External tuner boxes usually come with remote controls because the boxes are typically stored behind the monitor, which makes them hard to access once everything is connected. Plus, these boxes don't have room for numeric buttons (for channel-changing) or other television features such a volume controls and menu navigation buttons.*

Step 4: Connect the Tuner to Your Monitor and Speakers

Well, here's the tough part of this project. Let's take a look at the actual connections you'll need to make on your tuner. As this illustration shows, you will be inserting the tuner's power adaptor, the monitor, and the cable from the cable or satellite box or antenna. There will be other input and output options, but unless you're doing something beyond watching television, you won't need to worry about those.

Always follow manufacturer instructions, of course, but essentially things will go like this:

1. Take the tuner out of the box.

2. Plug the computer monitor into it as shown in Figure 5-4.

Figure 5-4

The monitor plugs directly into the tuner box.

3. Plug the tuner into the cable or satellite box or television antenna using a standard TV cable, as shown in Figure 5-5.

Figure 5-5

A standard TV cable plugs into the tuner from the television source.

4. Plug the tuner into a power source.

5. Turn on the tuner.

6. Turn on your monitor.

7. Start watching television (see Figure 5-6). You might need to use the remote control for your cable or satellite box as well as the remote control for the TV tuner.

Figure 5-6

You can be watching your shows within minutes.

There might be a lot of extra cords in the manufacturer's box that you are tempted to play with. Those are for your DVD player or games and other peripheral devices, and may even be to connect a PC to the tuner. You don't need any of them to watch plain old television, so don't let them confuse you as you set things up.

note *If you want to watch DVDs or videos or play games, just plug those peripheral items into the tuner box and turn them on. There are no special attachments required.*

Step 5: Connect the Tuner to Your Computer

If you prefer to have television as another feature on your desktop (or laptop) computer, there are just a few additional steps in the process. Your computer can be on while you perform these steps:

1. Take the tuner out of the box.

2. Remove the monitor cable from the back of the computer. Leave it attached to the monitor, though.

3. Plug the VGA cable into the tuner box.

4. Plug the other end of the VGA cable into the computer where you removed the monitor cable.

5. Plug the computer monitor cable into the tuner box (VGA out).

6. Plug the speaker out cable from the tuner into the line in jack on your computer.

7. Plug the tuner into the cable or satellite box or television antenna using a standard TV cable.

8. Plug the tuner into a power source.

9. Turn on the tuner.

10. Start watching television. You might need to use the remote control for your cable or satellite box as well as the remote control for the TV tuner.

tip *If you don't want the television picture to fill an entire monitor screen while you work, choose a tuner that offers picture-in-picture.*

Other Considerations

If you choose to use a CRT monitor, check the tuner to see the output resolution and refresh rates (the number of times, or "frequency," that the screen is redrawn each minute) it can produce and try to match the tuner's rates to your monitor's rates as closely as possible. Refresh rates differ depending on the resolution and most decrease as resolutions increase. The higher the refresh rate, the more clearly the picture will appear.

Some older monitors can only refresh at 60 Hz. This can provide a picture but can also cause a noticeable flicker. The flicker can cause eye strain and be an annoyance. Refresh rates of 72 Hz and above are considered "flicker free." Remember, even if the monitor can get to a higher resolution and refresh rate, the *tuner* has to be able to produce a picture at that resolution and rate also.

LCD monitors produce pictures differently than CRTs so there is no flicker. However, LCDs have an inherent property that is called "motion-blur." Each pixel or dot on an LCD screen is produced by lighting a specific cell or cells, which creates a sharper edge than a CRT pixel and makes an LCD picture crisper and the text easier to read. The drawback is that the cells in some of the earlier LCDs weren't able to shut off or change colors very quickly. So when something on the screen moved, the object tended to blur because the pixels or cells "faded" to the new color in the object's previous position. Newer LCD cells have become quicker at turning off or changing to a new color due to both enhancements in LCD technology and software algorithm improvements, making the blur almost unnoticeable.

Create an e-Shipping Center

What You'll Need

- Internet access: Yes
- Software: None
- Hardware: None
- Cost: $0
- Difficulty: Challenging

When you work from home, you can't take advantage of services that you would normally find at a standard business location. Things that you take for granted in a corporate environment—cafeteria, receptionist, shipping dock—are all part of your responsibility now. Since your cafeteria is probably your kitchen and the receptionist is now you, it's probably also time to get better organized with your own e-shipping department.

You don't have to send or receive much mail to take advantage of this project. It comes in handy whether you make one trip to the post office each year or trot down there daily. Just avoiding one lengthy stand in line is probably worth the time and effort it will take to set up your e-shipping center.

These centers work by taking advantage of the online services offered by the U.S. Post Office as well as other shipping companies, such as UPS and FedEx. You can print postage online, have boxes and other supplies delivered directly to your door, and arrange for front porch pickups whenever you need them.

An e-shipping center is helpful because you can typically log into your account from anywhere at any time, and there is no special software to install or update. Everything is handled on the carrier's web site. Almost all of the carrier's normal services are available to you when using online options, and the web sites are designed to make it easy for you to compare costs vs. delivery times per service. You can also obtain shipping reports, track deliveries, and store contact information in an online address book.

You only need Internet access to get started with this project—and a willingness to get your office a little bit more electronically organized.

note *The cost to set up an e-shipping center is a big fat zero. But actual shipping, of course, is not free!*

Step 1: Determine Your Shipping Needs

Most shipping providers are fairly similar, but since every home office has different needs, you should do some comparison shopping. Minor differences in address books or access to shipping records might be a major headache if you don't understand how those differences will impact you.

No matter which provider you choose, there are several benefits to setting up an e-shipping center in your home office:

- **Increased productivity** You can ship and track from any desktop with an Internet connection, and you never have to hop in the car to send an overnight letter or package again.

- **Improved client communication** Automatic e-mail notices are sent for you to alert others when a package has shipped and what the tracking number is.

- **Error reduction** The automatic address books improve shipping accuracy.

To make some determinations about the type of services you need from an e-shipping vendor, ask yourself: What's the largest number of contacts I might possibly need to include in my address book? How long do I want to access the vendor's shipping records? Do I send a lot of large boxes or overnight deliveries?

Vendors vary with the numbers of contacts that they allow you to maintain in their online address books; some are limited, some are not. Shipping records are typically kept on the vendor's web site, so vendors make records available online only for a limited amount of time because of space limitations. Shipping large boxes or items requires that your e-shipping vendor have a strong ground-shipping program. Finally, vendors vary in the options they offer for overnight deliveries. These options are discussed in more detail in the following section.

Take a few minutes to take a look back at the last 3 months and determine what you spent on shipping, too. If you spend large enough amounts on shipping on a regular basis, it could qualify you for a discount with some vendors.

Step 1: Learn About e-Shipping Options

No matter what you ship, as long as it's legal and not flammable, you'll find a carrier to ship it. Each carrier, however, offers slightly different e-shipping services, so it can literally pay to take the time to do your homework. You'll want to consider the shipping services provided, along with the types of products that can be ordered online and the types of tools the carrier provides to make it easy for you to track your shipments and related costs online.

Shipping Services

While there are local shipping services available, the four heavyweights in the industry are national carriers everyone has heard of. I'll be referring to these throughout this project since they are the most likely choice for most people. Here are the national carriers, along with some basic information about the services they provide. All except the U.S. Post Office will ship freight (packages typically weighing more than 150 pounds).

- **DHL Web Shipping, www.dhl.com** Arrange for pickup, print shipping labels on your printer, track shipments online, notify recipients via e-mail, save up to 300 customer addresses, and access shipping records for 99 days. DHL account required; no software to download.

- **FedEx Ship Manager, www.fedex.com** Arrange for pickup, print shipping labels on your printer, track shipments online, notify recipients via e-mail, save up to 300 customer addresses, and access shipping records for 45 days. FedEx account required; no software to download.

- **UPS Internet Shipping, www.ups.com** Arrange for pickup, print shipping labels on your printer, track shipments online, notify recipients via e-mail, save up to 2000 customer addresses, and access shipping records. UPS ID and credit card *or* UPS account required; no software to download. The UPS resource page for small business owners is shown in Figure 6-1.

Figure 6-1

UPS Internet Shipping has a variety of resources for small business owners, as do DHL, FedEx, and the USPS.

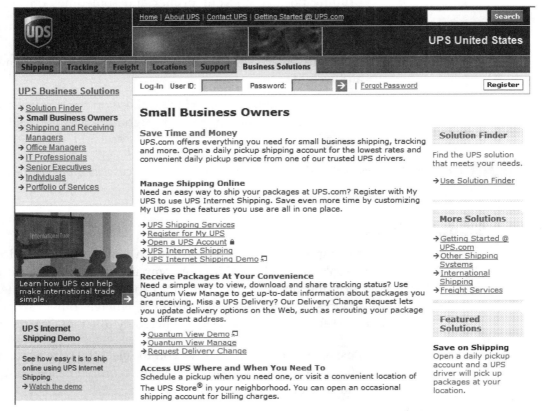

- **USPS Shipping Assistant, www.usps.com/shippingassistant**   This is the U.S. Post Office's service. Arrange for pickup, print shipping labels on your printer, track shipments online, notify recipients via e-mail, save customer addresses, and access shipping records on your own computer. Accepts postcards and letters. Free software download and user ID is required.

tip   *Packages heavier than 70 pounds cannot be mailed through the USPS.*

Shipping Products

When you choose a shipping service, consider the types of shipping products it offers, too. If one service offers free boxes, for example, but charges you more for shipping than the next carrier, then perhaps the free boxes aren't such a great deal for your needs. Products will vary based on the carrier, but here is a compilation of the types of products offered. You can order all of these online, depending upon the carrier.

- **Free materials**   Depending upon the service, you can ask for free boxes and other shipping materials, such as overnight envelopes, tubes, and boxes. These free boxes are delivered to your front door by several carriers.

- **Flat-rate boxes**   You can order most priority and express boxes and envelopes ahead of time with a flat-rate product. This eliminates the need for printing postage on your printer and sometimes offers a better rate than standard shipping options.

- **Prepaid shipping**   You can purchase envelopes and cards with postage already affixed. This is very useful if you typically send items of the same size and weight.

- **Free stickers and labels**   Having these on hand saves a trip to the carrier just to grab a small "urgent" or "signature required" sticker or something similar.

tip   *Items shipped in boxes should have enough room for complete cushioning around the item.*

Shipping Tools

Since this e-shipping center will be run from your computer and your home office, the online tools offered by a shipping company should be carefully considered. For example, printing labels or postage online can save you a lot of time. Be careful: some of these services are free with certain carriers, whereas other carriers charge a fee.

Here is a sample of the online tools offered by different carriers, and what they do:

- **Postage calculation**   Allows you to select the type of service for your shipping needs and calculate the postage required based on the size of the item and type of service chosen.

- **Print mailing labels**   Allows you to print mailing labels directly from your printer.

- **Print postage**   Lets you purchase postage labels with and without postage and print it out on your printer.

tip *The USPS offers Customized Postage through several vendors, which lets you add your own unique images and photos to your postage.*

- **Tracking and delivery confirmation**   Lets you verify the delivery of your shipment online.

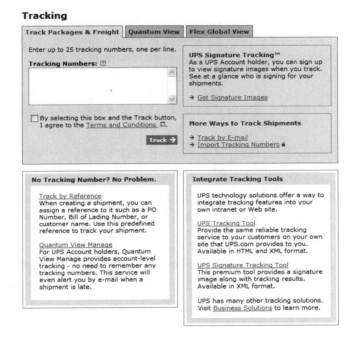

- **Rates and transit times**   By entering the weight and size of an item, as well as the delivery location, allows you to determine the postage rate as well as the expected delivery date and time for your shipment.

- **Order supplies**   Allows you to order shipping and packing supplies online for delivery to your front door.

- **Billing and payment**   Allows you to view and pay shipping bills online. Some carriers also offer rebilling and invoicing services as well.

- **Return services**   Lets your customers return items to you by completing an online form with their web browser. You can also preprint return labels when you know the recipient will have to return something to you.

- **E-mail notices**   Allows you to request that e-mail notices be sent to anyone you like—including yourself! These help recipients stay in the loop concerning delivery.

- **View, edit, or void shipments**   Allows you to see everything about your shipment online, and make changes as needed.

There will be other niche tools offered by carriers, but these are ones most commonly used for an e-shipping center.

note   *If you mail a lot of items through the USPS, you might want to consider a postage meter to help speed up mailing. The meter is a separate postage printing machine placed in your office; it prints postage directly onto your mail or onto an approved label.*

Insurance

Should you insure your shipments? Good question. Every shipment is different, and every carrier has different insurance options. They also vary in the types of delivery confirmation services they offer, although every carrier will offer at least a basic delivery tracking option.

If you are sending valuable merchandise through the mail, it might be worth the money to insure it against loss, damage, or theft. Remember, though, that you are only covering the item for the actual value—insurance won't cover any extra expenses involved in tracking the item or losses involved in a delivery that didn't make it on time.

Insurance can typically be purchased for a reasonable cost (the USPS, for example, offers insurance on items up to $500 for about $6.)

tip   *FedEx often runs online specials to save you money as incentive for using its online shipping services.*

Step 2: Create Your Profile

Once you decide upon a carrier, you need to create a profile or account with the carrier. This is pretty simple stuff; they will want your name, address, phone, payment information (so they can charge you for the services), and other basic business details.

Just fill in the blanks as the carrier instructs. You may be required to enter credit or credit card information to establish an account.

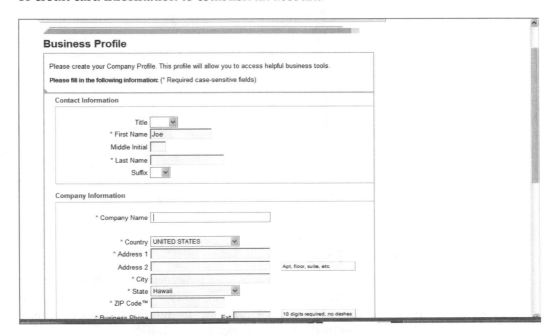

Once you enter this information and your account is created, the online system retains all the information you enter for shipments for at least a limited time. You also have access to all the online services offered by the carrier.

Step 3: Send Your Shipment

No matter which vendor you choose, there are some basic steps to follow every time you ship something.

Choose the Best Service for Your Shipment

Every shipment deserves the right service, so you want to find the best way to get your shipment to its destination on time. Even if you decide to use one carrier as your primary shipping provider, when you have urgent or bulky deliveries, it's a good idea to do a quick check online with a couple of carriers to make sure you're getting the best rate and delivery time for your shipment.

Each carrier offers an online service finder that helps you determine the right service for that carrier, and lets you find information quickly and easily. Don't be afraid to switch carriers once in awhile, even if you are convinced your chosen carrier is the best. You might be pleasantly surprised at new options a carrier is providing, or that your carrier's delivery time can be substantially beat by another carrier.

Choose a shipping service based on your budget and timetable.

Domestic Shipping   Calculate Domestic Rates

Service Options	Price	Speed *
Overnight Guaranteed Packages (Express Mail®)	$14.40 and up	Next Day
2-3 Day Packages (Priority Mail®)	$4.05 and up	2-3 Days
Ground Packages (Parcel Post®, Media Mail® & more...)	$2.81 and up	2-9 Days

* Days designed to be delivered depend on origin and destination.

International Shipping   Calculate International Rates

Service Options	Price	Speed *
Global Express Guaranteed®	$25.25 and up (documents) $38.00 and up (merchandise)	1-3 Days
Global Express Mail®	$16.25 and up	3-5 Days
Global Priority Mail®	$4.25 and up	4-6 Days
Global Airmail® (Parcel Post)	$13.25 and up	4-10 Days
Global Economy (Parcel Post)	$16.00 and up	4-6 Weeks

* Days designed to be delivered depend on origin and destination.

Use the Address Book

Online address books are provided by every carrier and are extremely helpful in saving time. With any carrier, however, delivery is only as good as the address provided. If your online address book is not up-to-date with proper names and addresses, your shipment can be delayed. Be sure to do a quick check of every recipient, especially if you haven't sent a package to that recipient for some time.

Adding new addresses to an online address book is very similar to adding them to your e-mail address book—name, address, and phone number are required, but beyond that, not much else is necessary, as you can see in Figure 6-2. You can add, edit, or delete contacts as needed. Each time you enter a new contact to create a label, the online address book will keep the information and store it for a limited amount of time (at least 90 days).

You can also keep a Ship From address online so that you don't need to keep filling in your return address information. Editing a Ship From address is easy and can be done with every individual shipment if you like, but the overall concept is to have one Ship From address that remains constant so that you aren't continually spending time on updates.

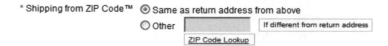

Figure 6-2

Each carrier offers easy-to-use online address books.

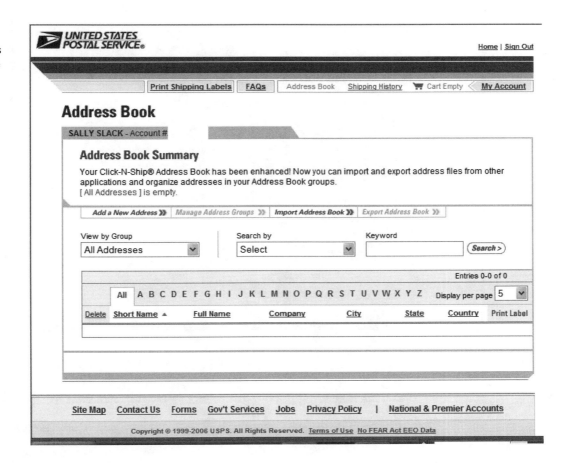

Creating online labels is very simple when you use the address book, too. The required information is dropped into the correct fields for you when you select a delivery address as long as you remember to mark the Save In Address Box check box, as shown in Figure 6-3. All you need to do is give the address a quick check the next time you use that address, in case information has changed.

Before you print a shipping label, you will be given a chance to review the label to ensure its accuracy. You will also have a chance to cancel the label completely before printing it. It's a good idea to print a sample label; most carriers offer this option so you can verify that your printer is able to print the label properly on the paper. It's a good idea to print two labels (one without postage) if your carrier doesn't offer packing slips. You can slip the second label into the package itself just in case the exterior label becomes damaged or unreadable.

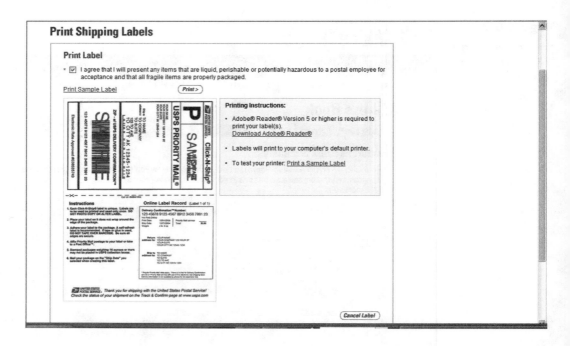

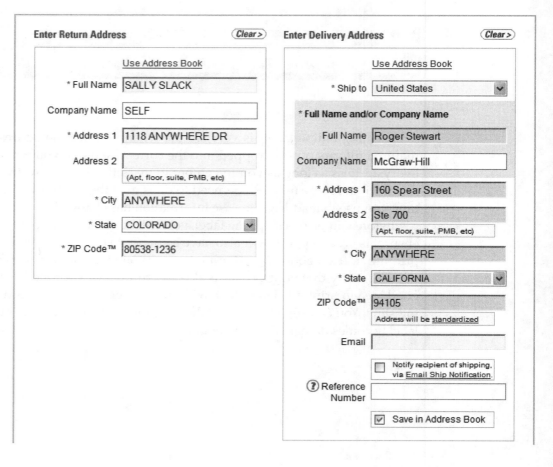

Figure 6-3

Checking Save In Address Book keeps the delivery address and contact information in your online address book.

tip   *Some carriers offer the option of importing address books or spreadsheets into the online address book.*

Prepare the Item for Shipment

If you can't use a standard box or envelope from your carrier, use a new box whenever possible to pack your items. The more often a box is used, the more it loses its shape and ability to protect your item. Any box should be free of punctures, rips, tears, or other damage. Every box should have a maximum gross weight printed on it somewhere; don't exceed that weight!

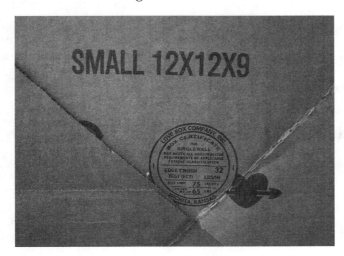

You should also be sure that previous labels or other previous shipment details are removed or at least hidden (use a big, thick black marker to cover old addresses) so that the carrier doesn't become confused about where the item should be delivered.

When you enter package information online (see Figure 6-4), you need to be as accurate as possible. Just because you underestimate the size or weight of a package doesn't mean the carrier won't come back to you for the extra postage required—or worse, ask your recipient for the extra postage.

Figure 6-4

Package information is easily entered online.

Enter Package Information

* Weight [   ] pounds [   ] ounces   Use total package weight

* Size Is your package larger than 84 inches in length and girth?   See Size Requirements
  ⦿ No ◯ Yes

* Shipping Date Thursday 01/11/07 ▾

* Shipping from ZIP Code™   ◯ Same as return address from above
  ◯ Other [   ] If different from return address
  ZIP Code Lookup

Note: If the weight you entered is less than the actual weight of the package, the Postal Service™ will require additional postage either at the time of mailing or delivery.

Special Guidelines

If you are shipping sensitive materials, be sure to follow the guidelines on your carrier's web site. Electronic media, for example, can potentially be damaged if not packed properly. Each carrier will have different guidelines for different types of items.

Heavy packages also have special guidelines. If the package isn't heavy enough to qualify for freight shipment but is still heavy (over 70 pounds or so), then you need to take extra care in preparing the item for shipment. Ideally, heavy items should be placed in boxes with stitched or stapled construction. Some carriers require the use of "heavy package" stickers to warn delivery drivers of the weight.

Freight shipments have completely different guidelines. Depending upon the shipment, you may be required to place your shipment on a pallet. If so, you are charged by the pallet instead of by the box. If you aren't sure whether your shipment requires the use of a pallet, contact the carrier's customer service.

tip   *UPS has strength guidelines for boxes posted on its web site.*

Schedule a Pickup

Scheduling a pickup is a pretty simple process no matter which vendor you use. While you can certainly deliver your packages to your vendor, you might want to go the next step and take advantage of this convenience.

- **DHL**   Enables you to schedule pickups for the same or next day. $3 per package is charged and an account with DHL is required (www.dhl.com.)

- **FedEx**   Enables you to schedule Express pickups for the same or next day; FedEx Ground and FedEx Home Delivery will schedule pickups for the next day and up to two weeks in advance. Freight services are available. Fees start at $4 per package and a FedEx user ID is required(www.fedex.com.)

- **UPS**   Offers same-day, next-day, and other scheduled pickups for all of its package delivery services. Up to 30 total UPS Ground and UPS 3 Day Select packages can be included in a single pickup. Between $2 and $4 is charged per package, depending upon the service selected, although extra charges could apply on weekends. Freight services are available, and anyone with a credit card can use the pickup services. Go to www.ups.com/pickup.

- **USPS**   Offers Carrier Pickup and Pickup On Demand Service. Carrier Pickup is free. You can schedule the service for the next postal day and include any number of packages in a single pickup. Anyone can use this service online, actually. All that's needed is the address so that the request can be sent to the proper mail carrier. Pickup On Demand costs $13.25 but allows you to send an unlimited number of packages in a single pickup. At least one package must be sent Priority Mail or Express Mail in either service to qualify the pickup, but you can include other letters and packages in the pickup. Same-day requests can be made and requests can be scheduled up to six days in advance as well. Both services can be set up online at www.usps.com/pickup.

> **tip** *If you primarily send packages locally, search the Yellow Pages for a local delivery service. You'll often get better rates than using a national carrier.*

Carrier Pickup

Send your package(s) with your carrier   *Please tell us what you think of Carrier pickup.* (Go >)

Next-Day Pickup (No account sign in.)

Pickup is needed the next Postal delivery day. (You may also schedule a pickup for the next Postal delivery day by signing into your account.)

Please provide a pickup address:

* Required Fields

* Address 1 [   ]

Address 2 [   ]
(Apt, floor, suite, etc.)

* ZIP Code™ [   ] ZIP Code Lookup

Edit/Cancel Next-Day Pickup   (Continue >)

Scheduled Pickup(s) (Account sign in required.)

Pickup is needed within the next three months. (You may also schedule a pickup for the next Postal delivery day.) Sign in to schedule, edit, or cancel pickups in the next three months.

Existing users: **New users:**
(Sign In >)   (Sign Up >)

Forgot your password?

Other Considerations

There are a few other things to consider when setting up an e-shipping center. For example, if you're ordering lots of plain boxes that must be purchased, consider ordering them online from a third-party vendor. Dozens of vendors are available and offer standard cartons, mailing boxes, tubes, mailing bags, and more online. Papermart.com, for example, offers nearly 800 different sizes of corrugated boxes (see Figure 6-5).

Figure 6-5

Numerous online stores offer boxes and other shipping materials at a discount and in bulk, including Paper Mart, whose web site is shown here.

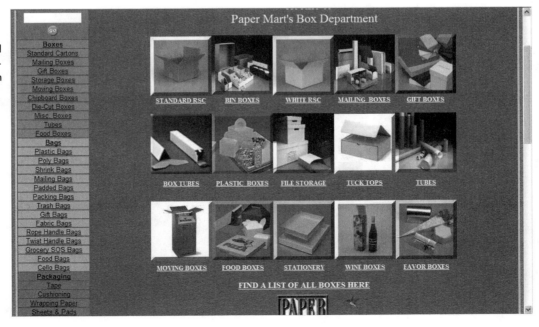

tip   *If you do a lot of bulk mailings, be aware that the USPS requires a permit for bulk mailings. You can obtain the permit online. Actual bulk mailing labels require the use of a postage meter.*

International Shipping

This chapter focused on domestic services but there may be occasions when you need to ship items internationally. Before you do, check with your carrier to be sure you understand its procedures. All four carriers mentioned in this chapter can handle international shipping on various levels, but some may be more practical for you than others.

For example, if an international customer needs to send an item back to you, DHL requires that you have a separate account set up to handle the return. Other carriers, such as FedEx, do not. Depending upon your needs and requirements, there may be other international factors that determine the carrier you choose. You may find that you want to use one carrier for domestic shipping and a second for international shipping.

Every single carrier mentioned here is anxious for your business. It's worth taking the time to look into the options they provide if you regularly mail items that require more than a stamp and a quick jaunt to the mailbox out front.

Part II

Take It On The Road

Get and Send
E-mail Anywhere

What You'll Need:

- Operating system: Windows XP, Windows Vista
- Software: None
- Hardware: Personal digital assistant
- Internet or cellular connection: Yes
- Cost: $0 to $40
- Difficulty: Easy

I know, you're addicted to e-mail. You want to check it all the time to make sure you haven't missed an urgent note from a client or your boss, and you want to send e-mails to show you are connected and responsive. This addiction is shared by millions these days—now that cell phones let us talk and send messages from anywhere a cell phone signal exists, we want to go to the next level with e-mail, too.

You don't need a twelve-step program for this addiction; you just need to know how to get and send e-mail no matter where you are. There are two pieces to this puzzle: you need a personal digital assistant (PDA) or a laptop, and you need to set up the PDA or laptop to send and receive e-mail. The PDA must be cell- or wireless-enabled.

With these two pieces in hand, you can be on the golf course and still working (it's true; my friend Joli does this all the time!) with no one the wiser. Let's face it, working from home has its benefits. One of those is freedom of movement—and if your movement happens to be away from your desk, that doesn't mean anyone else has to know.

tip *The price of smartphones dropped drastically in 2006, making them a reasonable purchase for home offices. Products with reduced prices include BlackBerry Pearl, BlackJack, Nokia E62, and the Treo 680.*

Step 1: Learn about PDAs

You've seen them. They are sitting around at Starbucks having coffee and typing furiously on a tiny device, confident and carefree. They are enjoying their work, and there is no reason you can't have one of those little devices, too. Personal digital assistants come in all shapes and sizes these days. They are handheld devices that started out as simple organizers in the 1990s but have evolved into devices that boast color touch screens, audio, Internet access, and wireless capabilities. It's literally computing functionality on the go.

Today, the devices becoming most popular are smartphones—mobile phones that send and receive e-mail as well as offer computing features such as word processing, spreadsheets, web browsers, and cell phone capabilities. Many people, however, prefer to use a separate cell phone with their PDA—they might use a BlackBerry or Treo, which have full keyboards as well as touchscreen input. The most current PDAs, such as the one shown in Figure 7-1, have an infrared port for connectivity and/or Bluetooth wireless capabilities. The use of PDAs is growing, with the most popular PDAs able to run either Windows Mobile, RIM BlackBerry, or Palm-based operating systems. Heck, you can even record your favorite television shows on some PDAs! That shows you how advanced these items have become since the early days of contact and calendar management.

Figure 7-1

T-Mobile MDA
smartphone

If you're doing a lot of work on large documents, you need a PDA that offers plenty of random access memory (RAM)—say, 64 to 128MB. If you just want to stick with calendars and reminders and a few e-mails, you'll probably be okay with 32 MB of RAM. Oh—always keep an extra battery on hand, too. There's nothing quite like running out of battery juice just before you hit Send.

You'll hear a lot of different terms for PDAs because a lot of different companies make them and want you to have their marketing phrase in your head. Pocket PC, for example, is a Windows Mobile PDA—but it's not a special kind of PDA.

Many PDAs have e-mail software preloaded, but if yours doesn't, you will need to add it. Typically, mobile phones and PDAs support POP3/IMAP services, methods that allow users to access e-mail from many different sources.

tip *Apple's iPhone can also be used to get and send e-mail through Internet connections.*

How PDAs Receive Data and E-mail

There are two primary methods for receiving e-mail on a PDA: real-time over the air and direct connection. Real-time access lets you connect directly to your e-mail account from your PDA. PDAs that use Pocket PC operating systems need ActiveSync software, which is typically included with your PDA. Direct connections download your e-mail from your PC onto your PDA; any replies or new messages you create on the PDA will be sent the next time you sync your device back to the PC. Data synchronization, or *syncing* as it's more commonly known, is the transmission of data to keep information current in two separate places. Syncing can be done in four ways:

- Through a cradle connected to a serial or USB port on your computer
- By an infra-red light beam
- Over a telephone modem
- Through a wireless or Bluetooth connection

In this project, we'll show you how to get your e-mail through a wireless connection.

tip *Sprint announced plans to launch the largest mobile wireless network (WiMax) in the United States by the end of 2007.*

Step 2: Create a Wireless Connection to the Internet for Your PDA

When you create a wireless connection to the Internet, you will likely need to pay for the service through your PDA provider. For example, the T-Mobile MDA smartphone that will be used in this project requires the addition of Internet services from T-Mobile for about $30 a month. That can be a bit pricey, but if you're on the road a lot and require real-time access to your e-mail, it's a useful service to have.

tip *More than 300 U.S. cities provide free or inexpensive wireless networks that run citywide. If yours is one of them, you won't need to hunt for a Wi-Fi hotspot again.*

Contact your service provider to set up the Internet services you need for your PDA. This can often be done online—go to your provider's web site and see if you can add it that way. T-Mobile, for example, allows you to add its Internet services package to your account online and then uploads the required software to your phone automatically. You shouldn't need to perform any setup or configuration tasks to get the Internet access, but you will need to initially enable it on your PDA using your service provider's instructions.

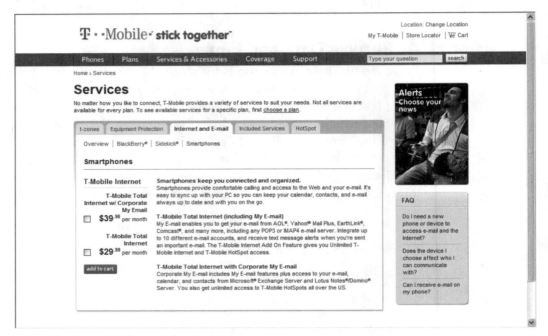

By the way, some of these Internet service packages include hotspot access, so you can use your laptop computer at wireless hotspots wherever you are. This might also include the ability to get certain instant messaging programs on your PDA, too. Other service providers have very simple packages for a few dollars a month that only provide limited Internet access; be certain that you understand exactly what's being offered before you sign up.

 Different packages work with different e-mail accounts. Be certain the one you sign up for will handle your account (Comcast, AOL, Earthlink, Microsoft Exchange, etc.)Both Windows XP and Windows Vista will work easily with most provider's Internet services packages.

Step 3: Set Up E-mail on a PDA

Mobile phone numbers often come with assigned e-mail addresses. If your PDA has this, you can already send and receive e-mail messages from anyone else with an e-mail address. This is a completely separate process from setting up your PDA to receive e-mail.

The process addressed in *this* project involves a direct connection to your regular e-mail inbox and outbox—the one that sits on your office computer and that you use every day. Different phones offer different ways to access your e-mail, so the steps for setting up e-mail on your particular PDA may differ from the ones provided here; you should check with your service provider for specific instructions involving your PDA.

There are literally dozens of e-mail providers just itching for your business, by the way. For most PDAs and home office users, you don't need to contract with any of them since your service provider already offers the same services.

It's helpful to see how simple the process can be on a PDA, so the steps to set up a T-Mobile My E-mail Mailbox on a T-Mobile MDA smartphone are given next as an example. Different e-mail providers have different setup instructions. Yahoo! Mail, for example, requires a subscription to a premium service to obtain remote or POP-3 access to mail accounts. Check with your e-mail provider if you run into any difficulties setting up e-mail on your PDA to be sure you have the proper account.

1. Turn on your smartphone.

2. At the Today screen, tap Set Up My E-Mail.

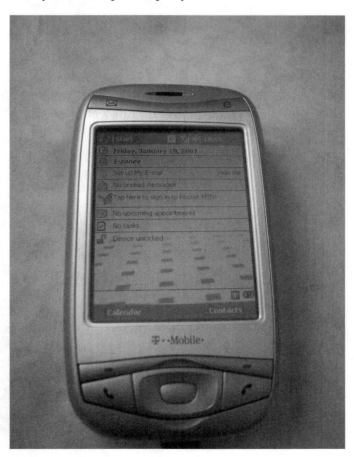

3. Tap Add A New My E-Mail Account.

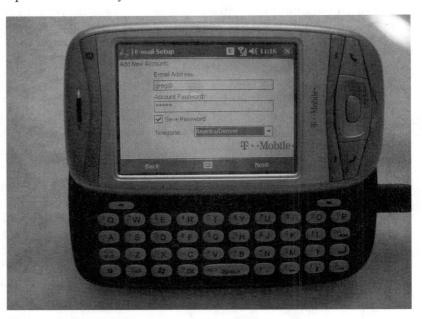

4. Tap Next.

5. Type in your e-mail address and the password you use for your e-mail account. The e-mail account you choose to use should be accessible using the POP-3 protocol, which is used to communicate between various mail servers like those from Earthlink or other Internet service providers (ISPs). Choose a time zone as well.

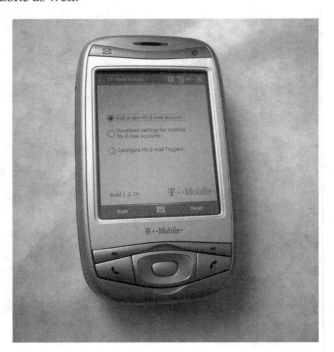

6. Tap Next. It may take several minutes while your account is set up, so be patient.

7. When the account has been created, tap Start.

8. Tap Messaging to access your account.

> **tip** Microsoft offers Direct Push wireless e-mail through Cingular. It is incorporated into Service Pack 2 for Exchange Server 2003 and used on some Windows Mobile 5.0 devices and above.

Step 4: Set Up Your Laptop to Get Wireless E-mail

If your e-mail is on an Exchange Server (common for corporate users) or you have the ability to get voicemail through your e-mail, you'll need to configure your laptop a little bit. This process isn't hard, but there are a few things you need to do before you can start typing away. First, your laptop must have a wireless card installed. Newer laptops come with these; older laptops require the purchase of one.

> **tip** If you have a web-based e-mail account such as Hotmail, Yahoo!, AOL, or Gmail, you don't need anything beyond a web browser and an Internet connection to access your e-mail.

1. Power on your laptop.

2. Check to see whether you're getting a network signal. This might be indicated by a green light on your wireless card or an icon on your screen.

3. Some locations configure the wireless networking card automatically. You will see a login screen, and required information (e-mail address, password, method of payment) will be required. Enter that information to obtain access to the wireless network you want to work on.

4. Click Start and click Programs.

5. Click Outlook Express.

6. Go to the Tools menu and click Accounts to open the Internet Accounts dialog box.

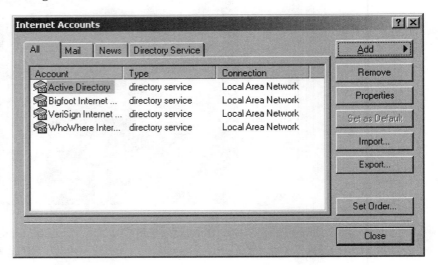

7. Click Add and then click Mail.

8. Type in a display name—this name will show on e-mails that recipients receive from you. Click Next.

9. Type in your e-mail address. Click Next.

10. Type in the name of the mail server that you use. (You might need to get this information from your ISP.) Click Next.

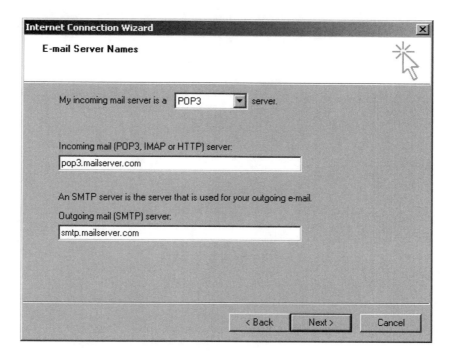

11. Type in the username and password you use to access the account. Click Next.

12. Click Finish.

You'll be back at the Internet Accounts window. Click the Mail tab; the account you just created should be there.

note *Learn how to set up your own wireless network in Project 23.*

This setup process might take as much as an hour or so, depending upon how explicit the instructions from your service provider are. My experience shows some of the providers assume you know an awful lot about technology; don't be afraid to give them a call and make them walk you through the process if you get stuck at any point. The ability to access your e-mail from anywhere will help you stay in touch as much as you want to—that's a big plus for anyone who works from home and wants to take advantage of the freedom that work environment can provide.

Set Up
a Mobile GPS

What You'll Need

- Cell phone, smart phone, or personal travel assistant
- Cost: $10–$799
- Difficulty: Easy

If you have ever become lost on the way to a client meeting, then you're a candidate for a mobile GPS. GPS stands for "Global Positioning System," a system that uses satellites to tell where a specific item is located on planet Earth. In most cases, the item is a person—you. GPS can instantly decipher your exact location on the planet and provide you with spoken and visual turn-by-turn directions to help you get to the next location you're heading to.

GPS navigation has been used for years in the marine industry and in the U.S. Armed Forces, but it's only been in, say, the last ten years that mobile GPS has become an affordable option for the rest of us. In the 1990s, for example, GPS maker Garmin offered handheld GPS devices for around $500 that the masses could place on the car dashboard. Car rental companies started offering cars with GPS a few years ago, which has given millions of drivers the opportunity to try GPS without buying their own device.

The options just keep getting better, however. Today, Garmin offers mobile GPS for your cell phone, smartphone, laptop, and PDA plus it has new products that it calls personal travel assistants. Other companies offer similar options and some products can even find you a hotel or a place to have lunch. Heck, even your dog can have his own GPS attached to his collar so you always know where he is.

The point to all this is that you, too, can have a mobile GPS. It doesn't have to cost a lot of money—although you can spend big bucks if you want—and it doesn't have to be difficult to set up. If you drive much at all, GPS navigation is a great option to add to your road warrior arsenal. For this project, we'll focus on GPS capabilities in cell phones, smartphones, and personal travel assistants.

tip *Cell phone navigation options link GPS satellites to phone company network coverage systems, so if you lose network signals, you lose your GPS capabilities, too. Choose a cell phone provider in your area with the lowest rate of dropped signals to get the best GPS coverage.*

Step 1: Understand the Options Available

There are dozens of providers and options available today for GPS navigation systems. GPS receivers rely on radio waves from satellites orbiting the Earth and use a combination of three satellites above you plus where you are in relation to those satellites to determine your exact location.

If your GPS receiver has a clear line of vision to the satellites, it works great. If it doesn't—if trees or tall buildings block it from any of the three required satellites—then it can't accurately locate your position or provide you with directions.

Cell phones and other devices work with GPS satellites through direct use or by downloading software that requires updates with the satellites.

Using Your Cell Phone for GPS Navigation

Cell phones operate similarly to landline telephones—you make and receive telephone calls on both. The difference is that cell phones work like stylish two-way radios—they send and receive radio signals from towers and base stations that are arranged into networks of cells. As you move around, you move from one cell to another with your signal strength increasing or decreasing depending upon your distance from a given base station. The towers transfer your signal from one base station to the next, as shown in Figure 8-1.

Figure 8-1

Cell phone signals are transferred between towers and base stations as you travel.

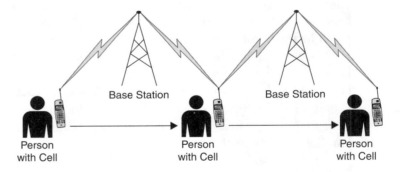

Almost every cell phone sold today has some sort of GPS receiving capability built into it, but not all phones have a full GPS receiver. Some cell phones understand programming languages and can subsequently offer turn-by-turn directions and information about businesses and attractions. A few even offer walking directions in addition to driving directions. Others don't understand programming languages and can only work like a tracking device. If you're not sure what your cell phone can do, contact your cell phone service provider and ask.

There are two basic ways to get GPS navigation coverage with your cell phone: by subscription, or by using specific software for your phone. Here are some examples of cell phone GPS subscription services at the time of writing:

- **Nextel/Sprint** Offers MapQuest Find Me with subscriptions starting at $3.99/month A sample cell phone with GPS is shown in Figure 8-2.

- **Verizon Wireless** Offers VZ Navigator through a download process and charges by airtime minutes used for navigation activities

- **T-Mobile** Offers GPS-enabled Google Maps through downloads and a combination of Internet services that start at $29.99/month

- **Cingular** Offers TeleNav GPS Navigator starting at $5.99/month

Figure 8-2

A wide variety of cell phones offer GPS navigation capabilities.

You can also download or purchase GPS software for your cell phone. TeleNav, for example, offers GPS software that can be used with each of the major cell phone carriers starting at $9.99/month. The type of phone you own makes a difference in whether a service like TeleNav can work for you, but it might be worth taking a look at. Go to www.telenav.com for more details.

tip   *The Federal Communications Commission (FCC) now requires that precise location information be provided for any cell phone used to make a 911 call. This means that cell phone manufacturers must incorporate a GPS receiver into every cell phone they offer. Cell phones manufactured prior to 2005 were not required to have this function.*

Using a Smartphone for GPS Navigation

If you haven't seen or used a smartphone, you're probably wondering what the big deal is. Essentially, smartphones combine the functions of a normal cell phone with a handheld computer. It has an operating system, local storage, and e-mail functions, and can make and receive phone calls—plus, it's programmable. These devices also typically feature a touch screen.

Carrying a single device that can handle all of these functions is appealing; more and more people are taking a look at these phones as they consider purchase options. They are offered by a variety of manufacturers, and a vast majority of new cell phones on the market today are actually smartphones, especially the more expensive products. Nokia, for example, ships more than 10 million smartphones annually.

Smartphones can integrate with GPS receivers or can be connected to existing portable GPS receivers. Because of its operating system capabilities and programming options, you can even create your own GPS software to use on your smartphone. It's much easier, however, to just use the GPS options already on the market unless you're a pretty skilled developer.

Here are some smartphones with GPS options available on the market:

- **Palm GPS Navigator Smartphone Edition for Treo phones**   Preloaded with TomTom Navigator 6 software and costs $299.

- **BlackBerry 7100i GPS Smartphone**   The addition of a GPS chip lets you download very detailed map imagery on-the-fly. It typically sells for $199 with a two-year service agreement.

- **Mio A701 GPS smartphone** An internal GPS receiver combines with MioMap 2.0 mapping software for a smartphone that retails for about $500.

- **Motorola Q Smartphone** You can download CoPilot Live 6 GPS software to avoid cell phone service fees. Retails from $199 to $419.

If you prefer to integrate your smartphone with a GPS receiver, it's pretty easy to do. Garmin, for example, offers the Garmin Mobile 20 (see Figure 8-3). This uses a phone mount that has a built-in GPS receiver and Bluetooth technology to work with Nokia, Windows Mobile, and Treo 650 smartphones. The phone mount attaches to your automobile windshield with a suction-cup; when you're in the car, you just drop your phone into the mount for navigation capabilities to begin. The phone mount also acts as a phone charger.

Figure 8-3

The Garmin Mobile 20, a sophisticated phone mount with a GPS receiver built-in, is shown here with a Treo smartphone.

Using a Personal Travel Assistant for GPS Navigation

Personal travel assistants are handheld GPS receivers that can be mounted in your car *or* carried easily in your purse or briefcase. Don't confuse them with the standard GPS receivers that simply mount on a dashboard and are not designed to be used out of the car. Personal travel assistants double as portable digital assistants in some ways, too—some offer MP3 player options, for example, and other features such as language guides or currency converters.

These products are completely separate from any cell phone service providers—you buy the personal travel assistant directly from a manufacturer like Garmin. However, some of these products do work with Bluetooth-enabled cell phones—Garmin's Nuvi 360, for example, can be used as a hands-free speaker for cell phones with wireless capabilities. It can also be used to make and receive phone calls but only when paired with your Bluetooth cell phone.

Personal travel assistants also work with your personal computer. For instance, you can typically download music and image files directly onto your personal travel assistant. Don't confuse these with fully loaded portable digital assistants, though. Personal travel assistants don't come with keyboards or other computer-like functions.

Because these items are relatively new on the market, they are also relatively expensive choices. By comparison, smartphones are a good choice if you need phone and GPS capabilities, but personal travel assistants offer much more than standard GPS navigation options. If you travel often and throughout the world, it might be a good idea to take a personal travel assistant with you.

Here are three examples of personal travel assistants:

- **Garmin Nuvi 360** Offers preloaded maps, alerts for speed zones, language guides, travel guides for restaurants and hotels, an MP3 player, and hands-free calling when integrated with a Bluetooth cell phone. Retails for about $800. See Figure 8-4 for a look at its interface.

- **Magellan RoadMate 860T** Offers a built-in MP3 player and photo viewer, and options include the TrafficKit, which provides live traffic incident reports and road work updates. Retails for about $800.

- **TomTom GO 910** Offers a built-in MP3 player, traffic updates, and text-to-speech options. Retails for about $550.

Figure 8-4

The Nuvi 360 from Garmin can be mounted on the dashboard of a car or carried in a purse, pocket, or briefcase.

Step 2: Map Your Next Trip

For this project, the steps really consist of determining whether you want a cell phone with GPS, a smartphone with GPS, or a personal travel assistant. Once you make that determination, you will work through your cell phone service provider (if using a cell phone or smartphone) to obtain the GPS software and services you need. Personal travel assistants require little set up, if any at all—you just buy the product and turn it on in most cases.

I wish it were harder so I had more to write about, but the process is truly that simple. That makes sense, however, since GPS is all about simplifying your life. If you are on the road much at all, why not take the time to explore these different options?

tip *GPS navigation products typically locate you initially by ZIP code. Entering your ZIP code also helps the system find the local restaurants, hotels, and other travel items you might be looking for.*

Project 9

Use Office Applications from Anywhere

What You'll Need

- Operating system: Any
- Software: None
- Hardware: None
- Internet connection: Yes
- Cost: $0
- Difficulty: Challenging

Has this ever happened to you? You're out of the office and realize you need to make a simple change to a document and mail it. So you get in the car, drive home, make the 30-second change, and send the document to whoever needs it. Then you get in the car and drive back to wherever you were—or you ditch the off-site excursion completely because it's now ruined.

Maybe it didn't happen quite like that, but I'm betting there have been times when you wished desperately that you could just access your documents quickly and easily from anywhere without a lot of hassle. If so, then you need to know about web-based applications.

There are ways to access your own computer remotely (see Project 10) but web-based applications are a very different concept. As long as you have an Internet connection, you can work—create and review documents online, collaborate with colleagues in real-time, and secure and back up your data. I know, it sounds too good to be true. But keep reading, and you'll see why web-based applications are poised to compete with Microsoft Office in a big way.

Every Major Desktop Function Is Online, Waiting for You

Most people today use Microsoft Office, and it's a great suite of office applications. Word, Excel, PowerPoint—these are all terrific programs that are easy to use. Expensive, but good stuff nonetheless. These types of desktop office applications are installed onto your computer, which means you can only use the application on that computer.

In contrast, web-based office applications are typically free and are *not* installed onto your computer. Instead, you access them by going to a web site on the Internet and working directly from that web site. The applications and your documents are stored on that site, which means they are instantly retrievable as long as you have an Internet connection, a keyboard, a screen, and a web browser.

Web-based applications are changing the way we think about data because the concept of owning a computer and its related applications and data is being replaced with the concept of simply owning the data. And if you access it through the Web, your data is never stuck somewhere that you aren't.

For every desktop application you now have, there is probably a web-based counterpart. There are five primary reasons to consider using these applications:

- No installation of software is necessary. You subscribe to the service to obtain access to the application. And no installation means there are no incompatibilities between the software and your operating system. Remember, the software doesn't run on your operating system, it runs on the Internet.

- The cost is substantially less than traditional software, and free in many cases. In fact, nearly every provider offers at least a free "test drive" to give you a taste of how the application works before you commit to anything.

- Storage and server space is provided.

- Sharing, editing, and collaborating in real time are standard features. Multiple people can access the same file at the same time through individual web browsers.

- Data is often more secure than on the average desktop computer because web-based application companies use highly reliable, redundant data storage farms to store your files and offer extensive data backup services.

It's only mentioned briefly, but the online collaboration aspects of web-based applications offer you the ability to work with multiple people at the same time, creating and exchanging in a real-time environment where ideas can be immediately exchanged and revisions instantly made. Working from home sometimes makes it difficult to work collaboratively if everyone doesn't have the same software—web-based applications typically provide you with a URL that you send to others. As long as they can access the Internet, anyone can collaborate with you.

The benefits make it hard to ignore these applications, especially if your home office is more of a base for you than a place where you spend your entire day.

note *So if everything's free, how do these companies make money? Simple—by offering you extended services and options that require ongoing subscriptions. The basics pull you in, and the ease of use keeps you coming back for more. At least, that's the bet these companies have placed.*

Step 1: Determine Your Needs

Once you decide to try a web-based application, you need to determine what you will use it for. For example, if you want to write documents that others can review online, you need a word processing program. But if you work on spreadsheets, you need a spreadsheet program. Maybe you give a lot of presentations, or you collaborate with people on documents and could use a space for online collaboration. There are two ways to go about finding the right approach for you: use applications on an individual basis from multiple providers or use a suite of applications offered by a single provider.

Either method is fine. Some people prefer the individual approach because they like the way a spreadsheet works from one place but don't care for the corresponding applications in the office suite. Others don't want to be bothered with finding a variety of different applications for the perfect item so they stick with the suite.

Either way, you will want to test drive applications to see which ones you prefer. At this writing, none has the complete power and agility of Microsoft Office, but several try to emulate the look and ease of those applications and include at least the best parts of them. If you can be flexible on certain features and functions, you'll have better luck finding a web-based application that suits you.

Step 2: Research and Choose Applications

Since even Microsoft is jumping into the web-based applications game with Windows Live, the level of competition is increasing in this space for your business. At this writing, however, Windows Live is a set of online services, not actual web-based applications. It won't be on the list for you to review as a result, but don't be surprised if Microsoft suddenly comes out of the woodwork with a web-based version of Office 2007 somewhere down the road.

Several of these applications are compatible with a variety of other office applications or allow you to save documents in industry standards such as DOC, XLS, or PPT. If you plan to distribute the documents you create on a wide basis, look for applications that offer strong compatibility features.

Here is the list of web-based applications for you to review; there are probably others you will find on the Internet. The idea is to take a look at each of these so you get the feeling for which applications offer the features and functions you need.

Web-Based Office Suites

When a group of applications works together and is offered by a single source, it is called a "suite" of applications. When the suite is typically used by office workers, it is called an office application suite. Three of these suites are worth reviewing: OpenOffice.org, ThinkFree and WebAsyst.

OpenOffice.org (www.openoffice.org)

This suite is free to download and includes five applications: word processing, drawing, presentation, database, and spreadsheet. It's a good choice for users with basic needs and limited budgets. One important feature is its compatibility with almost all other major office suites.

note *There are two different office application products with very similar names: OpenOffice .org and Open Office Suite. OpenOffice.org is the free application mentioned here; don't confuse it with other information you may see on the Internet about Open Office Suite. It may sound strange to call an application by a dot org name, but trademark issues require the differentiation between the two similarly named products.*

ThinkFree (www.thinkfree.com)

With this suite, you get three Microsoft Office–compatible applications: word processing (shown in Figure 9-1), spreadsheet, and presentation. Like OpenOffice.org, this suite is also free, plus it comes with 1 GB of free online file storage. ThinkFree's web site is user-friendly and offers a publishing feature that makes it easy to publish documents to web pages, blogs, and elsewhere.

Figure 9-1

ThinkFree's word processing interface looks very similar to Microsoft Word.

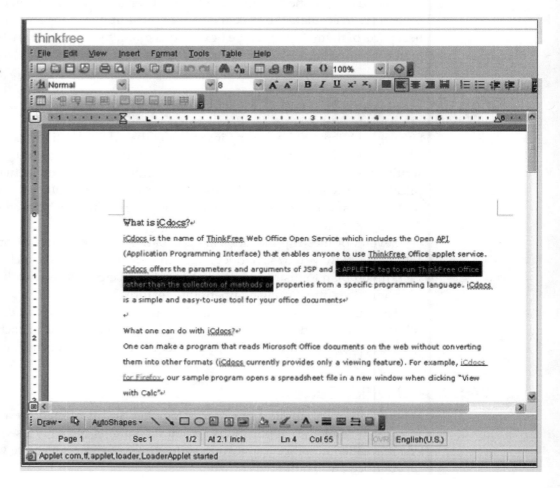

WebAsyst (www.webasyst.net)

Seven applications are offered by WebAsyst: a contact manager, e-mail, project manager, issue tracker, web publishing, online document management, and notes. Offers a free account that never expires although you will need to upgrade your account to a paid version in order to take full advantage of all the applications.

Individual Web-Based Office Application Providers

It's easy to try individual applications and mix or match them for your needs. If you go this route, you might find yourself using a couple of different providers, so weigh that fact against the ease of going to one place for everything. The following are listed in alphabetical order; this is by no means a complete list, as new providers are appearing regularly.

Google Docs & Spreadsheets (docs.google.com)

Google Docs & Spreadsheets lets you create basic word documents and spreadsheets. You can create documents from scratch or upload existing files (your formatting and formulas should come across intact). Google also offers Gmail—web-based e-mail with plenty of free storage and a good search engine (of course!) to help you find messages quickly.

Kiko Calendar (www.kiko.com)

Besides online calendar sharing, Kiko Calendar offers an integrated contacts list, iCal and vCard support (calendar file formats), appointment reminders, and instant messaging.

Num Sum (www.numsum.com)

If you need a simple, sharable web spreadsheet, check out this one. You can create the spreadsheet, designate others who can edit it, and even set it up as an RSS feed that publishes changing content automatically for you.

Plaxo (www.plaxo.com)

Try Plaxo if you create e-cards, want to search contacts and your calendar from your phone, or manage large numbers of contacts. Basic content is free but advanced features will cost you.

Remember the Milk (www.rememberthemilk.com)

To manage your life a little better, Remember the Milk is a decent task management program for setting due dates and reminders, generating maps to see where tasks are located, creating lists, and more.

Ta-da List (www.tadalist.com)

For simpler task management, try Ta-da List. It's not fancy but it lets you create simple lists to help remember tasks.

Thumbstacks.com (www.thumbstacks.com)

If you work with presentations very much, take a look at Thumbstacks.com. With it, you can create presentations and show them in Firefox or Internet Explorer browsers. It's a basic presentation program without frills such as slide transition, animation and actions, sounds, or video, but it gets the job done.

Writeboard (www.writeboard.com)

This is a minimalist writing application but it's so easy to use that many people don't care about all the features it doesn't offer. This is especially useful in collaborative environments, but caution: Writeboard is not compatible with other file formats except to export as a text file and can only be used with Internet Explorer 6.x, Safari, and Firefox browsers.

Yahoo! Mail (mail.yahoo.com)

Yahoo! offers a detailed address book, calendar, and notepad along with its e-mail services—it's free, and it's compatible with mobile devices.

Zoho Show (www.zohoshow.com)

Need more than Thumbstacks.com provides? Try Zoho Show. It lets you import existing PowerPoint and OpenOffice.org presentations, insert shapes, export to HTML for offline viewing, and use several other nice features.

Step 3: Try Out a Web-Based Application

Now that you know what web-based applications are and have had a chance to think about the type of application you might want to work with, it's time to try one out. Because it's so simple to use, we chose Writeboard for this exercise.

Create a Writeboard

To create a Writeboard, follow these steps:

1. Open your Internet browser (be sure you're connected to the Internet!) and go to www.writeboard.com.

2. In the Create A Writeboard box, shown in Figure 9-2, name your writeboard.

3. Assign your writeboard a password.

4. Enter your e-mail address.

5. Check the I Agree To The Terms check box. (Read the terms first.)

6. Click Create The Writeboard.

Figure 9-2

Creating a writeboard takes just seconds.

Your writeboard will appear on the screen and an e-mail will arrive in your inbox with the URL for your writeboard as well as the password you designated. Any time you need to locate the writeboard, you simply use the URL and password indicated in the e-mail.

Place Content on Your Writeboard

To place content on your new writeboard, place your cursor in the large empty text box and start writing (see Figure 9-3). If you want to format your text, use the formatting guide to help you make bulleted or numbered lists, headers, and bold or italic font. I told you this was minimalist—those are your only formatting options, and you'll get the hang of them very quickly.

When your content is entered, click Save This Writeboard.

note *If you want to keep the writeboard easily accessible, you can save it to your browser's Favorites.*

Access an Existing Writeboard

There are two ways to access an existing writeboard. The first is to click the URL in the automatically generated e-mail you were sent. Enter your password at the prompt and the writeboard will open.

The second method is to open it through your browser's Favorites if you saved it there.

Figure 9-3

You can start entering content as soon as the writeboard is created.

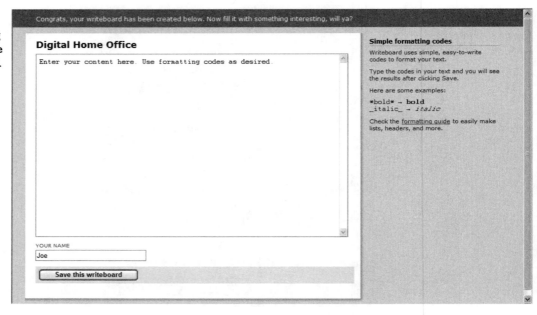

Collaborate with Your Writeboard

On the home page for your writeboard, notice that there are several links and a couple of buttons, as shown in Figure 9-4. Some of these links and buttons are described next.

Figure 9-4

Writeboards are easy to edit and use for collaboration purposes.

Invite People to Collaborate

Once you have added content to the writeboard and have saved it, others can add comments to it. But they can't do it until you let them know where your writeboard is, which do as follows:

1. Click Invite People.

2. Enter their e-mail addresses where indicated.

3. Click Send Invitation.

Recipients will receive an e-mail with the writeboard URL and password.

Edit this Page

Anyone who accesses your writeboard can make edits by clicking the Edit This Page button. They enter the new text or make changes as desired, and then click Save As The Newest Version.

If the edit was very minor, the editor can select Minor Edit, Don't Save A New Version. If this is selected, the Save As The Newest Version button changes to Save Over The Current Version and changes will not be logged as a new version in the version control pane. Try both options so you can see how version control appears on the screen.

Add a Comment

If readers don't want to edit the content, they can still make comments for everyone to see:

1. Click Add A Comment.

2. Add the comment in the text box provided.

3. Click Add This Comment.

The comment will now appear immediately below the original text.

Step 4: Start Using Web-Based Applications

It's not easy to change your mindset when you've been using desktop applications since you brought home your first personal computer. But if you work outside your home office very much—or want to!—then you owe it to yourself to give a couple of these applications an honest try. Start with one that you know you need onsite or offsite—a calendar, maybe, or a word processing application. Use it for a few weeks and gauge how often you were onsite and offsite, but still getting your work done from any location. If you're satisfied with that first application, build your web-based applications portfolio and get serious about working from anywhere.

Today's home office doesn't have to be located in the home, you know. No one *really* has to know that you're at Starbucks with your laptop or at an Internet café on a Greek island, do they?

Remote Control: Remotely Connect to Your PC or Get Help

What You'll Need

- Operating system: Windows 2000, Windows XP, or Windows Vista
- Software: None
- Hardware: None
- Cost: $0
- Difficulty: Advanced

So you're out of the office and you need a file on your computer because you don't use web-based applications. The file needs to be revised immediately and e-mailed to a client or boss, but you won't be back in the office for hours. Don't panic—I have a fix for you. It's Remote Desktop Connection, standard in more recent Windows operating systems.

If you have never used this type of connection, you're going to be surprised at how simple it is to set up. If you have used one of these before, you're going to be grateful I reminded you of it. It's a technology that allows you to sit at a computer in one place and connect to a second computer in a different physical location. You can see and use all the programs available on the second computer, just the same way you would if you were actually sitting in front of it. While you are connected remotely, the remote computer screen on the computer you are accessing will appear blank—so if you're at home working remotely on a computer at a downtown office, no one will be able to spy on you.

People use Remote Desktop Connection for a variety of reasons: working remotely, collaborating with others (try accessing your computer from a colleague's office, for example, so you can work together on projects), and console sharing, which is done when multiple users work on the same computer.

Cool, huh? Yeah, I like it too. There are a few prerequisites, though, so be sure to check those before you begin the actual connection steps.

note *The Remote Desktop Connection software is installed with Windows XP and Windows Vista. If you have a different Windows operating system (Windows 95—Windows 2000), go to www. microsoft.com/windowsxp/downloads/tools/rdclientdl.mspx to download the software needed (it's free).*

Step 1: Check that the Prerequisites Are Satisfied

Connecting to a remote computer is very easy as long as the following items are in place:

1. The remote computer must be turned on.

2. The remote computer must have a network or Internet connection.

3. Remote Desktop Connection must be enabled on the remote computer. We'll cover this in the next section.

4. You must be working on a computer that has access to the remote computer, via either the Internet or an actual network connection.

5. You must have permission to connect to the computer. This means you must be on the list of users for the remote computer. If it's your computer, you are probably on the list.

caution *Remote Desktop Connection has some limitations between operating systems. If you are using Windows Vista, for example, you cannot use Remote Desktop Connection to connect to computers running Windows XP Home Edition, Windows Vista Starter, Windows Vista Home Basic, Home Basic N, or Home Vista Premium. You can create connections from those editions, however.*

Step 2: Set Up the Remote Computer for Connection

Once your prerequisites are complete, you're ready to set up the remote computer for access. I'll give you two sets of instructions here: one for Windows Vista and one for Windows XP.

Using Windows Vista

1. Click the Start button.

2. Click Control Panel.

3. Click System And Maintenance. Careful here—it's easy to click one of the lines below (Get Started or Back Up) and think you clicked System And Maintenance, but you'll go to the wrong spot.

note *Depending upon how you have set up Windows Vista, you may be taken directly to Step 4 and be able to bypass Step 3 altogether.*

4. Click System.

5. In the left Tasks pane, click Remote Settings. This opens the System Properties dialog box.

6. Under Remote Desktop, select one of the following:

   - **Allow connections from computers running any version of Remote Desktop (less secure)**   Choose this option if you don't know which version of Remote Desktop Connection other people are using.

   - **Allow connections only from computers running Remote Desktop with Network Level Authentication (more secure)**   Choose this option if you know that connections to your computer will be made using Windows Vista.

7. Click Select Users. In the Remote Desktop Users dialog box, click Add. This opens the Select Users dialog box, where there are two actions to complete.

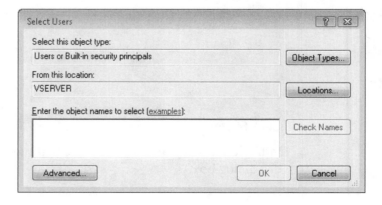

8. If the location shown is not the one you want, click Locations and browse for the location you want to use to search for users.

9. In the Enter The Object Names To Select section, type the name of the user you want to add. Click OK. If the name is not recognized by your computer, you may need to set up a separate user account for that person before they can be added. If it is recognized, it will be displayed in the Remote Desktop Users dialog box.

note *Remote Desktop Connection in Windows Vista uses Network Level Authentication (NLA). You can download NLA as a service pack for computers that run some of the earlier versions of Windows. Go to www.microsoft.com for more details.*

Using Windows XP

1. Click the Start button.

2. Click Control Panel.

3. In the Control Panel, double-click System.

4. In the System Properties dialog box, click the Remote tab.

5. Click Select Remote Users.

6. In the Remote Desktop Users dialog box, click Add. This opens the Select Users dialog box, where there are two actions to complete.

7. If the location shown is not the one you want, click Locations and choose the location you want to use to search for users.

8. In the Enter The Object Names To Select section, type the name of the user you want to add. Click OK. If the name is not recognized by your computer, you may need to set up a separate user account for that person before they can be added. If it is recognized, it will be displayed in the Remote Desktop Users dialog box.

note   *Remote Desktop Connection automatically locks the computer being accessed so that it can't be used in your absence. You can unlock the computer by pressing* CTRL-ALT-DEL.

Step 3: Access a Computer by Using Remote Desktop Connection

Once you've set up the computer for Remote Desktop Connection use, you're ready to go somewhere and use it. Just make sure the system you are using is compatible with the system you're accessing and then follow the directions here.

Using Windows Vista

1. Click the Start button.

2. In the Start Search box, type **Remote Desktop Connection**.

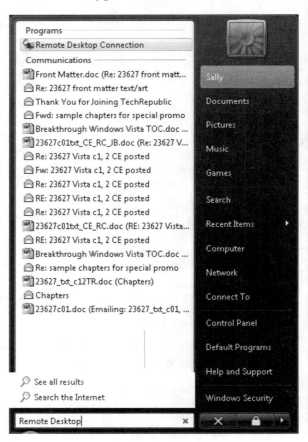

3. When the program appears, click it.

4. When the Remote Desktop Connection dialog box appears, type the name of the computer you will be connecting to. You can also type in an IP address here instead of a computer name.

5. Click Connect.

Add Users to Windows Vista

1. Click the Start button.

2. Click Control Panel.

3. Double-click User Accounts.

4. Click Manage User Accounts.

5. Click Add and follow the prompts.

tip *Don't know your computer's name? Click the Start button and then click Welcome Center. The computer name will be at the top of the window.*

Using Windows XP

1. Click the Start button.

2. Click All Programs | Accessories | Remote Desktop Connection.

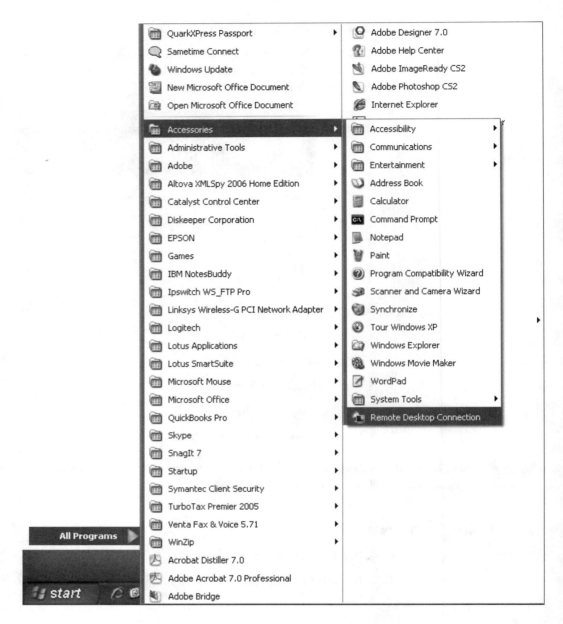

3. When the Remote Desktop Connection dialog box appears, type the name of the computer you will be connecting to. You can also type in an IP address here instead of a computer name.

4. Click Connect.

The remote computer's desktop will appear on your screen as shown in Figure 10-1.

Figure 10-1

The remote computer's desktop as it appears on your desktop—you can enlarge or reduce it as needed as well as open and use any programs or documents on the remote computer.

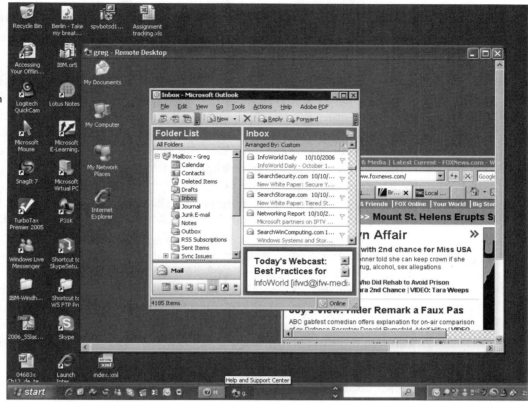

Add Users to Windows XP

1. Click the Start button.

2. Click Settings.

3. Click Control Panel.

4. Double-click Users And Groups.

5. Click Add Users and follow the prompts.

note *Depending upon the user account requirements for your computer, users may be required to use a password for Remote Desktop connections.*

There's nothing special involved once you have opened the connection—just start working and remember to save your files. One word of caution: the connection is a separate window on your desktop, so be careful when you're closing program windows if you're working on both desktops at the same time. It's easy to close the wrong window and discover you have closed out your remote connection.

Another Remote Control Option: Remote Assistance

There is another Windows feature that can come in handy when you need help with your computer or if you need to ask someone for help on a document or project you're working on. It's Remote Assistance, another built-in feature on more recent Windows operating systems.

This feature is perfect when you need help on your computer but are miles away from co-workers or anyone who can help. You just send an e-mail request for help and then both you and the other person can see your computer screen at the same time. You can even share control of the computer with the person you've asked for help, and both of you can control the mouse pointer. It works by connecting the two computers so that two people in different locations can work on the same computer at the same time.

For example, let's say that you are having trouble with a formula in Excel. You can send a request for assistance to a buddy who is an Excel expert and he can hop onto your computer, fix the problem for you, and then go on his merry way. Or maybe you want to work on a document with a friend but don't have collaborative software—this is a great collaborative tool because both of you can work on your computer at the same time. Friends or colleagues can also send requests to you for help, by the way—so if you start using this, be prepared for your buddies to catch on and ask for help in return. You can also offer to help others if you know they are having trouble with something. For purposes of this project, we'll assume you are asking someone else for help.

note *Both you and your helper must have Internet connections.*

Using Windows Vista

1. Click the Start button.

2. In the Start Search box, type **Remote Assistance.**

3. When the program appears, click it.

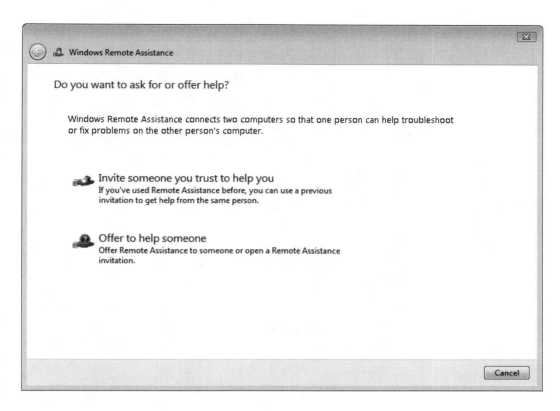

4. Click Invite Someone You Trust To Help You.

5. Click Use E-mail To Send An Invitation, unless you use web-based e-mail—then click Save This Invitation As A File.

6. Type in a password of at least six characters. Retype it for confirmation.

7. Click Next. Remote Assistance will open an e-mail for you with an attach-ment for the recipient to open to access your computer—it could take a minute or two if your e-mail program is not open.

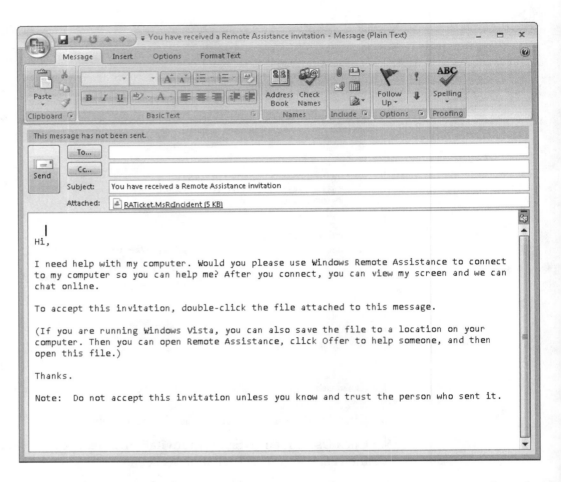

8. In the To box, type the e-mail address of the person you are sending the request to.

note   *You must add the password you specified to this e-mail. The automated process does not do that for you.*

9. Click Send. You'll see a Windows Remote Assistance window appear on your screen advising that you are waiting for an incoming connection.

> **tip** *You must remain connected to Remote Assistance while waiting for the other person to respond. If you cancel the request or close the Remote Assistance window, the invitation becomes invalid.*

If the other person receives your request for help, you'll be asked whether or not they can connect to your computer. Click Yes. To disconnect from the session, click Disconnect in the Connected To Your Helper dialog box.

Using Windows XP

1. Click the Start button.

2. Click All Programs.

3. Click Remote Assistance. The Help and Support Center window will appear.

4. Click Invite Someone To Help You under Remote Assistance.

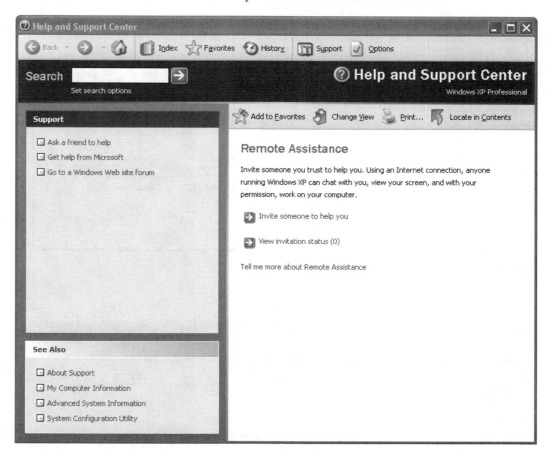

5. Choose a contact using Windows Messenger or e-mail.

6. Click Invite This Person.

7. You'll be prompted to enter contact information again, as well as type in a personal message. You do not need to enter this information if you don't want to.

8. Set a time limit for the expiration of the invitation.

9. Be sure Require The Recipient To Use A Password is selected. Then type in a password and confirm it. Don't forget to add the password to the invitation!

10. Click Send Invitation.

Your invitation will be sent to the recipient. They will receive an invitation as shown in Figure 10-2. After they accept, you will receive a notice on your computer as shown in Figure 10-3.

Figure 10-2

When someone accepts your request for help, they will be prompted to enter the password before being granted access.

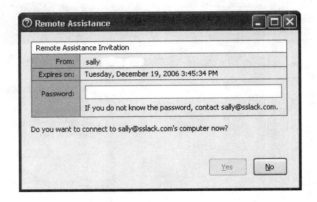

Figure 10-3

When your request for help is accepted, you will have one last chance to change your mind about allowing someone else access to your computer.

note *You may receive warnings that a program is attempting to access Microsoft Office Outlook if you chose the e-mail option. This is okay—it's just your system using Outlook to send the invitation.*

Other Options You Can Use

In both operating systems, Remote Assistance provides the ability to chat, pause, and send files. While it's not the most effective method for instant messaging, these options in Remote Assistance can be extremely helpful when you want to say something to the other person or perform another task. This feature is so under-used and unknown that most people won't have a clue what you're doing the first time you use Remote Assistance. It might be a good idea to give someone a quick heads-up before asking them to help you for the first time.

Don't be afraid to use this feature, or to try out Remote Desktop Connection. Both are great tools for working remotely and very easy to use. It may seem like a lot of steps to follow, but after the first time through, you'll be able to do either one very quickly. Now get to work!

note *Your helper can ask to take control of your computer. If this happens, a message will appear asking for approval before control transfers over. While he or she has control, you will see everything being done on your computer but you will also be able to work on your screen. When you want to stop sharing control, just click Stop Sharing.*

Part III

Communicate with Clients and Employers

Project 11

Turn Your PC into a Virtual Conference Room

What You'll Need:

- **Operating system: Any**
- **Software: Yes**
- **Hardware: None**
- **Internet or cellular connection: Yes**
- **Cost: $49/month or by per-minute basis (varies)**
- **Difficulty: Easy**

Got a meeting? Gotta talk face-to-face but you're in Aspen and the rest of the group is scattered throughout the country or world? No problem. Get your team together in an online video conference. These types of calls used to be quite complicated—video conferences needed special equipment that was very expensive, and the equipment had to be set up by specialists. Today, though, conference calling is as easy as setting up a webcam (see Project 3) and using powerful web solutions that make it easy to take care of business and launch meetings directly from your calendar or even instant messaging program.

Using simple software that pulls everyone into the same conference with simultaneous phone and web access, you can deliver presentations, share control of your desktop (and remotely control others), view attendees, and get the job done without spending thousands on travel.

Typically, not all attendees are shown at the same time in the conference call, but the presenter and anyone else who is speaking is typically shown. This type of face-to-face call is helpful because participants can see who is speaking and feel more comfortable speaking up themselves.

Now, let's be honest: Not everyone you work with will feel comfortable with a video conference call. That's probably because they don't realize just how simple these conferences can be to set up or just participate in—and they may not have a webcam yet. It's worth taking the time to hold some hands as you walk potential participants through webcam setup and an initial web conference. Plan for extra time (especially at the beginning of your conference) to allow for connection problems or people who might simply be resistive to learning a new process. But once you guide a group through one of these calls and participants see how painless the process really is, you'll have a gaggle of converts on your hands.

tip   *A web conference uses the Internet as a meeting room to share documents and collaborate online by allowing others to see your computer screen. Video web conferencing is the use of video during a web conference.*

Step 1: Research Providers

There are a lot of providers out there that can help you with online conferencing, although not all of them offer video. Some charge a flat monthly or annual fee, while others allow you to pay-per-use at a per-minute rate. The software that you'll download shouldn't take much time; each provider will supply any software required.

Take some time to look through several providers to determine which interfaces look the easiest to use, as well as to compare costs and features. Here are a few you can take a look at:

- **WebEx (www.webex.com)**   Offers web conferencing, video web conferencing, and online meeting services. Offers long- and short-term purchasing options, including instant pay-per-use with options between $0.02 and $0.33 per minute per person in the conference. Ten attendees are allowed for unlimited time; additional attendees can be added for a fee.

- **Windows NetMeeting (www.microsoft.com/windows/netmeeting/)**   Available as part of Windows XP and earlier versions of Windows only; offers web conferencing and video web conferencing. There is no cost to use this feature if you have it with your operating system. It can hold 30 or more attendees.

- **Microsoft   Office   Live   Meeting   (www.office.microsoft.com/en-us/ livemeeting)**   Offers web conferencing and online meeting services including Internet Audio Broadcast but does not offer video at this writing. Can handle up to 1000 attendees. Charges a $3000 one-time fee, plus additional fees depending upon the licensing option chosen.

- **Raindance (www.raindance.com)**   Offers web conferencing, video web conferencing, and online meeting services. You must call them for individual pricing and attendee information.

- **GoToMeeting (www.gotomeeting.com)**   Offers web conferencing and online meeting services but does not offer video. Monthly and annual plans are available starting at $39/month. The flat fee allows up to ten attendees per meeting.

tip   *Many programs also provide a transcript of the conference to all participants. The transcripts will include public meeting notes taken, as well as the agenda, starting and end times, a list of participants, and other details of the meeting.*

Step 2: Set Up a Meeting with WebEx

For this example, we'll use WebEx Meeting Center. You can try it out free for 14 days; a valid e-mail address is required to activate the account. When you've entered that information, you'll receive an e-mail from WebEx with your username and password information, along with a Start Meeting button. For the record, I set up this first meeting in less than five minutes.

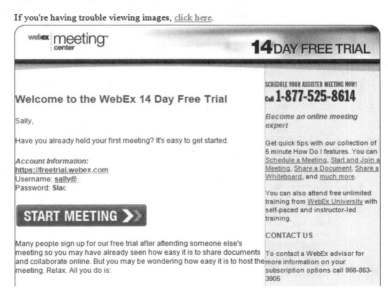

1. Click the Start Meeting button.
2. Click Install when the WebEx Client dialog box appears.

3. The Meeting In Progress window will appear. Do *not* close it. Continue to wait for the Meeting Manager to open. When it does, a Join Teleconference dialog box will also appear—note the call-in phone number, meeting number, and attendee ID number. You'll give these numbers to others to join the audio portion of your conference.

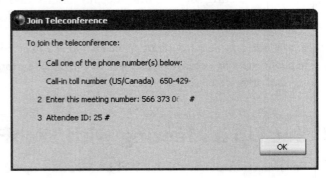

4. Click OK in the Join Teleconference dialog box.

The meeting is ready for others to join. Since this is a trial meeting, calendar invitations were not set up. If they were, others could simply join your meeting from that calendar invitation. In this case, however, participants will be invited by going to the Participants menu on the toolbar.

1. Click Invite.

2. Select By Email | Use Your Local Email Program. An e-mail invitation will automatically be generated with all meeting information included in it.

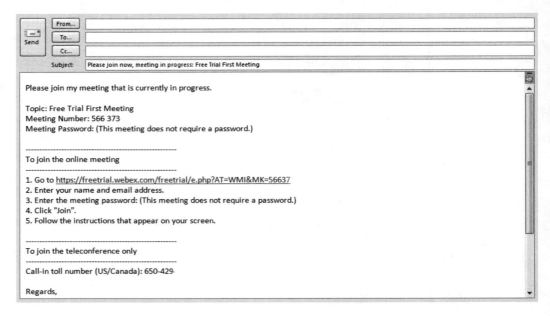

3. Enter the e-mail addresses of participants in the To line. Click Send.

When participants select the link in the e-mail, they will be taken to a web page that shows all relevant meeting information and allows participants to join the meeting by clicking a Join Now button. As each participant joins, their name will appear in the host's list of participants.

Including Video in Your WebEx Conference Call

With WebEx and other video conferencing software, you can turn video options on or off. In addition, there are two types of video that can be used in a meeting: single-point video or multipoint video.

Single-point video allows just one participant to send video images. The presenter or another person selected by the presenter are the only ones who can send live video in this case. Multipoint video allows several participants to send video images. This number is usually limited; WebEx, for example, allows up to four people to send video at one time. If this option is chosen, any participant up to the specified limit can send video.

To include video in a WebEx conference call, you must first be designated as a presenter:

1. Go to the Meeting menu on the toolbar. Click Options.

2. Select the General tab.

3. Select the Video box.

4. Select Single-point or Multipoint Video.

5. Click OK.

Your webcam needs to be set up before you can use video conferencing features. But once it's set up and you've selected the video options you want in your conference, there shouldn't be anything else you need to do—your computer and the web conferencing program should take care of launching the video during your conference.

tip *In the Video pane, select the Options button and increase the video frame rate if your video seems jerky. Changing video resolution to High will also give you a larger video picture in WebEx.*

Sharing Documents and Using the Whiteboard

If you want to show certain documents to all participants or even your desktop and applications on your computer, you can easily do it with the Share menu on the toolbar. Just click Share, then select the item you want to share. The Share feature also lets you open a whiteboard for collaborative conferencing—type or draw what you want, then let others in on the action too. The WebEx whiteboard can be displayed at various magnifications and can be saved or printed, too.

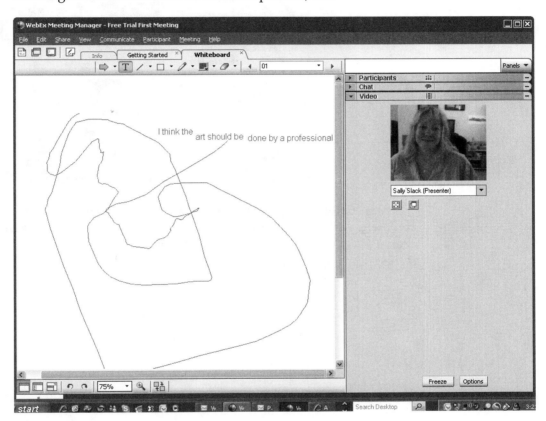

Chatting During the Conference Call

WebEx and other programs come with instant chat features that usually allow you to have private chats with other people in the conference. This feature is helpful because someone may have a quick comment or need to ask something that doesn't need to be shared with the entire group. You can also use this feature to send brief information to everyone in the conference or perhaps a certain group of participants in the call.

During a meeting, the presenter simply has to specify chat privileges for all participants; these privileges determine to whom participants can send messages. So, for example, as a participant, you might be able to send messages only to the host or to another participant on a private basis—settings can be established to cover a variety of situations.

To send a chat message, you simply type a message in the Chat panel, select the recipient, and click Send.

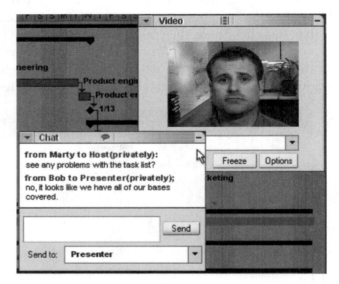

Web conferencing is truly so easy to use that once you participate in one of these conference calls, you'll never want to travel again. It may take a little pushing to get clients or colleagues on board with you, but be persistent. Sometimes all people need is the opportunity to try something new so they can discover the geek within.

Project 12

Talk for Free on Your PC

What You'll Need:

- **Operating system: Windows 2000, Windows XP, or Windows Vista**
- **Software: VoIP service software**
- **Hardware: Speakers and a microphone, webcam is optional**
- **Cost: $0–$50/month**
- **Difficulty: Easy**

If you are tired of paying the phone company for all your calls, listen up: You don't necessarily have to any more. It's called Internet-based telephony—Voice-over-IP (VoIP)—and it allows you to use the Internet connection you are already paying for to use your PC to make calls to other PCs or to landline telephones (a standard telephone). Best of all, this technology is now quickly becoming available for use on Wi-Fi and landline telephones—call a PC, have a PC call you, use your PC to call your grandma's house, whatever. You can make calls from your home office or down at the neighborhood Starbucks with the Wi-Fi phones; all you need is a wireless Internet connection (called a Wi-Fi hotspot).

Plus, you can use your PC or the phones for free conference calls and even send files through them as you chat. All of this is typically free, as long as you are calling PC-to-PC. Otherwise, services charge for PC calls to landlines. But if your business associates in, say, England or Mexico, have a PC, get ready to start taking business calls with your PC instead of a phone to save big bucks. As long as your business partners or clients are using the same VoIP service you are, you can call them free of charge.

Most of these services automatically encrypt your calls so that they can't be intercepted, by the way, and they typically offer video services, too. If you have a webcam (see Project 3), you can take advantage of the video options during your calls. Even if the other party doesn't have a webcam, they can still see you—which may or may not be a feature you like! Other service features typically include:

- Contact lists
- Basic or group chat

- Customized profile settings
- Conference calling
- Address book import options

Additional features (voice mail, call forwarding, etc.) are available depending upon the provider you choose. Interfaces (what you see on the screen) vary but, for the most part, are simple to use. Let's get started—it's never too early to start saving a little money!

note *VoIP establishes connections between users by using IP (Internet Protocol) "addresses." Every Internet connection has its own address—VoIP services track and log usernames and IP addresses so that all you have to do is click on a contact name and your computer handles the dialing process.*

Step 1: Choose a Service

When you choose a VoIP service, there are a few things to consider besides cost. For example, fax capabilities aren't standard with most of these services (some do have them, however, but typically charge for the convenience). Do you often make conference calls? If so, your service needs to be able to handle that. Do you need voicemail? Phone numbers to give out? Call blocking or forwarding? Different services offer different options but none seems to offer everything that a business could possibly need. It may be that you still need a dedicated fax line, for example, in combination with a VoIP service.

My recommendation is to take a look at the services you currently receive from your telephone provider, determine which ones you actually use regularly, and then search for a VoIP provider based on those needs. One other comment—consider what your business associates and clients use. If the majority use a particular service, it may be worthwhile to at least install that service even if it's not the one you primarily will use (calling within the same service, whether locally or internationally, is free, and right now some services don't offer the option to call from one service to another).

Here are some providers to consider, but remember that new ones are popping up all the time, so this is by no means a complete list. Conduct an Internet search for VoIP providers to see everything out there. Most work with any Windows operating system; if you have an older operating system such as Windows 95, however, you might need to perform some upgrades to take full advantage of the features a provider offers.

The following table lists providers that offer a minimum of PC-to-PC voice calling; other features are provided as shown. Some have additional features not listed here—Gizmo, for example, allows calls to multiple voice programs so you can talk PC-to-PC with people who are not using Gizmo. Use this table as a sample to get you started on finding the right service for you.

note   *VoIP is a highly competitive industry. Just because a provider doesn't have a service listed here doesn't mean that the service won't be offered soon—VoIP providers are constantly upgrading and offering new features.*

Provider	Video	Conference Calling	Instant Messages	Dial to a Landline	Dial from a Landline	Voicemail
Google Talk			X			X
Gizmo		X		X	X	X
Skype	X	X	X	X	X	X
Sunrocket		X		X	X	X
Vonage		X	X	X	X	X
Yahoo! Voice	X		X	X	X	X

tip   *Most VoIP services do not offer emergency dialing services.*

For your convenience, here are the web sites for the providers mentioned in this project:

- Vonage (www.vonage.com)
- Gizmo (www.gizmoproject.com)
- Yahoo! Messenger with Voice (www.voice.yahoo.com)
- SunRocket (www.sunrocket.com)
- Google Talk (www.google.com/talk)
- Skype (www.skype.com)

For this project, Skype (see Figure 12-1) is the VoIP provider of choice. Why? Many of my colleagues use Skype, which makes every call to them a free one for me whether they are in Europe, China, or the United States. It has pretty decent sound quality and a very simple interface that almost anyone can figure out without help, and the desktop and Wi-Fi phones available for purchase mean that I can literally use Skype anywhere there is an Internet connection.

Skype has partnered with companies that make both wireless and landline telephones. Some of these phones even offer both options in one phone—you can make and accept calls from computers or landlines from the same phone.

note   *This project can be done with Skype on a Macintosh, Linux, or Windows PC. At this writing, however, Skype still had video limitations for Macs, and contact lists, for example, couldn't be copied from one operating system to another on the Mac OS2.*

Figure 12-1

Skype is one of the most popular VoIP services available right now.

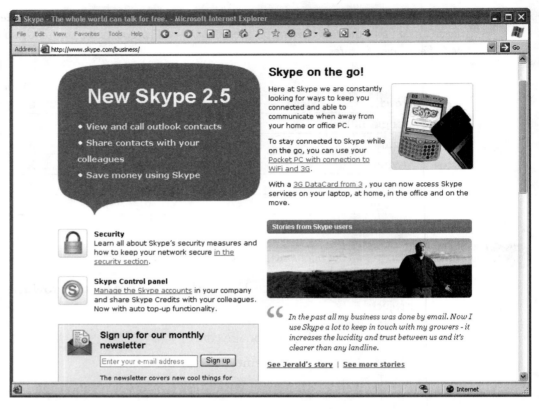

Step 2: Download the Software

Once you have selected a service, you need to download it from the Internet. Each service will have a Download section where you typically click a button and follow the prompts provided. Before you click the button, however, check the System Requirements section for the software.

Most VoIP services recommend a broadband connection for the best results—if you don't yet have that, you'll want to get it.

When you're ready, click the Download button and wait for the setup instructions. You may see a dialog box similar to Figure 12-2 that asks whether you want to run or save the file—click Run. When the download is complete, most programs provide a setup wizard of some sort. This is the easiest way to complete setup—follow the prompts to install the program, and click Finish or Close at the last prompt.

You now can open your program, either by accessing it through the Start button and selecting Programs or All Programs or by clicking an icon on your desktop or in your system tray depending on the options you selected during the installation process.

Figure 12-2

Follow the prompts to install your VoIP program properly.

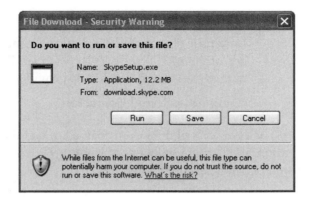

Step 3: Create a Contact List

Now that your program has been installed, you need to have someone to talk to, right? To do that, you need to tell your program the people you want to call. Every program has a toolbar menu (File, View, Help, etc)—in this toolbar should be a Contacts option. In Skype, the Contacts menu allows you to add, search, import, and send contacts. While the steps may be slightly different depending upon the software you have chosen, steps for adding a contact should go something like this:

1. Click Add A Contact. A dialog box like the one shown in Figure 12-3 will appear.

2. Enter the name (nickname or full name) or e-mail address of the person you want to add.

Figure 12-3

Potential contacts are shown according to the information you provide.

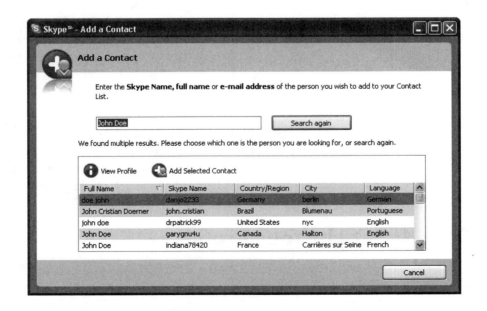

3. Click Search.

   Depending upon the accuracy of the information you entered—and the number of people on the service with similar information—you will see contact names that match the details provided. Find the name you want.

4. Click Add Selected Contact.

The contact will then appear in a contact list. Clicking a name lets you see information about that contact as shown in Figure 12-4, and you can make a phone call directly from the contact list.

Figure 12-4

With a contact list, you simply click a name to dial that person.

Importing contacts is a process that allows you to search your e-mail address book to find friends, family, and colleagues who already use your VoIP service (see Figure 12-5). The names and e-mail addresses are downloaded into your program and added to your contact list without much effort on your part.

Step 4: Set Up Your Profile

Every VoIP service has a Profile section. Profiles are the details that other users on your service see, for example, when they do a search and try to find you. In Figure 12-3, notice that most users have a country or city provided—that sort of information is entered

Figure 12-5

Skype allows you
to import contacts
from Microsoft Office
Outlook.

into your profile and helps others differentiate between you and your doppelganger in
another country. Profiles only offer the details you authorize, so you can enter as much
or as little information as you like.

In Skype, you can access your profile through File | Edit My Profile. This com-
mand brings up a My Profile window similar to that shown in Figure 12-6. Enter the
details you are comfortable with sharing publicly and click Update.

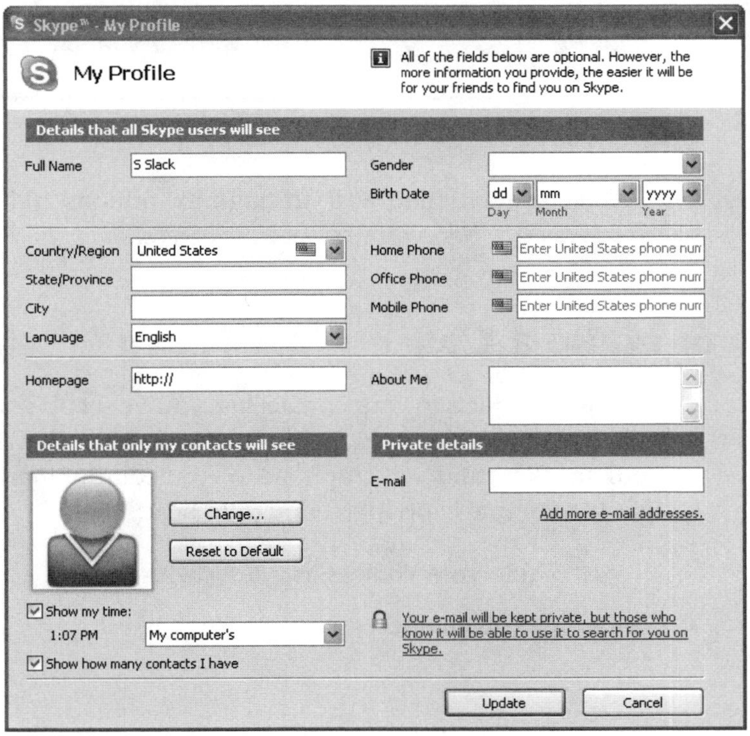

Figure 12-6

Entering details into
your profile allows
others to find and
contact you quickly
and easily.

Step 5: Establish Options

Another important section to review before making calls is the Options section. In Skype, go to Tools | Options to open the window shown in Figure 12-7. See the left pane that lists a variety of options, such as Sounds and Video? When you select an option in that pane, the information on the right side of the window provides you with choices for customizing all kinds of things, from the sound made when someone calls you to whether the program should automatically start when you start Windows.

Figure 12-7

Options are established according to your preferences.

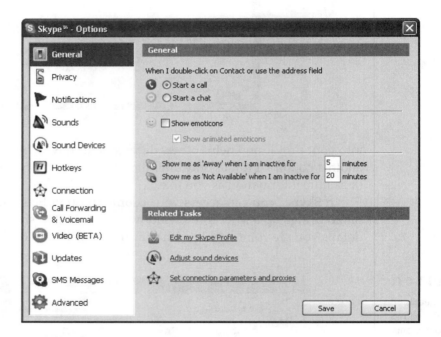

Take some time to walk through the options and make selections based on your preferences. When you're done, click Save.

Step 6: Make a Call

You have contacts in your contact list, you've set up your personal options, and you've established a profile . . . now it's time to make a call. First, be sure you have connected your speakers and a microphone to your computer and that they are turned on—and that the volume is up high enough to hear! Then:

1. Go to your contact list.
2. Select a name.

3.   You have three choices to dial:

●   Double-click the name to automatically dial.

●   Right-click to bring up a menu—select Start A Call.

●   Click the big green button at the bottom of the window as shown in Figure 12-8.

Figure 12-8

As you wait for the other person to answer, you will hear a ring just like you do on a landline.

4.   Wait for the other person to answer.

5.   Start talking.

If you wanted it to be more difficult, sorry. It's really that easy once your program has been installed. If the other person isn't available, they won't answer or the system won't put the call through. Most programs show a contact as unavailable if they are not online; simply pay attention to the icons next to a contact's name to determine their online status.

Make a Call to a Landline

If you are calling a landline and the person is not on your contact list:

1.   Go to the Dial tab.

2.   Be sure you have purchased Skype credit. If you haven't, click Buy Skype Credit and follow the prompts.

3. Enter or select the country you are dialing to.

4. Enter the phone number by using the onscreen dialpad or your keyboard.

5. Click the Dial button.

Answer a Call

Is your computer ringing? To answer it, simply click the Answer button on the incoming call window that has appeared on your screen and start talking, just as you would on any other phone.

Other Considerations

When you use a VoIP service like Skype, there are other aspects besides PC-to-PC calling that you'll want to consider taking advantage of.

Chat

Chat features are fairly standard across VoIP services. These are really just instant messaging programs that can be used whether or not you are talking with someone in a voice or video chat.

PC-to-Landline Calls

To call ordinary phones with Skype and other services, you typically need to buy credit with the service. This can usually be done with a credit card and sometimes even a PayPal account. Some services charge a flat annual or monthly fee to make PC-to-landline calls, while others charge by the call and number of minutes used. Skype offers North American users an "unlimited" option, which allows unlimited calls to any phone in the United States and Canada for $29.95 a year, for example.

Once you have deposited money into the credit account, you can make all the calls you want using a dialpad on your screen as shown in Figure 12-9. Replenish the account as needed.

Add Skype to Your Existing Phones

Skype offers a lot of phone products, but Uconnect is one product you may really want to look into if you decide to go with Skype for your VoIP service in your home office. It's a VoIP adapter that offers caller ID and connects to your existing corded and cordless phones.

Figure 12-9

Purchase credit and make your call with an onscreen dialpad to any phone in the world.

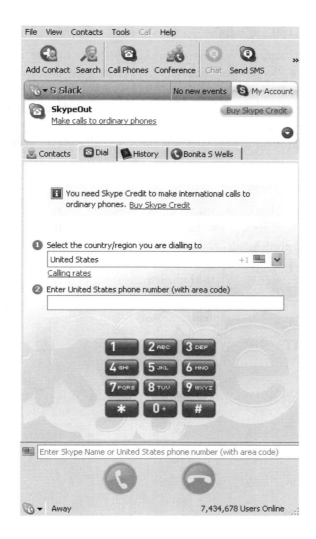

Get a Phone that Can Handle Skype and Landline Calls

The Products section of the Skype web site offers a variety of telephones that can connect to your laptop, be used in Wi-Fi networks, and make both free Skype calls and normal landline calls.

The Small Business section of the site also offers products designed for business users—landline telephones that can use Skype, speakerphones, headsets, Skype webcams (but you don't need a *special* webcam for Skype), and a Bluetooth wireless Internet Calling Kit.

note *VoIP phone services do not typically offer emergency calling (911).*

Landline-to-PC Calls

You can get your own standard phone number with Skype so that friends who don't have Skype can simply call you on their landline—and you can pick up the call on your PC or Skype phone. You do have to pay for this service (3- and 12-month subscriptions are available) but it comes with free voicemail. The best part is that you can choose any area code you want—give the "local" number to colleagues in another state and make it easy for them to call you for free.

Conference Calls

To make a conference call with Skype, go to Tools | Create A Conference Call. A dialog box appears with all your contacts. Select the contacts you want to include in the conference call, and click Start.

That's all there is to it—download the program that's best for you and start chatting for free. What are you waiting for?

Project 13

Create Your Own Wiki Collaborative Space

What You'll Need:

- **Operating system: Any**
- **Software: None**
- **Hardware: None**
- **Cost: $0**
- **Difficulty: Challenging**

Do you have a lot of ideas that you want to share with others? Are you knowledgeable in topics that others usually aren't? Do you enjoy collaborating with others? If you answered yes to any of these questions, creating a wiki might be a project for you.

A wiki is a web site you create that also allows others—strangers, people you know, *anyone*—to easily edit your pages. All these people tinkering in your wiki site are part of a community of volunteers who have an interest in your topic or project. Passwords can be applied to restrict edits to a certain group of people but most wikis allow anyone viewing the site to make edits.

Some people refer to wikis as databases because they typically have lots of pages connected via hyperlinks and offer some search capabilities, but a wiki is not a database, at least not in the truest sense of the word. A wiki is ridiculously simple to create—and requires zero knowledge of HTML, that pesky programming language that is typically the foundation for a web site. The use of minor text-formatting instructions is usually required, but those instructions are quick and easy to learn as you create your wiki.

Edits are usually made in real time so they appear instantly online. Every edit made is stored for the life of the wiki, which lets you check edits anytime you want. Incorrect edits can also be removed, however, with a simple move back to the original page.

There are lots of business uses for wikis—it can be a place to post project communications and milestones, for example; an interactive web site for your clients or employees to post comments, suggestions, files, etc.; or a company intranet. Typically, a wiki has unrestricted access (no registration required) so that it's easy for others to access. Of course, that means it's easy for anyone to see the information you're posting, so be careful when posting sensitive information.

Most wikis are based on web servers called *wiki engines*, although they can be part of a private LAN. There is also a version of wiki called a peer-to-peer (P2P) wiki where the wiki site is stored directly on your computer. P2P wikis are rare at the writing of this book but are expected to gain prominence in the next few years.

Some wiki engines provide strong content control that monitors every page in a wiki to maintain quality. This type of system automatically sends a notification warning of changes to wiki pages so validity of new edits can be verified.

note *The downside of wikis is that vandalism of a site can easily occur. Protections can be established, though, if you are worried about abuse. If you become aware of someone trying to vandalize your wiki, you can arrange for your wiki engine to block the user by IP address or username.*

Step 1: Choose a Wiki Engine

Once you decide to create a wiki, you need to choose a wiki engine to work with. I'm assuming now that you don't have a private server to work on, so this project focuses on creating a wiki on a public wiki engine. Many wiki engines offer the wiki software free to create a wiki, although some do charge fees. There are dozens of wiki engines to choose from. My recommendation is to take your time and search the Internet not only for wiki engines, but for sites that use them. Eventually, you will find one that satisfies your creative juices as well as fits your business needs.

Test Drive a Wiki

A guy named Ward Cunningham is credited with the creation of wikis. He describes a wiki as a "body of writing that a community is willing to know and maintain." If you are not sure what a wiki is, take a few minutes to browse these sites for examples. The chances are good you have already visited a wiki and just not realized it.

- **www.wikipedia.com** This site uses the MediaWiki wiki engine and is a simple, text-based wiki that allows embedded images, as shown in Figure 13-1.

- **www.ecologee.net/pmwiki.php** This site uses PmWiki as its engine, which offers advanced features such as "skins" to customize the look and feel of the pages, as shown in Figure 13-2.

Figure 13-1

Wikipedia's home page is a simple and effective use of text.

Figure 13-2

Some wiki engines offer "skins" to dress up wiki sites.

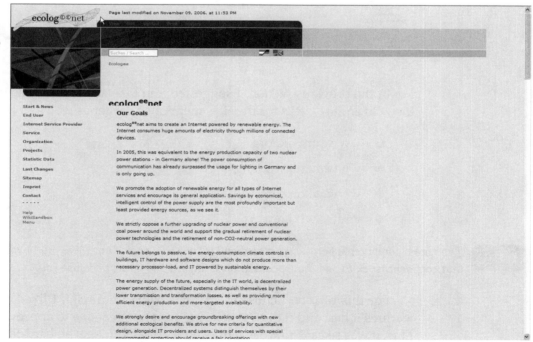

- **http://losangeles.wikia.com/wiki/Main_Page**   This site uses the Wikia wiki engine, which offers image integration and many other features, as shown in Figure 13-3.

Figure 13-3

The Los Angeles wiki is set up with tables, images, and text.

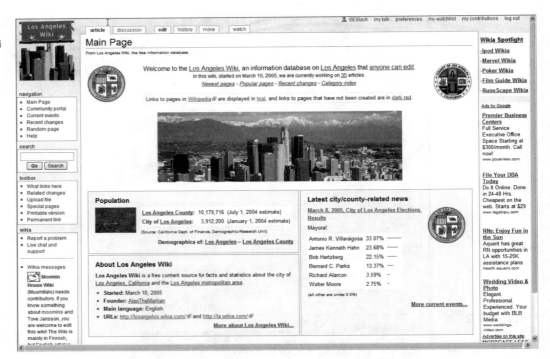

In the previous section, I suggested you take a look at a few web sites. Here are the wiki engine URLs for the sites mentioned earlier as well as a few more:

- www.pmwiki.org
- www.mediawiki.org
- www.wikia.com
- www.kwiki.org

note *If you are a computer superuser, go ahead and try any wiki engine out there. But if you're not that confident, stick to one that speaks in plain English and doesn't confuse you.*

For this project, I chose to create a Wikia mini-wiki. I liked all the options and features it has, and it didn't make me wait for someone to approve my wiki concept. Plus, it was so easy to work with—no coding language, no hard-to-follow installation instructions (there was nothing to install), and no strange languages to decode.

Considerations

When you review wiki engines, you need to think about the purpose of your wiki. Some engines expect your wiki to have a large potential audience; others don't care about that.

Next, what's your timeframe? A few wiki engines want to review your request for a new site over a period of weeks; others allow you to instantly download their software and get a site going within the same day.

A third consideration is the content you want to post. If you have a lot of images, then a text-based wiki isn't for you.

Finally, do you want to host the wiki or do you want it hosted somewhere else? Some wiki engines ask you to download software that will stay housed on your computer as you create and edit your site but others maintain all that on their servers. The more you place on your computer, the more complicated creating a wiki gets.

note   *A mini-wiki is created with a targeted or small audience in mind. If successful, they can become full-fledged wiki sites at the discretion of wiki engine administrators. These are great for project communications and working with individual clients.*

Step 2: Create Your Wiki

If you have chosen to go the long route and download software to your computer, you need to follow the download and installation instructions from your wiki engine. But if you're like me and simply want to create a site and see where it takes you, there is typically nothing to download. You do, however, usually have to create a user account and log onto the wiki engine. This lets the engine track you and confirm who you are.

To create a mini-wiki on Wikia, I followed these steps:

1. Go to the Wikia home page at www.wikia.org.
2. Log onto my account.
3. Click Try Out A Mini-wiki At Scratchpad Wiki Labs.
4. Type the name of the project in the box provided, shown in Figure 13-4.
5. Click Create.

Figure 13-4

Creating a mini-wiki can be done in minutes with Wikia.

help   discussion   edit   history   move   watch

Help:Make a new wiki

To make a new wiki within the Wikia **Scratchpad Wiki Lab** just type the name of your project in the box below and press "create".

Type your wiki title here
Create

See Scratchpad Wiki Labs for more info.

Want a new wiki in a right-to-left language? (Persian, Arabic, Hebrew, etc) - Use the new Right-to-Left Scratchpad!

Step 3: Add Content to Your Wiki

It's smart to read any tutorials your wiki engine provides. These usually offer tips for formatting text and adding things like bullets and numbered lists, as well as directions on how to link to other wikis or external sites.

Next, gather your thoughts about what you want to write. If you want to work on your text and come back to it later before posting, go ahead and do that in Word or some other word processing application. But if you're comfortable writing on-the-fly, just start entering your content, as shown in Figure 13-5.

Figure 13-5

To enter content, you just start typing in the text box.

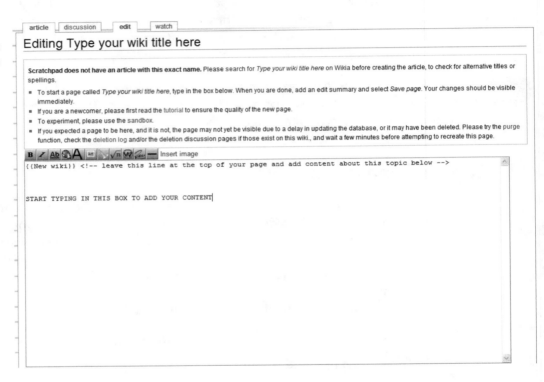

Keep your reader in mind! Nobody likes to read a full page of nothing but text—your eyes go cross-eyed and you get bored quickly. Separate your content into logical sections using headlines and horizontal lines, and bring keywords to your reader's attention by making them bold or italic.

tip *As you create your first wiki, start the tutorial and then create a new window so you can work on your wiki and flip over to the tutorial for reminders as you go.*

Consider using images, too. Those help break up text and add visual interest to your page. Be careful with images, though—if you don't own the copyright, don't post them.

One other item that can help your wiki: links. Both internal links to other wiki sites and external links to any web site are allowed. You can format the links so that when a reader clicks on one, the new site appears in a new browser. Each wiki engine has a different format for doing that, so just follow your engine's instructions. But opening new browser windows helps direct readers to new information while keeping your wiki open for them.

Wikis will automatically search your text when users type in search terms. For example, in my wiki shown in Figure 13-6, I use the term SOHO to refer to small office/home office workers. When SOHO was typed into the search box for the wiki engine, it instantly pulled up my wiki, highlighting SOHO in red. If you want a lot of people to find your wiki, be sure to use these kinds of "keywords"—words that are typically used by people when referring to your subject matter.

Figure 13-6

The Digital Home Office wiki was created in about ten minutes, including the creation of a logon account and the initial wiki content.

Contents [hide]
1 What is a Digital Home Office?
2 What's your digital home office story?
3 Resources for Digital Home Office Workers
4 Edit History

What is a Digital Home Office?   [edit]

Today's home office is much more than a desk and a computer, fax and phone. The 21st-Century digital home office is a **digital home office**: connected, collaborative, portable, and secure. Telecommuters, freelancers, and home-based businesses are all using wireless and Web-based technologies to create digital workspaces.

There are more than 40 million SOHO enterprises in the U.S. and about a million more are expected to join those ranks during the next year, according to Working Solo, Inc. The Small Business Administration says that 52% of all small businesses are home-based. Salary.com says one of the country's top trends in 2006 will be the expansion of work-from-home programs for employees. One study shows that, of those who work at home, 68% are employees. Just 19% are home-based business owners and 11% are non-home-based self-employed people. International Data Corp. estimates that by 2009, the United States will be the most mobile-enabled workforce in the world with more than 70% of workers working away from corporate offices.

Well-designed digital home offices can maximize free time for the owner, improve communication and collaboration between workers and colleagues, and save money through decreased phone charges, fewer IT equipment pieces and a reduced need for IT support. A connected, efficent workspace that helps people work smarter - not harder - is the hallmark of an true digital home office.

What's your digital home office story?   [edit]

I work from home as a full-time writer and author. My digital home office has one computer with three monitors, I store my files on an MS Exchange 2003 server, and I have the requisite fax machine and printer cluttering my desk. I use a webcam primarily for family but I do talk to colleagues with it as well via Skype. My favorite thing about working from home? The freedom I have to care for my young daughter! Plus, nothing beats the 30-foot commute from the bedroom to my office. - Sally

ADD YOUR STORY HERE! (Don't forget to click Save Page below)

My home office changes often, sometimes weekly. Some days I need to work on Vista RC2, some days Windows XP, and occassionally, I have to drag out my Mac. I even have a couple of Tablet PCs, a Blackberry, a scanner, a few printers, and a few sets of speakers around too. I have a lot of monitors, and they're configured to span data across them. Sometimes I feel I'm in a technological wonderland, and them I peek under the desk. At some point, someone's go to figure out how to get rid of all of these cables and wires. And going "wireless" doesn't seem to help much! Joli

My home office consists of 2 laptops, one for the my full-time insurance job, and one for managing my personal business and investments, 2 fax lines, 2 phone lines and 2 cell phones. My home office makes my old off-site office look tame! Still, having the ability to throw a load of laundry in, forego the office garb, and most importantly, be here for my family, is invaluable. My Company wins too, as my breaks and lunch are shorter, or non-existent, and I work as long as I need to to get the job done rather than picking up at 5 o'clock and going home. ~Carla

I work three jobs from home. In one corner, I plan the classes that I teach through a home-school co-op. In another corner, I'm a conference planner and registrar for a K-12 education group. And in MY corner, I help hopeful adoptive couples fix up their adoption profiles.

To do all this, I have a desktop, a laptop, a workhorse thumbdrive, and a printer/scanner/fax machine. My latest addition goes in my purse -- a smart phone that makes everything just a bit more portable and allows me to work anywhere. The only ones who DON'T like my home office are my kids -- they'd rather I be out in the backyard with them! -- Lori of www.profilesthatgetpicked.com

note *Want to check out my wiki? Go to http://scratchpad.wikia.com/wiki/Digital_Home_Office and add your comments about digital home offices.*

Step 4: Keep Your Wiki Active

Oh, sure, creating a wiki is fun, but maintaining it may not be as exciting if you aren't too interested in the topic. But if you're going to create a wiki, make it one that you and others will want to visit.

If you're creating one for colleagues, for example, set reminders for yourself to post regular updates to the wiki to keep colleagues coming back for more information. Clients, too, will continue returning if they find useful information about your products or services.

Remember, you can get as creative as you like with a wiki. The mini-wiki shown here was done in minutes; the full web site examples shown in the beginning of the project take much more time. Still, if your business could benefit from client or colleague interaction like this, it's a great project to try.

Set Up a Virtual Private Network

What You'll Need:

- Operating system: Windows Server 2003
- Software: None
- Hardware: Wireless access point with built-in router
- Internet connection: Yes
- Cost: $0
- Difficulty: Advanced

If you work at home for a large corporation, you may already have a virtual private network (VPN) connection to your company's corporate network. But smaller companies don't always have this kind of remote access set up—sometimes because of the lack of an internal IT department, sometimes because the concept just hasn't been introduced. If you own a small company, a VPN just might be the perfect way for you to keep the lines of communication open between your home office and those of your remote employees.

> **tip** VPNs use a tunnel system to send packets over a network.

Virtual private networks are private networks used to communicate confidential information over a public network, via the Internet or through the use of software. It's a pretty reliable method for maintaining fast, secure communications regardless of where people are physically located. Connections are sent through the Internet from a private network to your location, which lets you access the corporate network from anywhere. With a VPN, you or others can connect directly to your network and use the programs and documents stored on it.

> **tip** A firewall is a barrier between a private network and the Internet.

This kind of connection differs from traditional wide area network (WAN) connections because it doesn't transmit data over phone or other physical lines. As a result, VPNs are typically less expensive and easier to maintain than a WAN setup. There are multiple types of VPNs that can be set up; this project focuses on remote-access VPNs that permit secure, encrypted connections using Windows Server 2003.

A variety of methods are used to keep VPNs secure, including firewalls and encryption. Since there are no common standards for implementing a VPN, you'll find a variety of solutions on the market. In this project, we'll take a look at those solutions and show you the basics of implementing one.

tip *Encryption is a process between two computers. When one computer sends data, encryption takes the data and encodes it so that only the second computer can read it. Any other computer trying to read the data will be unable to.*

Step 1: Set Up a VPN

There are a couple of things you need before setting up a VPN using Windows Server 2003. The most critical piece is actually three pieces: three separate computers running Windows Server 2003. One will be configured as a domain controller, one will be configured as a VPN server, and one will be configured as a RADIUS server. Throughout this process, the domain controller computer will be referred to as the DC, the VPN server will be referred to as the VPN server, and the third computer will be referred to as the RADIUS server.

Then, you need a dedicated DSL line—VPN technologies use the same cabling and routers that public networks do, so to set up a VPN, you use the same service provider you use to access the Internet. Ideally, this is a dedicated DSL line.

tip *A router is a specialized computer that sends packets of information and allows information to flow between networks. Without routers, the Internet wouldn't exist.*

Anyone connecting to your VPN needs a VPN client—this is the software that allows a remote worker to connect to the VPN server. This software is included in Windows XP and Windows Vista.

note *The VPN server is what remote workers will connect to in order to obtain the information they need from your company network. There are a few different options for establishing a VPN server. For example, some routers have VPN server capabilities and can be used in place of a computer running Windows Server 2003. (That is not covered in this project.) Whatever you use, you need to ensure that the VPN server has two network interface cards (NICs). One NIC connects to the Internet, and the other connects to your private network. With Windows Server 2003, the necessary software for your VPN server is included.*

Step 2: Set Up Your Virtual Private Network

As you go through the steps to set up your VPN, you need items such as IP addresses and administrator passwords. If you are not the administrator for your network, you need to include them in this process or get the information you need from them.

A. Apply DHCP Services

Dynamic Host Configuration Protocol (DHCP) is just a set of rules. It allocates IP addresses (your computer's Internet address) and configuration options on your network. A few simple steps are needed to implement DHCP services on the Windows Server 2003 computer you have designated as the DC.

Set Up DHCP

1. Click Start and click Control Panel.

2. Click Add Or Remove Programs.

3. In the Add or Remove Programs dialog box, click Add/Remove Windows Components in the left pane. The Windows Components Wizard will appear.

4. Click Networking Services.

5. Click Details.

6. Select Dynamic Host Configuration Protocol (DHCP). Click OK.

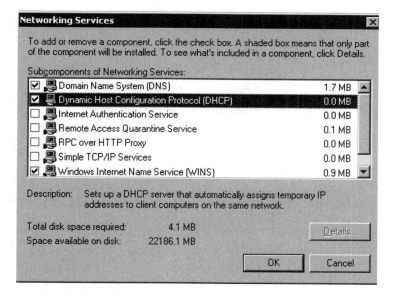

7. In the Windows Component Wizard dialog box, click Next. Windows will install the DHCP services.

8. Click Finish.

Create an Address Scope and Authorize the DHCP Server to Function on Your Network

1. Click Start and select Administrative Tools. Click DHCP.

2. In the DHCP window, right-click your server name under Contents of DHCP. Select Authorize.

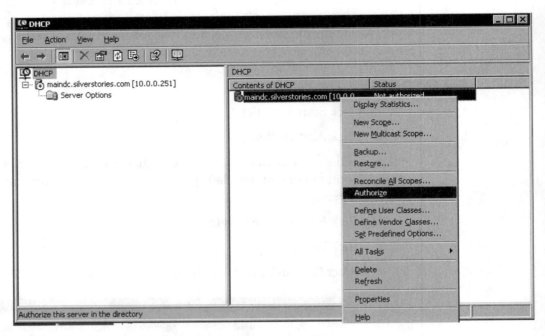

3. Right-click the server name again. Select New Scope. The New Scope Wizard will appear. Click Next.

4. Enter any name for the scope that you want to create. Click Next.

5. Now you need to enter an IP address range. This range should be consistent with the IP addressing scheme you already use but should not overlap any existing IP addresses. Click Next.

note   *The Length and Subnet Mask fields will be filled in for you automatically.*

6. Click Next. You do not need to worry about the Add Exclusions window.

7. Click Next. You do not need to worry about Lease Duration.

8. Click Next. Be sure Yes, I Want To Configure These Options Now is selected in the Configure DHCP Options window.

9. Click Next. In the Router (Default Gateway) window, enter the IP address of your network's default gateway. Click Add.

10. Click Next.

11. In the Domain Name and DNS Servers window, type in the name of your parent domain. Enter the server name and IP address for the DHCP server. Click Next.

12. Click Next to bypass the WINS Servers window.

13. In the Activate Scope window, select Yes, I Want To Activate The Scope Now. Click Next.

14. Click Finish. Close the DHCP window.

If you receive the error message that the DHCP service is not running on the target computer, you need to recheck your DHCP setup and walk through these steps again. Verify that all your IP addresses are correct. If all went well, you will have a new folder and subfolders under your DHCP server.

B. Create a Certificate Authority

The certificate Authority is a very big deal. Let's put it this way: If someone gets unauthorized access to your certificate authority, you no longer control your own network. This process sets up the proper protections for you on the DC:

1. Click Start and click Control Panel.

2. Select Add Or Remove Programs.

3. In the Add or Remove Programs dialog box, click Add/Remove Windows Components in the left pane. The Windows Components Wizard will appear.

4. Select Certificate Services. A warning window may appear advising you to ensure that the proper machine name and domain membership are configured. If you are satisfied that both are configured correctly, click Yes and move to the next step. Otherwise, click No and reconfigure one or both and then return to this process.

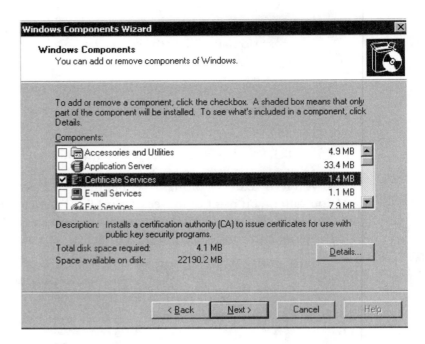

5. Click Details.

6. Select the CA subcomponent. (The actual name varies but it will have "CA" after it.) Click OK.

7. Click Next. Under CA Type, select Enterprise Root CA.

8. Click Next. Enter a common name for the certificate authority as well as a certificate validity period.

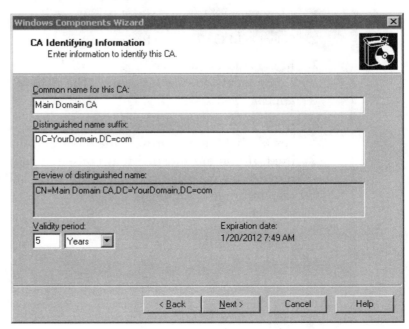

9. Click Next. Windows generates cryptographic keys and sets key protections.

10. A prompt appears asking you to enter a location for the certificate database. Keep the default location unless you prefer a different spot. Click Next.

11. Click Finish.

If you see a message indicating that Windows must restart the IIS services, click Yes and Windows will install the necessary components.

C. Install Internet Authentication Service (IAS)

This process will authenticate users who enter your network through the VPN connection. Move to the computer you have designated as your VPN server to complete these instructions.

1. Click Start and click Control Panel.

2. Select Add Or Remove Programs.

3. In the Add or Remove Programs dialog box, click Add/Remove Windows Components in the left pane. The Windows Components Wizard will appear.

4. Double-click Networking Services.

5. Select Internet Authentication Service. Click OK.

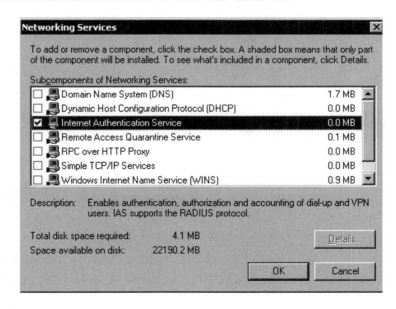

6. Click Next. The wizard will install IAS for you.

7. Click Finish.

D. Configure Internet Authentication Service

This process will completes the authentication for users who enter your network through the VPN connection. You will use the computer you have designated as your VPN server to complete these instructions.

1. Click Start and click Control Panel.

2. Select Administrative Tools and click Internet Authentication Service.

3. In the Internet Authentication Service window, right-click Internet Authentication Service (Local).

4. Select Register Server In Active Directory.

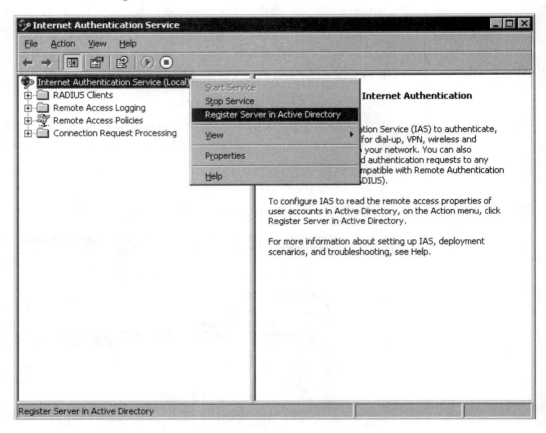

5. Click OK when asked to confirm the authorization.

6. Click OK if the Service Registered window appears.

7. In the Internet Authentication Service window, right-click RADIUS Clients.

8. Select New RADIUS Client. This will be the IP address of the server that the VPN server will be configured on.

9. Enter a name in Friendly Name and enter the IP address of one of your computers. Click Next.

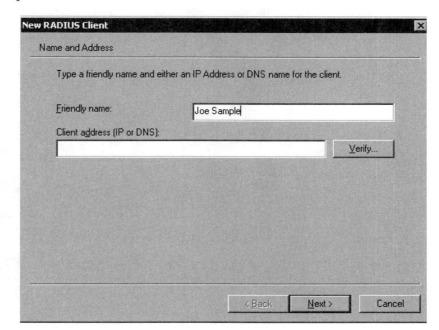

10. Under Client-Vendor, be sure RADIUS Standard is selected. Enter and confirm a shared secret (any word or character set that you can remember, like a password).

11. Click Finish.

note *Do not close the Internet Authentication Service window. You need it for Step E.*

E. Create a Remote Access Policy

This process sets up the conditions under which users can connect to your VPN. Prior to this step, if you have multiple users who will need access, be sure you have an Active Directory group established that includes all the users who will access the network through the VPN. The group creation process was covered in Project 20, Step 5.

1. In the Internet Authentication Service window, right-click Remote Access Policies.

2. Select New Remote Access Policy. The Remote Access Policy Wizard will appear. Click Next.

3. Be sure Use The Wizard To Set Up A Typical Policy For A Common Scenario is selected. Next to Policy Name, enter **VPN Access Policy** (or choose a different name). Click Next.

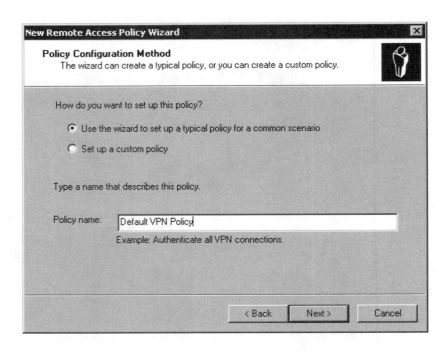

4. Select VPN. Click Next.

5. On the User or Group Access screen, select User Or Group. Use the Add and Remove buttons as needed. Click Next.

6. In the Authentication Methods window, select Microsoft Encrypted Authentication version 2 (MS-CHAPv2). Click Next.

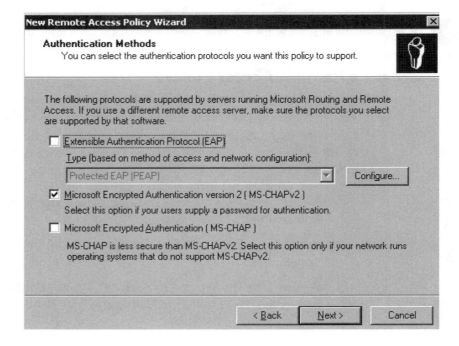

7. On the Policy Encryption Level window, be sure only Strongest Encryption (IPSec Triple DES or MPPE 128-bit) is selected. Deselect Basic and Strong options. Click Next.

8. Click Finish.

9. Close the Internet Authentication Service window.

F. Configure Your VPN Server

You need to create or check a few settings now. You will use the computer you have designated as your VPN server to complete these instructions.

1. Click Start and click Control Panel.

2. Click Network Connections. Rename the connections to something that is easy to recognize, such as Internal and External. This will help you identify which NIC is connected to which network.

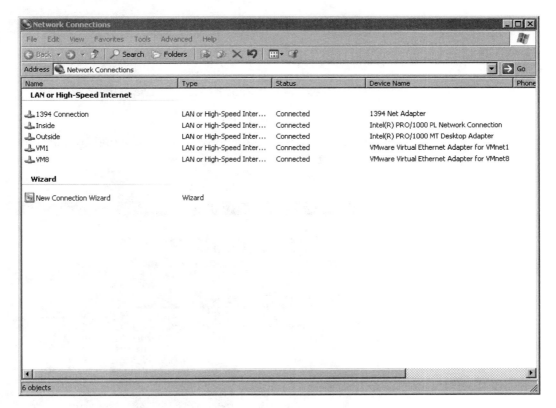

3. Go back to Start and click Administrative Tools.

4. Click Routing And Remote Access.

5. Right-click your VPN server in the left pane. The Routing and Remote Access Server Setup Wizard will appear.

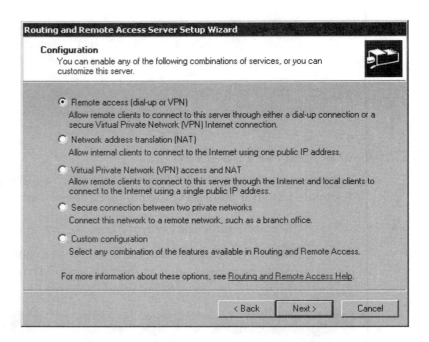

note *If a warning window appears, follow its instructions before returning to this configuration process.*

6. Click Next. Select Remote Access (Dial-Up or VPN).

7. Click Next. Select VPN.

8. Click Next. Select the network interface that connects the VPN server to the Internet. You should see the common names you entered in Step 2 of this process.

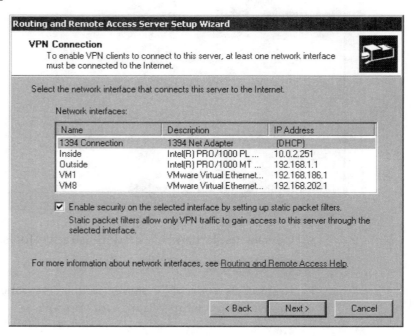

9. Select Enable Security On The Selected Interface By Setting Up Static Packet Filters. Click Next.

10. In this step, you are selecting the interface that the VPN users will use to access your internal network. Select the appropriate connection from the list provided. Click Next.

11. Select Automatically. Click Next.

12. Select Yes, Set Up This Server To Work With A RADIUS Server. Click Next.

13. Enter the primary RADIUS server IP address. This was set up in Step C. Enter your shared secret from Step D. Click Next.

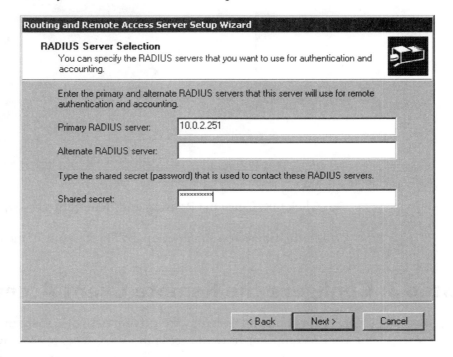

14. Click Finish.

Keep the Routing and Remote Access window open. You need it for the next step.

G. Associate the DHCP Server with the VPN Server

You're getting very close to the end! This step will complete the VPN configuration steps. Stay on the VPN server for these next steps.

1. In the Routing and Remote Access window, right-click DHCP Relay Agent and click Properties.

2. Enter the IP address of the DHCP server you configured in Step A. Click Add.

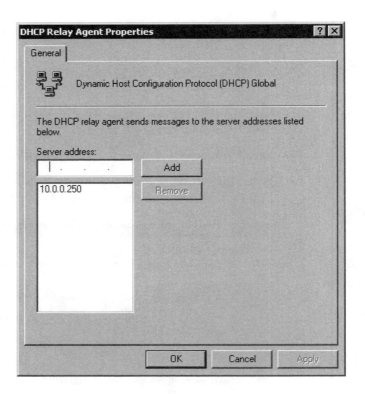

3. Click OK. Close the Routing and Remote Access window.

Congratulations! You have set up a VPN for your home office.

Step 3: Configure the Remote Client Access

In order for someone to access the private network, there must be instructions to tell the user's computer how to access the VPN. This process will set up those instructions. For this process, use a computer you might use to access the VPN from another location. This could be a laptop computer or a desktop.

1. Click Start and click Control Panel.

2. Double-click Network Connections.

3. Click New Connection Wizard. Select Connect to the Network at My Workplace. Click Next.

4. Select Virtual Private Network Connection. Click Next.

5. Type in a name for the connection. Click Next.

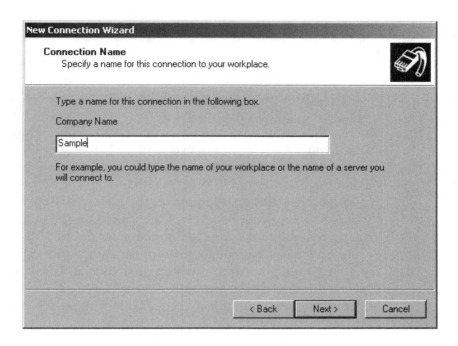

6. Type in the IP address of the VPN server you set up in Step F. Click Next.

7. Select Do Not Use My Smart Card. Click Next.

8. Select Anyone's Use. Click Next.

9. Select the option to place a shortcut on your desktop for the VPN server. Click Finish.

Step 4: Test Your Connection

You just need to test the connection now to be sure everything is set up correctly. On your desktop of the same computer you just configured, perform these steps:

1. Double-click the shortcut on your desktop.

2. Enter your username and password.

3. Click Connect.

If the connection doesn't work, you will see an error message. You will need to go back through the steps of this process to determine where your error was made. Otherwise, the connection will be automatic and you will see this message on your taskbar:

Step 5: Consider Managed VPN Options

If you don't want to worry about all the details but still like the idea of having a VPN for your employees, consider using a managed VPN provider. Managed VPN services are just what the name implies: they manage the entire VPN process for you, taking care of all the details and providing technical support, too. You will still need to install software from the provider, but additional equipment shouldn't be necessary if you already have a network set up (see Project 23).

Try checking with your phone company or other Internet service provider to see if they offer a managed VPN option, too—you'll be surprised at how many providers of Internet services are jumping on the managed VPN bandwagon. Managed VPN services charge subscription fees for the hosting of your VPN, plus most typically charge a monthly fee for each remote user on the VPN. Fees depend on the type of services you subscribe to, the numbers of locations involved, and the broadband width size used, but they can start at as little as $100 per month and go as high as several hundred dollars a month.

Here are a few providers; there are many more available:

- Blue Ridge Networks (www.blueridgenetworks.com)
- Internap Network Services (www.internap.com)
- New Edge Networks (www.newedgenetworks.com)
- Positive Networks (www.positivenetworks.com)

The entire process of setting up a VPN is a detailed one, but the benefits of providing this kind of network to employees or business colleagues can be many. Congratulations on completing the toughest project in this book!

Part IV

Enhance Your Sales and Marketing

Earn Advertising Incomes from Your Blog or Web Site

What You'll Need:

- **Operating system: Any**
- **Software: None**
- **Hardware: None**
- **Web site: Yes**
- **Cost: $0**
- **Difficulty: Easy**

Business web sites are critical in today's online world. Customers and clients are more apt to ask for your web site address than your business card because they know that with it, they can get all the information they need from the comfort of their home or office. If your web site is set up well, it generates new and repeat business for you. That's all well and good but there's another thing your web site can do silently for you: add a new revenue stream to your business.

Advertising income generated from web site traffic is one of the most overlooked revenue streams in small business. Essentially, you sell advertising space on your web site and earn money based on the number of times an ad is clicked. Once you have set up the advertising program, you don't need to monitor it—ads are updated and changed routinely based on the code you have added to your web site.

tip *A bonus to these advertising programs is that several offer additional features that can help improve your web site—search functions, podcasts, etc.*

Most people assume that advertising is difficult to set up or that the ads will somehow compete with the business messaging on the web site. The truth is that it's fairly simple to set up and the ads can be targeted to complement your web site's content, the user's geographical location, and other key factors. Payment will vary depending upon the amount of traffic your web site receives and the number of clicks on the ads. Readers don't have to *buy* anything from the ad's sponsor for you to make money but they must actually click the ad for payment to be generated. The real beauty of this system is that it's free for you—there are absolutely no fees to host ads on your web site because you're the one selling the space. It does take a tiny bit of work, however . . . it might take you the better part of an hour to set the whole thing up.

You paid a small fortune to create that web site; why not make some of that money back by letting the site do double duty as an online location for your business and an advertising space for others?

note   *Contextual ads are ads matched to what visitors on a particular web site are looking for. The ads appear based on the content your web site provides and are usually triggered by keywords on the web site.*

Step 1: Choose an Advertising Partner

There are several companies that offer advertisements for your web site. Each one has benefits and drawbacks; look for one that will pay a fee you are happy with and that updates ads as quickly as possible when your content changes.

Here are a few advertising partners for you to consider but keep in mind that many, many more are available:

- **Google AdSense (www.google.com/adsense)**   Provides competitive ad filters, default ads if a targeted ad can't be provided, and ad customization to match your web site, and offers Google AdSense for Search, which lets you place a Google search box on your web site—as people use your search box, keyword advertisements appear. If the ad is clicked by someone from your search box, you get paid.

- **Clicksor (www.clicksor.com)**   Offers text or graphical banners, pop-under advertisements, search boxes, contextual inline links, layer ads, and XML feeds.

- **BrightAds (www.kanoodle.com)**   Uses a topic- and segment-based approach instead of keywords to target advertising and allows you to customize ads for your site.

- **Yahoo! Publisher Network (http://publisher.yahoo.com)**   Enables you to choose the color, layout, and size of the ads, get filtering of competitive ads, and offer your readers ads in RSS.

- **ValueClick Media (www.valueclickmedia.com)**   Formerly known as Fast-Click, provides video advertising along with text and banner ads. Requires a minimum of 3000 impressions (web site visitors) per month.

- **MSN ContentAds (www.adcenter.microsoft.com)**   In beta testing at the end of 2006; expected to heavily compete with Google AdSense.

tip *Payments for web site ads are typically made on a cost-per-click (CPC) or cost-per-1000-impressions (CPM) basis. If your site doesn't have a lot of visitors, go with a CPC payment.*

Step 2: Sign Up for Your Advertising Program

Every advertising program has policies it will ask you to abide by. Some programs may restrict you from using two different advertising programs on a single web site, for example, or may prohibit you from instructing readers to help you earn money by clicking advertiser links (this skews advertising numbers to your benefit). When you sign up for a program, check the program policies first to be sure you can stick with them.

Once you're ready to sign up, go to the home page of your chosen program and follow the instructions. I decided to use Google AdSense on my writing web site, so I'll use that as an example of how the process goes. Here are the steps I followed:

1. Go to www.google.com/adsense and click Click Here To Apply, as shown in Figure 15-1.

2. Complete the application. (Under Product Selection, I chose both AdSense for Content and for Search.)

3. Click Submit Information.

Figure 15-1

Google AdSense is one of the most popular online advertising programs for web site publishers.

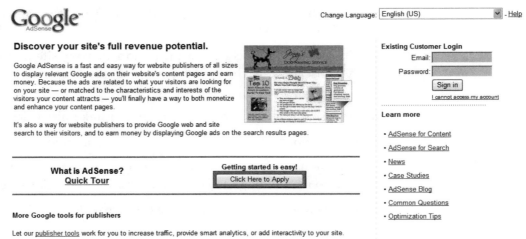

4. Double-check the information on the summary page—you can't change the payee name or country/territory later. Click Continue.

note *If you do not have an account with Google, you need to create one now. Selecting I Do Not Use These Other Services will automatically provide you with the option for creating your account.*

5. Wait for the e-mail from Google. When it arrives, click the link provided to activate the application review by Google.

It could take 1–2 days to receive approval or declination from Google, although I received mine in just a couple of hours. If you receive approval, go to Step 3. If you don't, try a different advertising program that allows content from your web site.

note *Most advertising programs will review your site and its content before allowing you to join the program. Sites with pornography, gambling, excessive profanity, and similar types of content are often not accepted—be sure to check site content restrictions before taking the time to sign up.*

Step 3: Get Started with Your Program

When your application is approved, Google sends a congratulatory e-mail with instructions for logging in and implementing the advertising code. It also includes a link to a detailed video walkthrough. Other programs provide similar options; just follow the instructions provided for the program you choose. With any program, you need to determine where the ads will be placed on your web site and what they should look like. Carefully consider these two aspects before you generate ad code and place it on your web site.

For Google, the next steps are to log into the account so the AdSense code can be generated and added to your web site:

1. Upon login, you need to accept the terms and conditions of the program.

2. Once that's done, the Google AdSense Overview page appears. Click the AdSense Setup tab.

3. Choose the product you want to add to your site: AdSense for Content, AdSense for Search, or Referrals. For this example, I chose AdSense for Content.

4. Choose the ad type you want (ad unit or link unit). Click Continue.

5. Choose your ad format and colors. Click Continue.

6. Choose ad channels (these help you monitor ad performance—take some time to read through the details provided by Google). Click Continue.

7. Get your ad code by copying the code provided.

Choose Ad Type > Choose Ad Format and Colors > Choose Ad Channels > **Get Ad Code**

Wizard | Single page

Click anywhere in this box to select all code.

You may paste this code into any web page or website that complies with our program policies. Once the code is live on your site, relevant ads should appear within 48 hours.

For more help with implementing the AdSense code, please see our Code Implementation Guide.
For tips on placing ads to maximize earnings, see our Optimization Tips.

Your AdSense code:

```
<script type="text/javascript"><!--
google_ad_client = "pub-8059647079616453";
google_ad_width = 728;
google_ad_height = 90;
google_ad_format = "728x90_as";
google_ad_type = "text_image";
//2006-12-06: Writing
google_ad_channel = "7298471299";
//--></script>
<script type="text/javascript"
  src="http://pagead2.googlesyndication.com/pagead/show_ads.js">
</script>
```

[<< Back]

<< Back to AdSense Setup

8. Paste the ad code into your web site wherever you want—once the code is live, ads should begin appearing within 48 hours as shown in Figure 15-2. (Mine appeared within a minute or two.)

```
365     <td valign="top" width="1245" height="100%" style="border-right-style:none; border-right-width:medium; border-top-style:none; border-t
366      </td>
367   </tr>
368 </table>
369 <script type="text/javascript"><!--
370 google_ad_client = "pub-8059647079616453";
371 google_ad_width = 728;
372 google_ad_height = 90;
373 google_ad_format = "728x90_as";
374 google_ad_type = "text_image";
375 //2006-12-06: Writing
376 google_ad_channel = "7298471299";
377 //--></script>
378 <script type="text/javascript"
379 src="http://pagead2.googlesyndication.com/pagead/show_ads.js">
380 </script>
381 <p align="center"><i><small>This site was last updated
382 <!--webbot bot="Timestamp" S-Type="EDITED" S-Format="%m/%d/%y" --> </small></i>
383 </p>
384
385 </body>
386
387 </html>
```

When you choose the ads to display, keep in mind that sometimes there might not be ads that exactly meet the filtering criteria for your web site. You should be prompted at some point to designate replacement ads in case contextual ads are not available.

Figure 15-2

Sample ad appearing on the author's web site immediately after pasting in ad code

Staff Leasing - Denver
Denver Based Staff Leasing
Over 20 Yrs Exp, Excellent
Service
DiscoveryOutsourcing.com

Ads by Gooooooogle

Your Own Nursing Agency
Achieve Financial
Independence Profit From the
Nursing Shortage
www.medstaffbook.com

Hospital Staffing
Revenue Cycle Staffing
including PFS, Pt. Access, Med.
Records
www.hrgpros.com

When Quality Counts
Accounting temporaries who
get the job done right!
www.accountdata.com

Advertise on this site

In Figure 15-3, you can see the public service announcement that appeared on my web site when a contextual ad wasn't available—I had requested that PSAs appear whenever the other ads didn't.

Figure 15-3

Ads will change based on the criteria you assign.

> **Make Your Donation Today**
> Help Rebuild Lives & Communities in Hurricane Affected States.
> www.BushClintonKatrinaFund.org
>
> Public Service Ads by Google   Advertise on this site

tip   *Most advertising programs allow you to place your code on multiple sites as long as you own each site. Take advantage of this if your program allows it!*

Step 4: Maximize Your Ad Revenue

If you find that you like this method of revenue generation, you'll want to increase the traffic on your web site. Here are six tips for doing that:

- *Place valuable content on your site.* Include content that attracts advertisements higher-paying consumers will find irresistible. Keep updating the content, too. Visitors will return more often to web sites that have continually changing and time-sensitive information.

- *Use copy on your site that encourages people to click ads.* While programs like AdSense will prohibit the phrase "Click my AdSense Ad to help pay for this site" it will allow phrases such as "Sponsored Links" or "Advertisements."

- *Use a tool to help improve your site's ranking on search engines.* Tools such as Search Engine Optimizer evaluate your web page and give you suggestions for improving its ranking on search engines.

- *Use keywords on your site that search engine users enter when looking for information.* Programs such as Wordtracker can help you determine the most used keywords by various target audiences.

- *Cross-link with other logically connected businesses in your area.* For example, if you are an insurance broker, place a link on your site for a local mortgage broker—and ask them to place your link on their site.

- *Use a web site traffic analysis program.* Know who is visiting your site—and what they did while they were there. Try StatCounter.com, ClickTracks, or similar programs.

note   *Regardless of the program you use, you also need to be sure you have provided the proper financial account information so that you can be paid according to the terms of your agreement. Some programs pay biweekly, some monthly. Some pay only when your payment reaches a certain level, so if you don't have a lot of traffic to your site, you might not see any money for a few months.*

Project 16

Establish an eBay Store

What You'll Need:

- Operating system: Any
- Software: None
- Hardware: None
- Cost: $15.95 to $499.95/month
- Difficulty: Challenging

What exactly is your business? Do you sell products or services? Do you have inventory on hand? Are you interested in generating more income over the Internet? One more question: Do you have an eBay store?

Lots of businesses have web sites. Some are informational sites, some are commerce sites, and some are not worth the space they take up on the Web. If you are a small business, it's not easy to build a web site with worldwide reach, yet local reach often doesn't mean much in terms of product sales. If you have products to sell, however, you must be on the Web—consumers that do show up expect you to be there in full force, and tend to distrust businesses that don't have a presence. As a result, more and more businesses are finding that eBay—with its steady stream of customers looking for products to buy—is a viable addition to their web portfolio.

One reason businesses are turning to eBay is that buyers on eBay are increasingly coming from international locations—the strength of other currencies against the dollar encourages them to buy American products. And, with an average of thousands of unique visitors daily, even skeptics must admit that eBay is ripe with sales opportunity.

tip *eBay offers discussion boards, an Answer Center, chat rooms, and other tools for sellers.*

167

Step 1: Set Up Your Accounts

You need to have a user account to sell on eBay. It's just like setting up an account anywhere else; follow the prompts and fill in the information as requested.

1. On the eBay home page, click Register, as shown in Figure 16-1.

2. On the next page, you have the option to register as a business or individual. Choose the option you prefer, and fill in the required fields.

3. Click Continue and follow all prompts until your registration is complete.

Figure 16-1

The registration process starts on the home page of eBay.

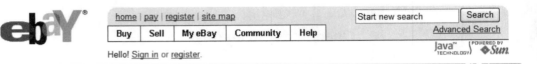

To make customers happy, you also need to have a PayPal account so you can accept payments with that method. A huge number of eBay buyers use PayPal; if you want them to buy from you, you'd better offer it.

PayPal will require that you provide them with a checking account (for depositing your payments) along with other normal registration information. Go to www .paypal.com and click Sign Up Now! on the home page to establish your account. Once your account is established, you can add a PayPal logo to your eBay store, plus receive a variety of seller protections such as fraud prevention, dispute resolution assistance, and coverage for qualified chargebacks. Another handy feature in a global economy: PayPal allows you to accept payments in 16 different currencies and automatically converts payments to your currency.

 PayPal offers fee eBay sales and marketing tools and can help you with shipping payments as well as tracking shipments.

Step 2: Create Your eBay Store

Once you have registered, log on to eBay and go to My eBay. In the Related Links section on the bottom right of the page, click Selling Resources.

This will take you to the Selling-Related Links page. On the bottom right, click Create An eBay Store.

eBay Stores:
Learn About eBay Stores
Create an eBay Store
Edit Your eBay Store
Close Your eBay Store

Even if you are already signed in to eBay, you may be prompted for your user ID and password again. Go ahead and enter those if necessary and click Sign In Securely. Then follow these steps:

1. Choose your subscription level. (You can always upgrade later.)

2. Choose a store name.

3. Click Continue.

4. Select additional products as desired. Click Continue.

5. Read and accept the terms of service.

6. Click Subscribe.

That's it—your store has been created. Any active sales listings you might have had prior to creating a store will automatically flow into your new store. You will receive a confirmation e-mail from eBay. There is still a bit more work to be done, however. I'll explain in the next section.

note *Be careful when naming your store—you cannot use a name that is identical to or could be confused with a company name protected by trademark law.*

Step 3: Design Your Storefront

When you reach Subscribe to Stores: Congratulations, click Start Quick Store Setup. You have two options: to accept all of the recommended settings (just click Apply Settings) or to customize the settings the way you want.

You can customize your store settings in five areas:

- Store color and theme

- Store description

- Item display

- Promotion boxes

- Store marketing

Click Edit under any area you want to customize. When you have made the changes you want in each area, click Save. When you are done with all changes in all areas, click Apply Settings.

Next, you'll see the Manage My Store page. This shows you the URL assigned to your store (you can use this on your business web site to link buyers to products, for example) and a variety of information about your store. Take some time to read through this page; eBay wants its sellers to succeed and thus offers a variety of customer support options and tips for increasing buyer traffic to your store.

> **tip** You can always go back and edit your store's appearance at any time. Play around with designs and colors until you find the combination that works for you.

Step 4: Start Selling Your Products

Now the real fun begins—and it *can* be fun. On the Manage My Store page, find the Start Selling Now! section. Click Sell Your Item Form. You may be prompted to reenter your eBay user ID and password.

> ☼ **Start selling now!**
> Use the Sell Your Item Form or any of our Selling Tools to start your listings today.

Select a Selling Format

The next page asks you to determine the selling format you want to use. There are four formats:

- **Sell Item at Online Auction**   The standard method used by the majority of sellers on eBay. This allows bidding for the item but you still set an initial price. You can also add the Buy It Now option, which is a price you establish for anyone willing to forgo the auction process and simply purchase the item outright.

- **Sell at a Fixed Price**   Just like it says, a price is set and buyers can purchase the item only at that price. No bidding is accepted.

- **Sell in Store Inventory**   Items are listed at a set price and no bidding is allowed.

- **Create an Ad Format Listing**   Items are listed as a method to generating multiple leads; no transactions are completed online. This listing is good for services and real estate offerings.

Choose a format and then click Continue.

For this project, we will walk through selling an item at online auction. Once you understand that process, it's very simple to try one of the others—the processes aren't terribly different although your specific content may be different in each process.

Choose a Category for the Product

Take your time with this section—choosing categories is critical to seller success. The best way I've found to select the right category for my items is to do a quick keyword search for the item I plan to list, then take a good look at where other sellers have listed similar items. As shown in Figure 16-2, entering the keyword is one of the first sections shown to you.

Figure 16-2

Searching by keyword can help you quickly establish the right competitive category for your product.

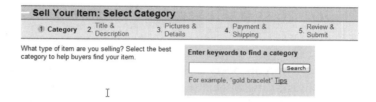

In my case, I'm going to list a copy of Microsoft Office Professional Edition 2003. I entered that title into the keyword search and the results popped up clearly showing that Computers & Networking/Software was the place for my product (see Figure 16-3). If you choose this method, you can simply click Sell In This Category and continue.

Figure 16-3

The results of a keyword search are clearly displayed with the percentages of similar items in various category listings.

Find a Main Category		
Top 10 categories found for Office 2003 professional edition		
Category		
⦿ Computers & Networking > Software > Business & Productivity > Business Suites > Microsoft > Office 2003 Professional		(32%)
○ Books > Nonfiction Books		(6%)
○ Computers & Networking > Software > Business & Productivity > Business Suites > Microsoft > Office 2003 Standard		(6%)
○ Books > Textbooks, Education		(4%)
○ Computers & Networking > Software > Business & Productivity > Business Suites > Microsoft > Office 2003 Other		(4%)
○ Computers & Networking > Software > Business & Productivity > Business Suites > Microsoft > Office 97		(4%)
○ Computers & Networking > Software > Business & Productivity > Business Suites > Other		(4%)
○ Computers & Networking > Software > Operating Systems > Windows > Windows XP Professional		(4%)
○ DVDs & Movies > DVD, HD DVD & Blu-ray		(4%)
○ Computers & Networking > Software > Business & Productivity > Business Suites > Microsoft > Office XP Professional		(3%)

You can select a suggested main category below and click **Sell In This Category**, or use different keywords to refine your search.

Enter item keywords to find a category
[Office 2003 professional editi] [Search] Tips
For example, "gold bracelet" not "jewelry"

[Cancel] [Sell In This Category] 🔆 **Tip:** Add a second category to increase your item's exposure. You can do this at the bottom of the main category page.

Let's assume, however, that you didn't want one of the categories shown in the keyword results list. Click Cancel to return to the Select Category page. Under Browse Categories, click a category from the list in the first box on the left.

Once you choose an initial category, subcategories appear in the second box. Now that you can see categories in the second box—select a subcategory. Continue this process as long as new categories appear for your product. Some products have multiple subcategories; others may have just one. When there are no more subcategories, the final box will be light gray and indicate that you should continue below.

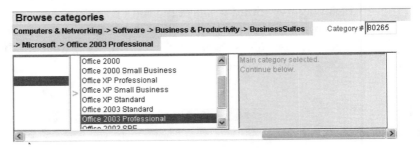

Now you need to decide whether or not to list the item in a second category. While adding a second category can expand the number of buyers who see your listing, it also adds to the fees eBay imposes. For your first item, try one category—you can always use this feature as you get more familiar with listing items.

Click Continue.

Describe Your Item

Here's where the fun comes in: creating a description that will catch a buyer's eye. If you have items that everyone else is describing identically, take a minute to find a new way to describe the item. "MS Office Professional Edition 2003" is the name of the product I'm selling; the title and description I'm entering on this page is "NEW & SEALED IN BOX! MS OFFICE 2003 PRO Great Gift!"

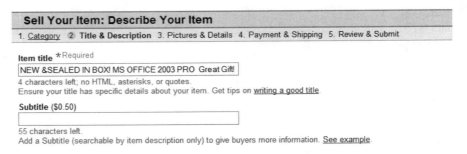

You also have an option on this page to add a subtitle for a small fee. Plus, you need to indicate the item's condition—new or used.

Now, scroll down the page and you'll see an Item Description box. This is where you can get really creative. If you've interested the buyer enough to look at your product, you really need to hook them in this section. Use the font, color, and other text buttons to make your text really pop.

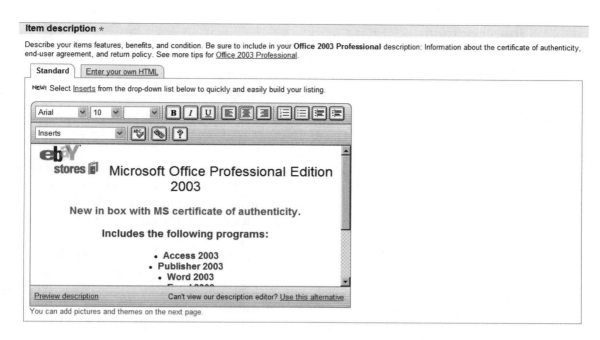

Click Preview to see how your listing will look; when you're satisfied, click Continue.

Add Pricing, Pictures, and Other Details

At this point, you'll enter pricing, pictures, and additional details for your listing. Select the main store category for your item (you can choose a second category as well if you like) and then move to Starting Price. While a lower starting price can offer more bids, don't make yours so low that you'll never make the price you expect for the item. Check similar listings to see where their bids started to help you get an idea of a good starting point. Unless I really think bids will go crazy, I like to choose a starting price as well as a Buy It Now price. The starting price simply starts your bidders off; the Buy It Now price is the price you agree to sell the item for if someone is willing to buy the item for the indicated price.

Under Duration, select the time limit for your auction (between 1 and 10 days) and the start time for the auction.

Under Quantity, don't forget to select how many of the items you have for sale *in this auction.*

note *Quantity auctions can be a little confusing. If you have 50 drills you want to sell for $5 each, list a quantity of 50 and a starting price of $5. Bidders will specify both the offered price and the number of drills they want. The highest total bid value (bid price multiplied by the number of items bid on) will win; other bidders get that price and whatever quantity is left.*

Item Location

This is important—you need to be sure the ZIP code and location of your product are included in your auction. These two items help bidders determine whether or not the shipping costs and potential mailing time for the item are worth the time and effort to bid.

Add Pictures

The first picture for your item is free; use the opportunity to display a photo that says everything. If you need to use multiple photos to get the sales point across, that's fine—a small fee will be added for every picture included. eBay Basic Picture Services is fine for most listings although you can take advantage of an enhanced picture service if you like.

Download any pictures to your hard disk and then click Browse to add the picture(s), as shown in Figure 16-4. You can add 12 pictures per listing. eBay offers some options like supersizing pictures and a picture show—take advantage of any offers that are free, and think twice about any that require a fee. The fees seem small but if you keep adding fee-based options to your listing, your profit will be reduced accordingly.

Figure 16-4

Up to 12 pictures can be added to support your listing.

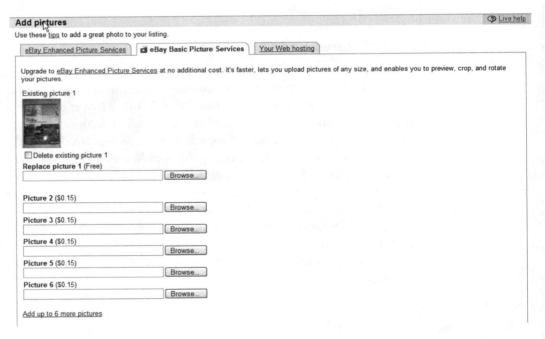

Listing Designer

The standard layout for your listing is text on top, picture on the bottom. If you want to change that, you need to select Listing Designer. This option offers a variety of backgrounds and frames for your item's page, along with the choice of different layouts. This is a totally personal choice; I typically stick with the standard layout and have sold plenty of items that way.

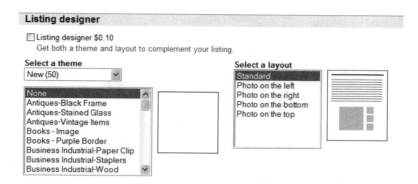

Increase Your Item's Visibility

If you want to bundle some of the options you have chosen, the Value Pack might be a good choice for you. It bundles photo gallery, subtitle, and Listing Designer charges into one package so that you save a few pennies.

The Pro Pack is a much bigger package at a much bigger price. I don't recommend it unless you have an extremely high ticket item.

In this section, eBay gives you one last chance to select options such as bold text in your headline or promotion and gift services. Choose them if you wish, then click Continue.

Choose Payment and Shipping Options

The Payment and Shipping section is pretty self-explanatory. Choose the payment methods you'll accept from buyers (PayPal, money order, cashier's check, personal check, etc.) and then move down the page.

Payment Address

Be sure the payment address listed for you is correct and decide if you want to offer any buyer financing options.

Set Shipping and Sales Tax Costs

Specifying shipping costs is a smart thing to do—these stay on your profile so you don't have to continually update them with every item you list. You have three shipping cost options here: Flat, Calculated, and Freight. Each has a drop-down menu (shown in Figure 16-5) you can use to simplify your shipping selections but you can also add other shipping methods.

- **Flat**   You establish the full cost for shipping and the cost is the same to all buyers regardless of location. It's easy to include handling costs with this one.

- **Calculated**   The cost is based on the buyer's address and the type of shipping service they choose. You can specify the shipping services you agree to use.

- **Freight**   This is used for large items over 150 pounds.

Figure 16-5

Selecting shipping
methods on eBay is
fast and easy.

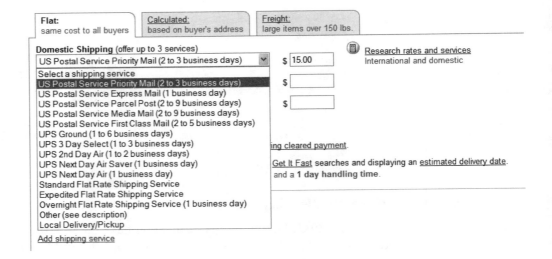

Use the shipping calculator whenever you can—this helps buyers see accurate shipping costs and often encourages sales.

Payment Instructions

There are other sections on this page to complete but the most important is the Payment Instructions section. This is where you can clearly state your return policy, how items will be shipping, what you want international buyers to do, etc. For example, my payment instructions read:

> Payment is expected within 72 hours of purchase. If you do not submit payment within that time, items will be relisted and buyer feedback will be submitted accordingly. No returns. I do my best to describe items as accurately as possible. ASK QUESTIONS BEFORE BIDDING! All items shipped at buyer's expense and risk. Please obtain shipping insurance if you are concerned about shipping risks. INTERNATIONAL BUYERS (Outside U.S.) Please email for shipping rates before sending payment.

I want buyers to be crystal clear that I do not accept returns, that shipping insurance is their problem, and that shipping rates shown do not apply to buyers outside the United States.

Complete any other sections on the page and then click Continue.
Just one more step to complete!

Review and Submit

This section starts with personalized recommendations from eBay to help improve your listing's chances of success. Take those under consideration but follow your instincts.

Below that, you can review your actual listing. You can preview how your item will appear to buyers, make edits where desired, and confirm pricing, shipping, duration, and other details.

Review the Fees and Submit Your Listing

Remember all the little fees that I mentioned can really add up? This is where you will see the total amount of those fees. Plus, a Final Value Fee is charged if your item sells—you can check here for details on that fee.

Click the Button to Actually Submit the Listing

When you are confident your listing is complete, click Submit Listing. When Sell Your Item: Congratulations appears, your item will be listed on eBay and the indicated fees will be charged to your account. It might take a few minutes for your listing to appear on eBay, but it will, just as mine did in Figure 16-6.

Figure 16-6

Here is my new store with its first product!

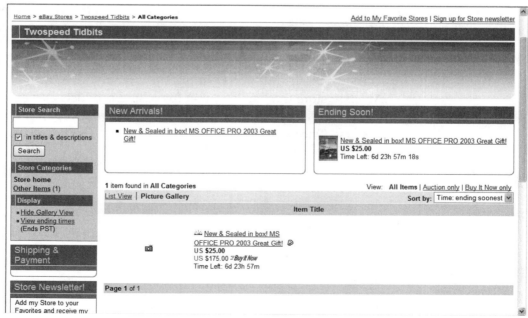

tip *If you don't want to do everything all at once, don't stress. You can access your store account by going to My eBay from the eBay home page, then clicking Seller Account.*

You will receive a confirmation e-mail from eBay showing that your listing has been posted. Go ahead—list something else! The first one took a lot of time, but now the process will go much more quickly since you're used to it and you have already entered several details that eBay will retain for your next listing. Good luck!

Other Considerations

Now that your eBay store has been established, there are a couple of other considerations for you.

First, you can link your eBay store to a commerce web site. This is particularly helpful if you already have products listed on your personal web site and want to use eBay to supplement the sales activity. Check under Seller Account to find out how to link the two together.

Second, PayPal. PayPal, PayPal, PayPal! You can link a merchant account to your eBay store if you already have one established but keep in mind that many, many eBay buyers use PayPal. If you don't have a PayPal account for them to use, you are losing buyers you never even dreamed of. I can't stress enough the importance of it, especially in the global atmosphere of this selling site.

tip *PayPal lets you accept credit card payments even on your own web site (U.S. only) just like you would with a merchant account. Your customers don't need to have a PayPal account, either. Check out Website Payments Standard or Pro on the PayPal site for more details.*

Third, check the Selling Manager Summary under Seller Account for reports and updates on your sales activity. This monitors all your listings, shows your payments, disputes, and shipping status, and provides details about a variety of other aspects of your store.

Fourth, check out all the marketing tools eBay provides. You might find some tips for your own brick-and-mortar store!

An eBay store is a viable option for selling products and even services online. If you're nervous about setting up a full store, get your feet wet with a few individual listings first. Once you see how easy it is to list and sell on eBay, you'll wonder why you haven't tried this avenue before.

Set Up a Commerce Web Site

What You'll Need:

- Software: Yes, depends upon solution chosen
- Hardware: None
- Web site and Internet connection: Yes
- Cost: $10/month and up
- Difficulty: Advanced

Most business owners have a simple, informative web site that offers information about the company and general details about products and services provided. That's great, but it's a good bet your web site could be doing more for you by selling your products and services 24 hours a day, 7 days a week. Sites that sell products and services are called commerce sites, or e-commerce sites.

If you don't already have commerce capabilities on your web site, you're potentially missing out on sales to people who prefer to shop anonymously, online, and at all hours of the day or night. And if you don't have a web site at all, well, you're just sending potential buyers to someone who does.

Now, you might be saying that you "only" provide services to clients, or "just" one or two products—why bother with a commerce site? Obviously, the final decision to sell online is up to you but if you're in business, the objective is to sell whatever you're offering. *Why bother with a commerce site?* Because it can sell almost anything you offer. Not everything, of course, is appropriate for sale online. But many, many items are.

Services can be sold the same way products are, for instance. You might offer packages consisting of hours of your expertise. For example, a financial planner might offer an introductory package that consists of a one-hour consultation and a three-page financial recommendation. Additional packages offered might be a full financial plan with a certain number of consulting hours included or a set number of consulting hours at a discount if purchased online. The possibilities really are endless; it's up to you to decide how your services could be marketed and sold online.

Consumers, by the way, are increasingly accepting e-commerce business models. Although there are still concerns over security, safety improvements in the last few years have reassured many buyers that Internet shopping is a reasonable alternative to hopping in the car and driving to the store.

When you add commerce capabilities to a web site, you don't really deal with the credit information—the Internet merchant provider you select will house all card-holder information and process the sale, providing you with an approval and then placing the money into your bank account. The assumption for this project is that you already have an online presence; if you do not, you'll want to take advantage of some of the commerce options that offer web site setup as well as commerce capabilities. Both will be covered in this project. There is a lot of research and thought that will go into this project; you'll have to make many decisions on your own. But ultimately, you'll learn how to determine which commerce option is best for you and the process for setting it up on your web site.

note *The 2006 holiday season was good for online retailers—comScore Networks reported that Internet shopping increased by 26 percent over 2005. The overall year was a good one, too. Annual online spending in 2006 surpassed $100 billion for the first time, with Internet sales comprising 7 percent of all U.S. retail revenue.*

Step 1: Consider All Your Options Before You Begin

Beyond determining which of the products or services you have that are appropriate for sale online, there are several other considerations to keep in mind before setting up commerce capabilities on your web site:

First, your web site must be attractive and easy to navigate. A good graphic designer can help with this but there are plenty of services that offer web site design services along with commerce options.

Second, your ability to deliver the product or service in a timely manner is critical. If you can't back up your online sales with prompt service or product delivery, you'll be dealing with complaints and unhappy customers instead of counting the dollars in your bank account.

Third, payment options need to be as varied as those offered by traditional brick-and-mortar retailers. That means offering options along with credit and debit card transactions, such as e-checks or PayPal.

Fourth, and possibly most important, your business model must be a sound one with strong market research and analysis to determine what buyers want from you. Online sales won't improve a poor business model.

Now that you have these items to consider, also take some time to determine exactly what you want to sell online and how much those items will average in cost. Some credit card merchants charge fees based on the average product sale from your site (see Figure 17-1 for an application example); you need to have at least a general idea of that average number as you set up commerce capabilities. You also need to be able to anticipate what you think the credit card volume might be on a monthly basis—guessing is fine, but make it an educated guess since your fees may be tied to it.

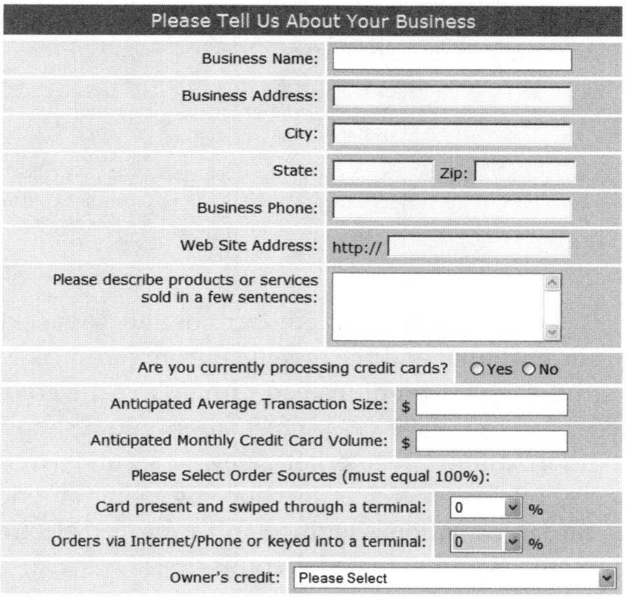

Figure 17-1

Most applications require you to include information regarding anticipated average transaction size and monthly credit card volume.

Another good idea is to have photos available of your products or that somehow illustrate your services. Most commerce options allow you to upload photos and business logos, so have these ready before you jump into the online retailing game.

Every e-commerce solution will differ in its merchant solution requirements. For example, some will require that your web site clearly list a return/refund policy and a customer service contact phone number. Others may require that you be in business for a certain amount of time before a merchant account will be approved. As you look at all your options, check the merchant account requirements before applying to be certain you qualify. Even though you might not qualify with one provider, you might be eagerly accepted at the next.

tip *PayPal links to buyer bank accounts to directly transfer money from the buyer to the seller. Wildly popular on eBay, this payment option is now becoming used by a variety of online retailers who have no links to eBay at all.*

Step 2: Understand the Components of Online Credit Card Processing

Online credit card processing differs from its brick-and-mortar counterpart in a couple of very distinct ways: the shopping cart, the Internet gateway, and the Internet merchant account.

When you use a credit card in a retail store such as Macy's, you hand it directly to the merchant for processing. The merchant sends the card information for approval, approval is received, and the transaction is complete. Funds are sent to the merchant's designated account. Fraud is safeguarded against by a face-to-face check of the buyer and the buyer's signature.

When you use a credit card online, some extra steps are required to protect both the customer and the merchant from fraud, as well as to make the experience simple and easy for both. Instead of handing the credit card directly to the merchant, the buyer inputs the card information into a shopping cart that also holds the product information. An Internet gateway securely transfers the credit card information to the Internet merchant account by using an encryption process to foil thieves. The card information is verified and approved electronically and funds are placed into the merchant's designated account.

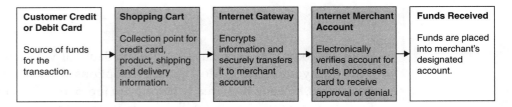

Even though there are additional steps involved in the online credit card process, the steps are invisible to you and your customers. The extra items are all handled electronically behind the scenes in real time.

What *isn't* invisible is the initial setup of the extra steps. When you add commerce capabilities to your web site (or build a new site with those capabilities), you need to be sure you have a shopping cart, an Internet gateway, and an Internet merchant account. With those three items, you can sell online. As you read through the following sections, you'll see how all these items are offered by providers—either individually or in bulk—to give you the needed processing features for completing a sale online.

 If you already have a merchant account for your business, don't assume you can accept Internet orders. Many banks require separate merchant accounts for brick-and-mortar transactions and Internet transactions.

Step 3: Add Commerce Capabilities to an Existing Web Site

When you add commerce capabilities to any web site, you don't really deal with the credit information—the merchant provider you select houses all cardholder information and processes the sale, providing you with an approval and then placing the money into your bank account as shown in previous illustrations. However, it's important that you select a solution provider that meets your needs.

Ideally, the merchant provider you select will offer the shopping cart, Internet gateway, and Internet merchant account capabilities you need. Some providers do this by placing all these items into your site; others do it by allowing you access to their capabilities or by linking you instantly to third-party providers. A few providers fall short of providing all three, however, so it's imperative that you do your homework before making a final choice. For example, some providers offer an Internet merchant account but not a shopping cart or Internet gateway. If you select one of these providers, it's not necessarily a setback to get to the final solution but it creates more work on your part since you need to find other providers for the missing pieces.

My recommendation is to work with a provider that offers all three pieces you need. If you find one that only offers one piece of the puzzle and doesn't have an easily integrated process for the other pieces, keep searching.

How e-Commerce Solution Providers Work

Every e-commerce solution provider is different; some require lengthy applications and several days to grant approval while others can be up and running within a few hours. Each one, however, requires your bank account information as well as basic information about your business so that payments can be properly made to you. Don't be surprised if you're asked for the following information on any e-commerce solution site:

- Your social security number, driver's license number, or other identifying information

- Bank account and routing number of your checking account

- Information about your business, such as a tax identification number and location information

Just like the bank on the street corner, every merchant account solution provider offers different processing terms, too. That's a big factor to consider when making your selection.

Application fees can vary from very low to very high (international accounts typically have higher fees overall), and monthly fees just to have the account open can range from $2 to more than $20. Other fees to be aware of are also standard in the industry: discount rates and per-transaction fees. Each online transaction is typically charged a percentage of the total dollar amount charged (this is a discount rate) *as well as* a fee for that transaction (per-transaction fee). Both can vary wildly, so shop around!

Whether you are a low- or high-volume seller, you'll want the best possible combination of the three fees: monthly, discount, and transaction. It's a good idea to find at least three potential candidates for your business, then compare their rates on a line-by-line basis to see which one works best in your particular situation. The more you sell, the more willing banks are to offer you better rates.

Other fees can be charged as part of a merchant account: a reserve fund, which covers charge-backs, and chargeback fees, similar to the nonsufficient funds fees charged for bad checks.

Popular e-Commerce Solution Providers

There are hundreds of e-commerce solution providers available to add to your web site. Fees vary by provider. Here are some popular online options to consider:

- **Google Checkout (www.google.com/services)**   Offers merchant solutions and shopping cart functions and money back for users of its AdWords program. Users need a Google ID and password.

- **PayPal (www.paypal.com)**   Offers gateway and merchant solutions, including e-mail and credit card payments. Integrates with many shopping carts. Customers do not need a PayPal account for web site payment options.

- **Authorize.Net Payment Gateway (www.authorize.net)**   Accepts a variety of payments including e-checks, gift cards, signature debits, and Internet auctions. It also integrates with dozens of shopping cart solutions.

- **First Data (www.firstdata.com)**   Offers several solutions, including Tele-Check acceptance and shopping cart functions.

 It's a good idea to check with your local bank to see if it offers e-commerce solutions. Banks sometimes have very lengthy qualification applications to complete but you can often get special rates if you are an existing customer.

Popular Shopping Cart Options

Dozens of shopping carts are available, all with varying fees. If you choose an e-commerce solution provider such as PayPal that integrates with shopping carts but doesn't offer its own, you need to add a shopping cart to your site before you can use the solution provider for the merchant and gateway features. However, many e-commerce solutions include shopping carts, such as the one shown in Figure 17-2, so it's important to decide upon the solution provider you want before worrying about whether or not you need a shopping cart. If you do need one with your provider, the provider will give you instructions for how to add the shopping cart to your web site as well as tell you the shopping cart solutions that the provider most easily integrates with.

Figure 17-2

This example from McGraw-Hill shows a book added to a simple shopping cart.

Shopping Cart

Step 1 of 3

Title	Quantity	Extended Price
CNET Do-It-Yourself iPod Projects By: Hart-Davis, Guy	1	$ 24.95

Format   Paperback
Your Price   **$ 24.95**
REMOVE ✕   SAVE FOR LATER

UPDATE QUANTITIES   Subtotal: $ 24.95

CONTINUE SHOPPING   CHECKOUT

Shopping cart solutions vary in many ways: layout, real-time shipping rates, coding required to add the cart to your site, and more. Some may integrate with Quick-Books, for example, to help you with accounting. Others may only allow certain types of products to be sold, while some have no limitations. All, however, will perform the same basic steps and require information similar to that shown in Figure 17-3.

Each shopping cart provider charges a fee; some charge by the month, others charge a one-time licensing fee. Here are some places to start:

- **1ShoppingCart.com (www.1shoppingcart.com)** $29/month.

- **ClickCartPro (www.clickcartpro.com)**   One-time license fee of $179.

- **eMartCart (www.emartcart.com)** $14.95/month.

- **X-Cart (www.x-cart.com)**   One-time license fees dependent on cart chosen; $199–$499.

- **eCart (www.webassist.com)**   Offers both a one-time fee ($249.99) and a monthly subscription fee ($19.99).

- **SecureNetShop (www.securenetshop.com)**   Starts at $19.99/month.

As you search for a shopping cart, keep in mind the type of products or services you sell. Some cart options might work better for your particular sales needs; don't just choose a shopping cart because your buddy has it.

Figure 17-3

As customers move through the shopping cart process, they are asked for billing, shipping, and credit card information before the transaction is processed.

> **Billing Information**
>
> Your billing address and phone number must be entered exactly as they appear on your credit card statement.
> * fields are required
>
> Country   United States
> First Name *
> Middle Initial
> Last Name *
> Company
> Address line 1 *
> Address line 2
> City *
> State / Province *
> Zip / Postal Code *
> Phone *
>
> ⊙ Ship to my billing address
> ○ Ship to a different address
>
> **Shipping Method**
> Next Day Air and Second Day Air are not available to P.O. Boxes. All AFO/FPO orders, as well as orders from all US Territories including Pueto Rico and Guam, must use the International Shipping option. For more information, please read the International Orders FAQ.
>
> The order total does not reflect shipping charges. Contact International Customer Service to determine the total of your order.
>
> **Why is My Personal Information Being Collected?**
> McGraw Hill Professional is collecting this information to fulfill your order. Your privacy is important to us. Read our **Privacy Policy.**

Step 3: Create a New Web Site with Commerce Capabilities

There are so many providers offering to help create a new web site with commerce capabilities that it might take an entire book just to go through them all. If you don't have the technical know-how to create a web site from scratch and add the e-commerce solution you need, these all-in-one solutions are a terrific way to start selling on the Web quickly and easily. Some even claim you can have a commerce web site set up within five minutes.

Since 1998 **Merchant Accounts Express** — Click Here To Apply It's Fast, Easy & FREE ▶

100% Risk Free Guarantee — click for detail

Site Builder Express - Ecommerce Website Builder

Have a great looking web site like this in 5 minutes with full ecommerce shopping cart and merchant account capability built in!

These solutions offer you customizable templates—just choose a design from the ones offered, and fill in the blanks as you walk through the process steps. Before you know it, you'll have a completely personalized web site.

For some solutions, you may need to work with your Internet service provider (the service you use to connect to the Internet, such as your phone or cable company), whereas other solutions can even set you up with a domain name and anything else needed. Keep your ISP phone numbers handy as you go through this process so that you can make a quick call if necessary.

The beauty of using one of these options is that everything is integrated for you—from choosing a domain name to adding your products, the steps are all-inclusive. This is particularly helpful if you just want to start selling online without worrying about how all the pieces fit together.

Popular All-in-One e-Commerce Solution Providers

Here are the five well-known providers; you can find hundreds more with a simple online search. Each of these allows you to create a web site complete with full commerce capabilities.

- **Yahoo! Small Business (http://smallbusiness.yahoo.com)** Offers web hosting and e-commerce site solutions with 24-hour phone support.

tip   *Look for a provider that offers 24-hour telephone support.*

- **Merchant Accounts Express   (www.merchantexpress.com/ecommerce_website_builder.htm)**   Offers a web site builder with a full e-commerce shopping cart and merchant account capability built-in.

- **GoDaddy.com (www.godaddy.com)**   Provides simple web site builders as well as a QuickBooks merchant solution and shopping carts.

- **MonsterCommerce (www.monstercommerce.com)**   Offers web site templates and graphics, shopping cart, and integration with PayPal merchant and gateway solutions.

- **MIVA (www.miva.com)**   Offers MIVA Merchant, which integrates with PayPal merchant and gateway solutions and offers 400 modules to tailor your online store.

tip *Managing and fulfilling orders is key to online sales success. Look for a commerce provider that will send automated faxes or e-mails when new orders are received.*

Step 4: Add the Commerce Option of Your Choice

This is where things get a bit tricky. Because of the multitude of choices available, I will only review the basics of this process instead of showing you detailed steps. The nice thing is that the most popular online options are designed with the novice in mind. That means the process is fairly simple and easy to understand. If you decide to use different providers and integrate them yourself, you might find the going a little more difficult. But don't despair! You *can* do this. Just allow yourself extra time if you plan to do the integration on your own.

1. Research and decide upon an e-commerce solution provider.

2. Sign up with that provider and obtain necessary approvals, passwords, and account information.

note *Step 2 can take 3 to 5 days depending upon the solution you have chosen.*

3. Download and install the solution according to the provider's instructions.

4. Add a separate shopping cart if necessary by signing up with a shopping cart provider and following its installation instructions (not required by all-in-one solutions).

5. Build the web site if necessary (not necessary if you already have a web site).

6. Add products or services to the e-commerce solution you have selected, according to its directions.

7. Begin selling products online.

So many of these providers offer setup wizards that the actual steps involved—while they may be lengthy—should be relatively simple to walk through. Expect to spend several hours of actual work on this, though. It's better to move slowly through the process your provider outlines than to rush and become confused.

tip *Use the technical support your solution provider offers if you run into any problems or don't understand a step in the process. These technical teams are there to help you get things set up correctly; if you don't, they lose a customer and revenue. Don't be afraid to use them as often as necessary during the process.*

Other Considerations

Security is a huge issue with Internet sales. No matter who you choose as an Internet merchant provider, be sure that they use the Address Verification System (AVS).

This system compares the home address entered by the customer to the one on file with the customer's credit card company. If the two don't match, AVS detects the disparity for you. This helps you avoid unsavory types who use a stolen card and request products be shipped to a false address.

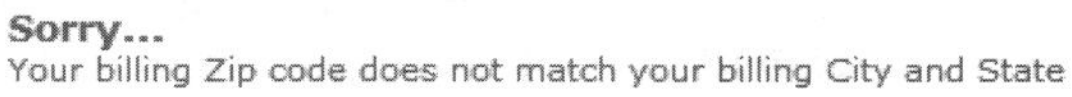

Sorry...
Your billing Zip code does not match your billing City and State

Sorry...
YOUR CARD WAS REJECTED :

Payment Information
Your billing address and phone number must be entered exactly as they appear on your credit card statement.
* fields are required

We accept the following	VISA MasterCard DISCOVER
Credit Card Type	Visa
Card Number	
Security Code	
Expiration	January (01) 2006
Name on Card	

Business licenses are typically not required to obtain an account with a commerce solution provider, but they can make the application process easier. Trade name registrations, dba certificates, and other identifying business documents are also helpful in speeding up the process.

Consider using a provider who offers Virtual Terminal (see Figure 17-4) if you sell your products and services away from your home office. Virtual Terminal allows you to manually process credit card transactions by phone and by mail, just like a physical

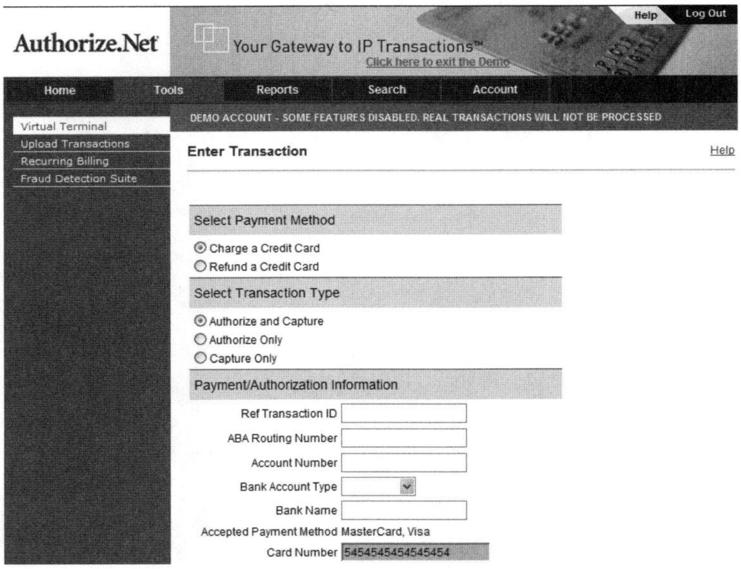

Figure 17-4

Virtual Terminal allows you to process credit cards from any Internet connection.

Authorize.Net — Your Gateway to IP Transactions™
Click here to exit the Demo

Home | Tools | Reports | Search | Account

Virtual Terminal
Upload Transactions
Recurring Billing
Fraud Detection Suite

DEMO ACCOUNT - SOME FEATURES DISABLED. REAL TRANSACTIONS WILL NOT BE PROCESSED

Enter Transaction

Select Payment Method
◉ Charge a Credit Card
○ Refund a Credit Card

Select Transaction Type
◉ Authorize and Capture
○ Authorize Only
○ Capture Only

Payment/Authorization Information
Ref Transaction ID
ABA Routing Number
Account Number
Bank Account Type
Bank Name
Accepted Payment Method MasterCard, Visa
Card Number 5454545454545454

terminal that sits by the register in a retail store. It can be accessed using any Internet connection, which means you can physically be almost anywhere and conducting sales—at the same time your web site is conducting sales online.

If you want to create your own web site but don't want to tie it to an e-commerce solution provider, try using a template service such as Web.com or Microsoft Office Live Basics (see Figure 17-5) to create the site. These services help you build a simple site with a domain name. Then just follow the instructions for adding an e-commerce solution to your web site.

Figure 17-5

Simple web site templates are offered by a variety of providers, such as Microsoft.

Whatever your business, the chances are high that you could be selling your products online. Take the time to do some research and you just might be pleasantly surprised to discover how quickly you can add an online revenue stream to your bottom line.

Project 18

Create a Podcast from Your Home Office

What You'll Need:

- **Operating system: Any**
- **Software: Yes**
- **Hardware: Microphone with noise-canceling features**
- **Cost: $0–$100**
- **Difficulty: Advanced**

So your first question probably is, "What's a podcast?" Don't feel out of the loop if you don't know what one is; most people don't. But next to blogging (instant online publication of your thoughts), podcasts are quickly becoming the hottest way to reach audiences with your message. They are simply voice recordings published on the Internet as downloadable MP3 files. Think of a podcast as your own personal radio show—you control the content, the Internet helps distribute your show. The term is a combination of Apple's iPod and the familiar term "broadcasting"—some credit podcast creation to an MTV VJ who was searching for a way to download recorded interviews to his iPod. He created a program that would meet his needs and the first podcast was born. As long as you have a computer, a microphone, an Internet connection, and some software, you can produce your own podcast.

Your next question might be, "So why do I need to know how to create a podcast?" Depending upon your reasons for working from home, you might not need to know. But if you're a business owner of any kind, then you should know because podcasts can be used as high-tech marketing tools. You can create your own radio show, distribute it, and convert new customers—all for free. Think of the possibilities! If you own a construction company, you might want to create a show that tells listeners what to do when a tree falls on a home—then add a plug, of course, for your business. Or perhaps you are a financial planner working from home. How about a radio show that targets your customers with information about retirement planning, using your products as examples throughout?

Podcasting does have different demographics than radio broadcasting, that's true. But if you're seeking a new audience—younger, more hip, and more technology-oriented—then you need to start rethinking any radio or television ads you're running and consider podcasts as an alternative. Or, at the very least, you should consider podcasts as a complement to your current advertising. Younger generations live on the Internet, and if they are any part of your target audience, then you need to live where they live. Listeners can hear your shows individually or subscribe to your podcast so that new shows are automatically downloaded for them.

Podcasting may sound a little difficult, but once you get through the first one you'll realize it's not as hard as it seems. You might even have a little fun with it. Heaven forbid! Work that's fun?

Step 1: Get and Install the Right Tools

Since podcasts are just online broadcasts, it makes sense that you need some recording tools to get the job done. You need the following items:

- Headset with a noise-canceling microphone. Don't cut corners here; if your sound is of poor quality, listeners won't return. Many MP3 players actually have built-in microphones, by the way, which will work just fine for this project.

- Podcasting software, such as Audacity (free), Propaganda. You can get Audacity at www.audacity.sorceforge.net or Propaganda at CNET's www.download.com. There are lots of other choices on the Web, too. In fact, some podcast directories now offer podcast software (see "Step 4: Upload Your Podcast to the Internet").

- Computer with an Internet connection.

In some cases, a portable MP3 voice recorder is used, but for this project, you won't need one. I created a podcast using free trial software (Propaganda) that I downloaded off the Internet and a headset I happened to have lying around; if you have headphones already, go ahead and use them for your first podcast test and see how the sound comes across.

Speaking of software, I recommend choosing one that touts its simplicity. Podcasting does not have to be difficult; the software you choose will make the difference between a tough project and a very simple one.

note *Podcasts can include music, too, as a background or as the main content in your podcast.*

Step 2: Create Your Content

Do yourself a favor and at least write down an outline for your first podcast. Unless you're a skilled public speaker, you're likely to lose your train of thought as you record your first podcast. An outline can help you keep your wits together, stay on track, and keep listeners connected as your podcast plays.

Before you can write an outline, however, you need to have an idea of the topics that might work for your podcast. While every home office runs a different business, here are some general topics that might spark some ideas for you. Just plug in your business where it's appropriate. You can talk about:

- Your business topics
- A local sports team
- Current events and the latest news
- Seasonal activities in your area (hunting, snowboarding, waterskiing, etc.)
- The latest movies or television shows
- Interesting people in your demographic (conduct interviews with them!)
- *Anything* that applies to your target audience (cooking, shopping, automotive tips, college life, animals, children, etc.)

tip *Listen to a few podcasts to get an idea of how and why the successful ones work. Go to http://podcasts.yahoo.com or www.podcast.net and poke around to see what interests you—and others.*

Also, try researching podcast directories as shown in Figure 18-1. Those can help you get a good idea of the podcasts already out there, and might spark some ideas for you. If you work for a corporation, take a look at their marketing materials for ideas, too. Play up an advertising campaign with a podcast of your own or come up with a new one. The only important thing to remember is that the podcast complements both your business and your own personal interests. Otherwise, you'll get bored—and so will your listeners. But if a topic is close to your heart, the passion will come across in your podcast and hook those listeners long-term.

tip *Give listeners a preview of the next show at the end of your podcast. This reminds people to tune in and gives them something to look forward to.*

Figure 18-1

Several web sites offer podcast directories to help listeners find the podcast that's right for them.

Step 3: Record Your Podcast

The first item to consider when you begin recording is the location you're in. You want to find a quiet spot for the actual recording; background noise will turn off listeners fast. Get comfortable, be sure your headset is plugged into your computer (and is situated nicely upon your head), then open your sound recording program. For this project, we will use Propaganda—the free trial software downloaded off the Internet.

1. In Propaganda, choose File | Record to open the Record dialog box, shown in Figure 18-2.

2. In the Record dialog box, select Maximize Volume and Apply Noise Filter if they aren't already selected.

Figure 18-2

Propaganda's Record dialog box shows you information about your microphone and recording levels.

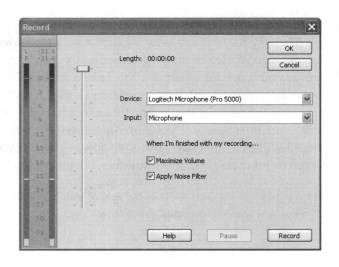

note *If your microphone is not recording sound, check all connections and try bringing the microphone closer to your mouth. If that doesn't work, check the input controls to be sure you have the proper levels set for your microphone. As a final step, check the instruction booklet for your sound card. You might need to add an auxiliary power supply to your microphone port.*

3. Click Record when you are ready to begin speaking. Notice the recording level bars on the left side; those move as you speak. Also, the word "Recording" appears in red letters to remind you that you are recording.

tip *At any time during the recording, you can click Pause. This gives you time to gather your thoughts or just take a break. When you're ready to begin recording again, click Record.*

4. When you're finished, click OK.

5. In the Label Recording dialog box, fill in the information requested (Title, Artist, Show, File Name) and click OK.

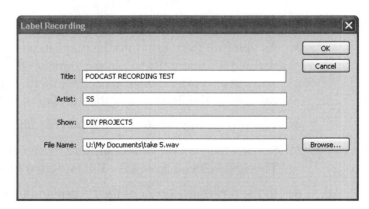

Your recording will appear in the Title/Transition pane on your screen as well as in the Library. Now you are ready to create a playlist, which will then be exported to the Internet:

1. Choose File | New Playlist.

2. In the Library pane, click and drag the recordings you want to add to your playlist, as shown in Figure 18-3.

Figure 18-3

A simple click-and-drag action creates a final playlist.

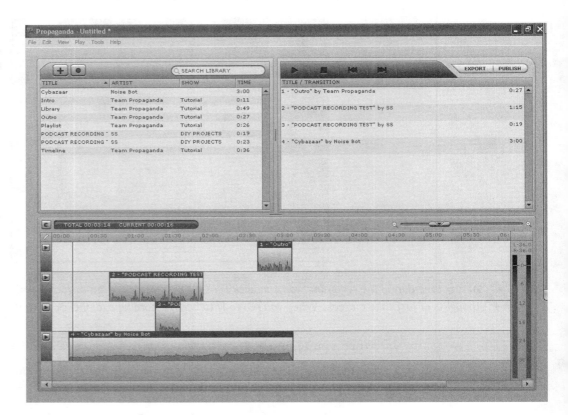

3. As you pull the items onto the playlist, you can click and drag each recorded segment horizontally to place it exactly where you want in the final playlist. You can also extend or crop each segment, as shown in Figure 18-4. The vertical lines in the figure show the number of times the segment was extended.

4. When you're ready to save the playlist, choose File | Save Playlist.

5. Select a location on your computer to save it to, name the file, and click Save. This ensures you have saved the original files.

6. In the top-right corner of the Propaganda window, click Export.

Figure 18-4

In segment 2, the segment has been extended to more than twice its original size.

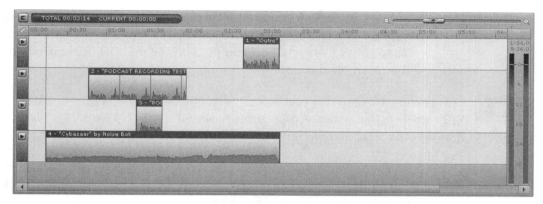

7. In the Export Options dialog box, select Export My Playlist To One Or More Files. Click OK.

8. In the Export Playlist to Files dialog box, type the filename for your file. If you plan to do many podcasts, it's a good idea to date the file in the title. For example, "My First Podcast 6_12_2007" helps you identify the podcast quickly and easily.

9. In the Save As Type drop-down list box, select Mixed MP3 File (*.mp3) and click Save. This creates the actual sound file for the podcast. You'll need this sound file to publish your podcast to the Web.

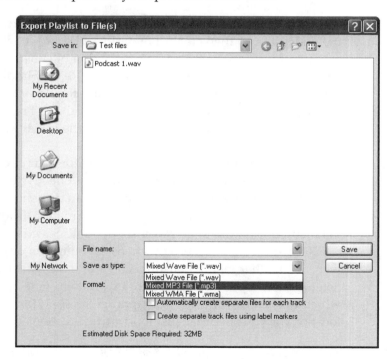

You can choose other file formats, such as WAV or WMA. These formats have a tendency to consume a lot more space per minute of your podcast, so MP3 is the best size to choose, especially if you plan on the podcast being used on an iPod, Zune, or other portable device.

> **tip** *If you have trouble converting your podcast to an MP3 file, you might need to add an MP3 encoder to your system. A popular free encoder is LAME MP3 Encoder, available at www.free-codecs.com/Lame_Encoder_download.htm.*

There are plenty of things you can do with a program like Propaganda to spice up your podcast—you can overlay sound, increase or decrease sound at certain points, and take advantage of other nifty features. These are all great features, and as you become more comfortable using your software, you can get more creative. But essentially, your podcast recording is now complete.

Step 4: Upload Your Podcast to the Internet

Propaganda offers a web syndication service and methods for publishing your podcast to your own web site. However, I chose not to use Propaganda to publish my podcast to my web site. Instead, I placed the MP3 file created in the previous section into my web site folder on my hard drive. Then I simply added a link on my web site to the MP3 file—viewers could just click the link to hear the file.

To add a link to your web site, follow the instructions of your web publishing software. Essentially, however, you will create a short line of text such as "Listen to the podcast" and then create a hyperlink to connect listeners to the MP3 file.

If you want to offer listeners the option of subscribing to your regular podcasts, you need to create an RSS feed. RSS means Really Simple Syndication—it's the format used by web sites and blogs to distribute regularly updated content. A bonus with RSS feeds it that they bypass spam filters and don't require you to deal with subscription management issues. Once you set up the initial RSS file, you can distribute your ongoing content with minimal effort.

It's worth setting up a syndication feed for your podcast if you're serious about attracting new customers. Syndication is cost-effective and a great way to build awareness of your business and brand, plus it can drive traffic to your web site and make it easy for existing customers to get information from you. Project 20 offers more detailed information to help you set up an RSS feed for your web site and podcasts.

Regardless of whether you choose syndication or just post your podcast to your web site, neither method ensures you will have listeners. You need to go where your listeners are, too. Podcast directories can help you find them; you'll need to decide which one works best for your particular situation. When you choose a directory location for your podcast, just follow the directions for adding a podcast.

> **note** *Most podcast directories expect you to have an RSS URL for your podcast.*

Here is a sample of sites and directories that will accept your podcast.

- **Google Base (http://google.com/base)** Accepts links to your own web site or hosts the podcast and provides you with a unique URL for it.

- **Podcast Alley (www.podcastalley.com)** Accepts podcast listings and indexes them to make it easy for users to find.

- **Yahoo! Podcasts (http://podcasts.yahoo.com)** Accepts podcast listings and has good advice for creating podcasts.

- **Podblaze (www.podblaze.com)** Offers users podcast software with the ability to create a podcast station with a podcasting web site and corresponding domain.

- **Digital Podcast (www.digitalpodcast.com)** Offers users podcast software and accepts podcasts for its directory.

- **Podcast.net (www.podcast.net)** Offers a directory that accepts podcasts.

Step 5: Advertise Your Podcast

While podcasts are a relatively new phenomenon, they are gaining popularity, especially among college-age listeners. This means that as these listeners age, they will expect to hear your messages in the formats they prefer. Establish these potential clients as listeners now, and you're looking at holding onto them as clients for a long time. Advertising your podcast is a good way to reach these listeners.

The podcast directories mentioned in the previous section are a great way to advertise your podcast. If you list a podcast in one of these directories, be sure to take some time to enter genre and content categories (such as "comedy" or "movies") that will help your listeners find you easily. But there are other ways to grab attention for your podcast.

Podcast forums, for example, are often provided by podcast directory sites. Don't be afraid to jump into a forum and plug your podcast! The directories also feature specific podcasts on a weekly or monthly basis. Check with the directory to which you belong to see how your podcast can qualify as a featured podcast.

Another way to advertise your podcast is to add it to your business cards. While it might be fun to have listeners all around the world, if your specialty is selling insurance in a particular state, then you need to be sure you're reaching local listeners, too. Include the podcast in any other local advertising you do, and on any marketing materials.

Other Considerations

On the Web, attention spans are short. Keep that in mind and create your podcast accordingly—if you don't come across with your relevant business messages early and often, they will be lost to listeners who click in for just a few minutes. Another good rule of thumb to keep listeners hanging on is to tell them what they will hear in your podcast as well as what they won't. Tell them that at 2 minutes and 30 seconds, you'll discuss XYZ, for example. Those who want to listen to your entire podcast will wait, while those who want to hear a certain section can skip forward quickly. Either way, you've kept all your listeners and given them the opportunity to find what interests them quickly.

As far as recording goes, keep at it until you have a perfect take. No one will want to suffer through your stops and starts, coughs, or lengthy pauses, let alone a recording that squeaks or has static or background noise.

If you feel funny talking into a microphone by yourself, why not podcast with someone else? Having a partner can help you stay motivated and on task; plus it's just more fun.

It's okay to use background music, but keep it simple. If your podcast is about financial planning, listeners are tuning in to hear about that topic—not your favorite song. Speaking of favorite songs, be cautious when using copyrighted music. If you don't have the legal rights to use the music, don't use it.

tip   *Record in small sound bites. It's easier for you to get it right with small bits of dialogue, and the end result will be a high-quality recording.*

How you produce your podcast is ultimately up to you. But keep this in mind: which radio shows do you enjoy listening to the most? Analyze what makes those shows interesting. Is it guests? Banter? Detailed information? Music? Whatever it is, don't be afraid to copy the format. At the same time, don't be afraid to change your show until the format is exactly what you want. If you're not happy, listeners won't be happy. Keep adjusting until things feel right, then keep the format going so listeners can bond with you.

Podcasts can be fun and very, very simple to produce. The question is, what are *you* going to talk about on yours?

Set Up an RSS Feed for Your Web Site

What You'll Need:
- Web site or blog: Yes
- Software: None
- Hardware: None
- Cost: $0
- Difficulty: Advanced

Really Simple Syndication—that's what RSS stands for. It's a syndication format for web content that anyone with a web site can offer free to readers, and it is a great way to keep visitors coming back to your web site. RSS feeds come in all shapes and sizes; in fact, you can probably find one for any hobby or interest you can think of. With more and more people today subscribing to RSS feeds, take a few minutes to think about your business and the information you might be able to share with others in this format.

For any web site, a steady stream of traffic is necessary to keep the site successful in terms of product and service sales. You can have an informational web site, of course, that doesn't sell anything, but even those sites need visitors to make it worth shelling out the money to keep the site operating. That's where the business knowledge you have can come in handy. It can become the source of an RSS feed that others subscribe to—and that keeps them thinking about you, your web site, and your business every time they read it.

tip *RSS feeds help keep search engine spiders returning often to your site to index your pages because of continually changing information on your site.*

The information doesn't necessarily need to be in written format; podcasts, discussed in Project 18, can easily be used for RSS feeds, as you'll see in this project. These feeds offer information of all kinds. As you read through this project, put a creativity hat on your head. You just might be surprised at the ideas that come to you for creating an RSS feed that offers your web site readers great information and acts as a consistent marketing tool for your business.

note *Syndication has been around for decades in the newspaper industry. Cartoons and columns (Dear Abby, for example) are created, then made available to any newspaper that cares to run the item. The newspaper pays a fee for each syndicated item it runs. RSS syndication operates on a similar concept, except that the content is always free.*

Step 1: Understand How RSS Feeds Work with Your Web Site

An RSS feed is just a file that contains items. The items are the web pages that you want others to link to. When you publish new content to your web site (a podcast, an article, new products or services—anything!), your goal is to have others know about it, right? By listing that new item's location on your web site as an "item" in your RSS file, the new item's information appears to anyone receiving your RSS feed. Readers just click to follow the link to your new content.

You need three pieces of information to add your item into an RSS file: the title of the item, a description for it, and a link to it. These items are created using HTML (hypertext markup language).

HTML Introduction

To create an actual RSS feed, you do need to know a little bit about how your web site is coded. Typically, web sites use a language called HTML to produce the site that everyone sees. However, there are plenty of programs available that make it easy to create a web site without ever knowing any code. Microsoft FrontPage, for example, allows you to drop in pictures, text, and other content in a design view that never shows you the coding that occurs every time you drop in that picture or text (see Figure 19-1). Microsoft Expression is another equally simple-to-use web design tool that keeps coding out of the way unless you want to specifically see it. At the same time, these programs almost always offer you the option of switching views so you can see the code involved (see Figure 19-2).

All that code looks pretty frightening, I know. But you don't need to worry about *all* that code, just a small part of it. That's because there are tools on the Internet that help you out: RSS code generators. Some of them require you to enter small amounts of the code from the page you want to designate as an RSS feed; others don't.

Here's the real deal with HTML code: you need it to tell the Internet where things start and stop on your web page. For example, if you include a title on your web site ("Sally Slack's Web Site"), you need to indicate somehow that it's a title instead of a simple phrase. You do this by using code that precedes the title, and by using code at the end of the title. As HTML is translated to other computers, the title appears the way you want it to. But if you leave off the code, the title can't appear. It's the same

Figure 19-1

A web page shown in Microsoft FrontPage design view.

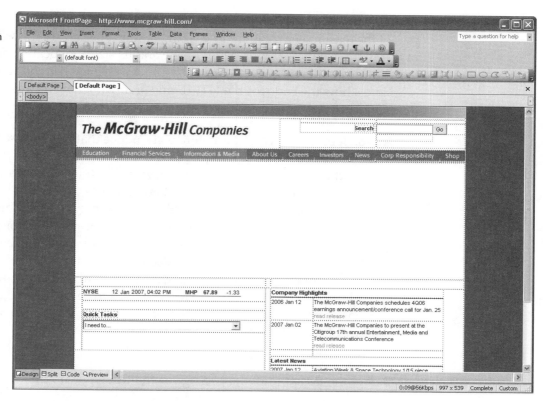

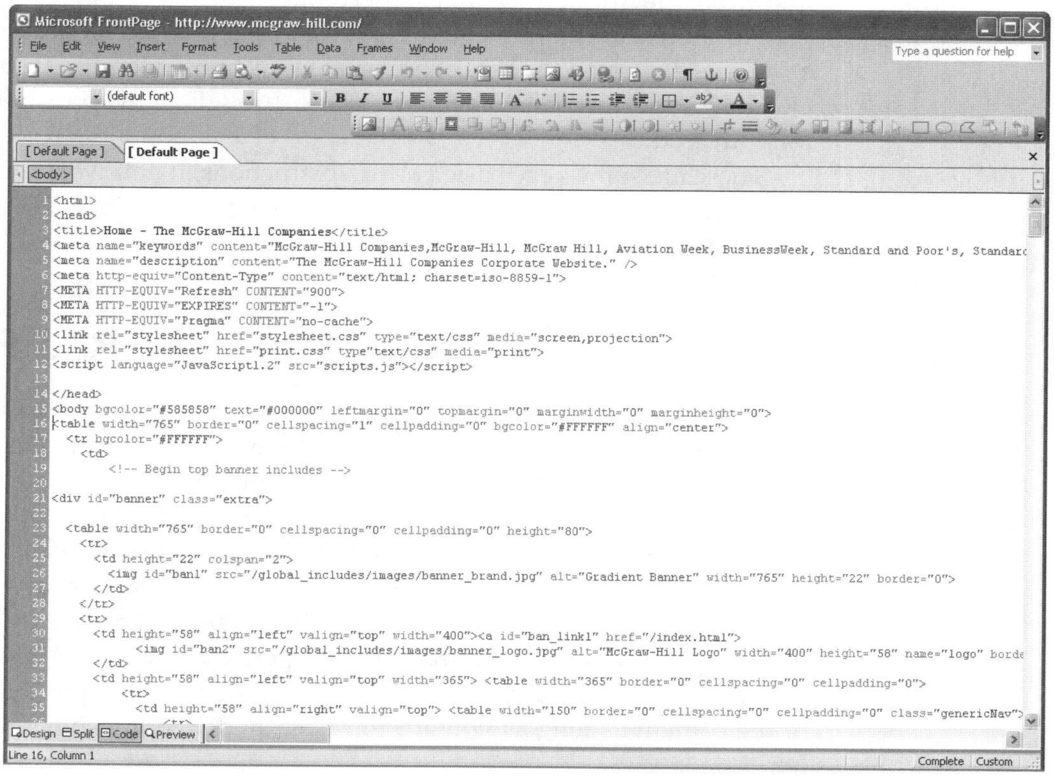

Figure 19-2

The same web page, shown in Microsoft FrontPage code view.

with any other content on your web site—HTML codes appear for everything. That's part of the reason seeing Figure 19-2 is frightening: you can see the code for every piece of text in bold, italic, or color; every image and its size and location on the page; every headline; every paragraph, etc. *Everything* on a web page has code attached to it.

Here's how the code for the HTML title on my main web page looks:

```
<title>Sally Slack's Web Site</title>
```

As you look at the word *title* before Sally, notice that it is enclosed by angle brackets. In the first appearance of *title*, there is no forward slash within the angle brackets. In the second instance of *title*, there is a forward slash within the angle brackets. The presence of a forward slash after the first angle bracket "closes" the coding information, whereas the lack of one "opens" the coding information. This open and close feature of HTML language tells computers what information is contained within the angle brackets. Any HTML code placed in the angle brackets will be read correctly as long as the angle brackets and forward slash are used appropriately.

This is important to understand as you work with HTML code. Whenever you open a code, you need to close it. Codes also need to be closed in the order they were opened. For example, if the title for my web page included code to bold all the letters, the code would look like this:

```
<title><bold>Sally Slack's Web Site</bold></title>
```

Before the actual title, the coding for the title appears first, then coding for the bold text appears second. But after the actual title, coding for the bold text appears first while the title coding appears second.

For more information about HTML coding, take a look at HTML Code Tutorial, a web site dedicated to HTML coding, at www.htmlcodetutorial.com. It has an HTML Quick List and tutorials to help you wade through all the possibilities you could use for your feed.

These are some very basic HTML instructions; if you want more details, it might be useful to buy a separate book on building web sites with HTML coding. You won't need it, though, to complete this project.

Step 2: Decide on the Content for Your RSS Feed

Decisions, decisions! What kind of information should you share with readers in this format? The first thing to consider is the time you have available for any kind of ongoing content. Since RSS feeds rely on continual updates to keep readers happy, it's critical that the content you provide be something you can do on a regular basis.

Do you have 10 minutes a week to devote to this or 4 hours? Ten minutes might dictate that you offer a simple bulleted list of information every week or month; 4 hours could mean you have time to write a 500-word article. If your time may vary depending upon workload, that's okay—perhaps you offer that simple bulleted list one week, an article the next, and a podcast the next. It's okay to change the actual form of the content as long as you are consistently delivering something to your readers (or listeners).

Once you determine the amount of time you can devote to continuing content, it's time to think about the actual information you want to share. Considering that this feed will likely be for your business (rather than personal reasons), think about the kind of questions that you receive from clients or customers. The chances are good that you can identify several themes that will be of interest to readers. If you are affiliated with a corporation, be sure to check its marketing materials for ideas, too.

Here are some examples of business-related RSS feeds already in existence (don't be afraid to create a competing feed, by the way—yours could be bigger and better!). Some titles are self-explanatory, some are not, so I've included brief descriptors in parentheses.

- Straight Talk: Small Business News
- How to Save the World (environmentalist)
- Arts/Crafts Business
- Beauty Dish (beauty products distributor)
- The Work of Photographers
- Halo Babies (comic strip artist)
- FreshFinance
- Moreover—Automotive Industry News

These examples, which barely touch on the feed topics available, show that every industry and every type of business person has information to share. When you title your feed, keep in mind that "Mike's News" isn't going to attract as many readers as say, "Mike's Nissan News" might. No one knows who Mike is, but they will recognize a brand name such as Nissan. As you create the title for your feed, keep those types of details in mind.

tip *If you are affiliated with a corporation, see whether it offers an RSS feed. You might be able to place the feed on your site or connect to the corporate feed and maintain your individual identity for feed readers.*

Step 3: Create an RSS Feed for Your Content

Now it's time to start creating your actual RSS file. There are a couple of different processes associated with this; we'll take each one step by step. As mentioned earlier in this project, you need three pieces of information to add your item into an RSS file: the title of the item, a description for it, and a link to it. *The item itself is a web page.*

Create or Identify the Web Pages to Be Used in Your Feed

The first step is to identify or create the web pages that will hold the content for your RSS feed. Each web page can be a separate item in your RSS feed, but you can't make multiple RSS feeds from a single web page—the feed will only recognize one web page at a time, not the various elements on the web page.

As an example, I decided to create a separate web page for every new book I have coming out in the next six months. On my main web page, as shown in Figure 19-3, I have a section called "Book News" and limited information about each book.

Figure 19-3

The author's home page with the Book News section.

But I wanted to create a feed that updated each book's news separately. For each book—there are currently three—I created a new, individual web page with more details about the book and when it will be available. These individual web pages (as shown in Figure 19-4) will become the items in my RSS feed.

There's no need to create a special web page; just create them the way you normally would.

Create the RSS File

Once you have created or identified the web pages you will use in your RSS feed, you need to create the RSS file. The easiest way I've found to do this is to use Notepad, which is a simple word processing program available in any version of Windows. In Windows XP, follow these steps to open Notepad:

1. Click Start and select All Programs.

2. Go to Accessories and click Notepad to open it.

Figure 19-4

An individual web page from the author's web site, which is used as an item in her RSS feed.

tip   *WordPad puts in additional formatting characters that might disable your XML. If you need to use WordPad instead of Notepad, be sure to save the file in text-only format.*

Enter the Code in Your RSS File

Next, you'll enter the code for your feed. This is where that brief lesson on coding earlier in this project will help you out. I'll show you line by line where to put the code using the code I have used on my own web site. Where text is in bold, you should change it to meet your web site and item information. *Do not* change the code associated with a line. Lines 1–6 are identifying information for the feed and your main web site; the following lines are specific items you want included in the feed. In my case, those were specific books and their related web pages.

tip   *If you're working in code view, it can be difficult to find the text you want. Use the Edit/Find tool to locate the first word of any phrase you're looking for.*

In Notepad, enter the following code *including and between* the angle brackets (< >) symbols (do not include Line X or the dashes preceding the code). Line 1 shows you an example of the highlighted code. In other lines, change anything in bold to meet your personal needs. Otherwise, leave the coding the same as shown here.:

```
Line 1 -- <?xml version="1.0" encoding="UTF-8"?>
Line 2 -- <rss version="2.0">
```

```
Line 3 -- <channel>
Line 4 -- <title>Sally Slack's Book News</title>
Line 5 -- <description>Get the latest news on publication dates!
</description>
Line 6 -- <link>http://www.sslack.com</link>
Line 7 -- <item>
Line 8 -- <title>PC Magazine's Office 2007 Solutions</title>
Line 9 -- <description>This well-organized guide is perfect for anyone
upgrading to Microsoft Office 2007!</description>
Line 10 -- <link>http://www.sslack.com/booknews.htm</link>
Line 11 -- </item>
Line 12 -- <item>
Line 13 -- <title>Breakthrough Windows Vista</title>
Line 14 -- <description>Find your favorite features and discover the
possibilities!</description>
Line 15 -- <link>http://www.sslack.com/booknews2.htm</link>
Line 16 -- </item>
Line 17 -- <item>
Line 18 -- <title>CNET Do-It-Yourself Digital Home Office Projects
</title>
Line 19 -- <description>Use the latest wireless and Web technologies to
create a digital workspace!</description>
Line 20 -- <link>http://www.sslack.com/booknews3.htm</link>
Line 21 -- </item>
Line 22 -- </channel>
Line 23 -- </rss>
```

See Figure 19-5 for how this exact code looks within Notepad. You can certainly add more items to your feed; just continue coding as shown in Figure 19-5.

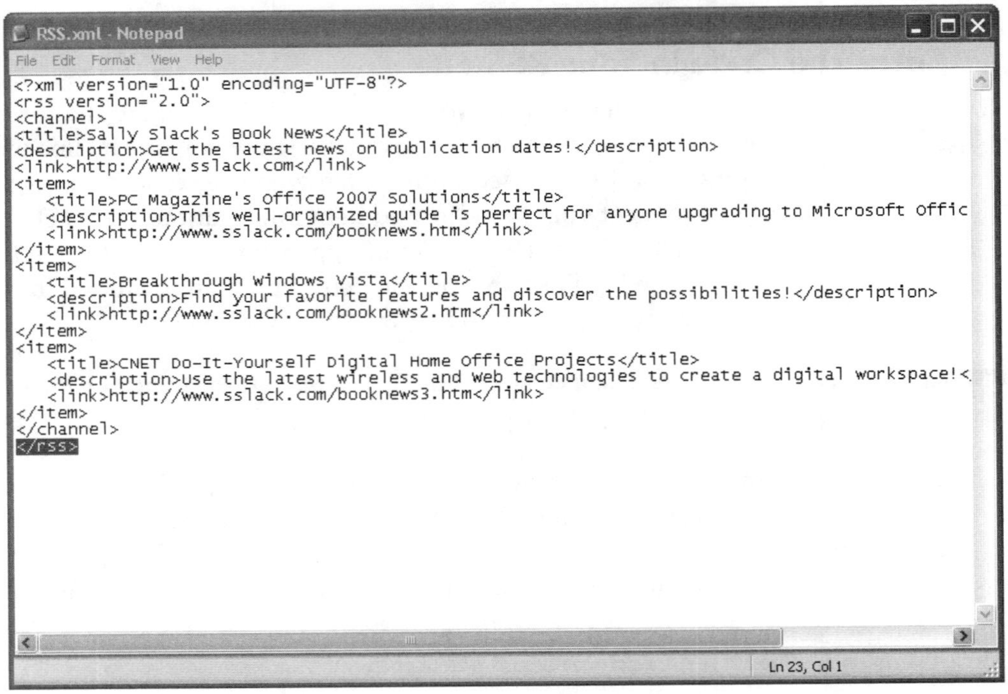

Figure 19-5

RSS code as it appears within Notepad

As you look at the code in Notepad, you can easily see how each item contains a title, description, and link—all the requirements for an RSS feed.

```
<item>
     <title>Breakthrough Windows Vista</title>
     <description>Find your favorite features and discover the possibilities!</description>
     <link>http://www.sslack.com/booknews2.htm</link>
</item>
```

note *Project 18 shows how to create a podcast. To add that podcast to your RSS feed, be sure the podcast file is located in the root folder for your web site. Create a page for it just as you would any other informational item you want to add to your RSS feed, providing a link somewhere on the page to the actual podcast file. Then simply follow the same coding steps for adding that podcast web page as a new item in your RSS feed.*

The additional coding at the beginning and end of the RSS file is necessary for the Internet to recognize other aspects of the RSS feed, such as the version. Don't sweat it, just copy what's shown here and you'll be fine.

tip *You can purchase software such as FeedForAll (www.feedforall.com) to create your feeds if you don't want to take the time to learn how to do it.*

When your code is complete, you need to save the Notepad document as an XML file:

1. Choose File | Save As.

2. In the Save As dialog box, select the root folder for your web site.

3. In the File Name list box, type **RSS.xml.**

4. In the Save As Type list box, select Text Documents (*txt).

5. Click Save.

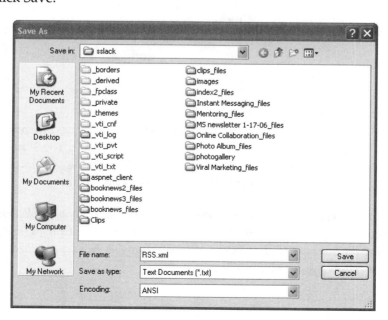

tip *Channels appear in a file to show how items in the feed relate to each other.*

The RSS file should now be saved in the same file as all your other web pages. As a final check here, go to Feed Validator at www.feedvalidator.org and enter the main URL for your feed (the one you used in Line 6). RSS file validation is always changing, so you might see some comments or a warning suggesting you place additional code in the file. Don't worry about that *unless* the validator also indicates that your code is not valid. For example, my validation request returned with a warning saying I needed to add a guid element—an element really only necessary for weblogs, not web pages.

As I scrolled down the page, the validation also said "Congratulations! This is a valid RSS feed."

Congratulations!

Take warnings with a grain of salt but do pay attention if the validator can't find your feed or doesn't see the items within it. You'll need to go back and double-check every line to find the mistake, although the validator sometimes returns error information targeting a specific line of your code.

tip *Having trouble saving your RSS file as an XML file? Occasionally, a Windows default causes this problem. Choose Start | My Computer, select Tools/Folder Options, and go to the View tab. Be sure the box next to Hide Extensions For Known File Types is not checked. If it is, it's probably the cause of your saving problem.*

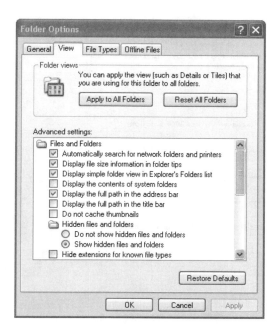

You're ready to move on to adding the feed to your web site.

Step 4: Add the RSS Feed to Your Web Site

Relax—you've made it through the toughest parts of this project. Adding the feed to your web site is actually very simple: you just place text or an icon on your web site (the home page is fine) the same way you would add any other content and then add a hyperlink to the RSS file you already placed in your web site's root folder.

For mine, I found an RSS feed icon online that was free. I also decided to place text next to it just in case folks new to RSS didn't recognize the icon. Once the icon and text were in place, I just added the hyperlink to the RSS file.

When someone clicks the link, they are taken to the RSS feed for the site, as shown in Figure 19-6.

Notice that the headlines on the feed are exactly the same as the ones in the code shown earlier. Readers can click each headline to go directly to the correlating page. However, by clicking Subscribe To This Feed in the box at the top of the page, readers can have the feed automatically added to their web browser and even some e-mail providers—any program that uses the Common Feed List.

🍁 Subscribe to this feed

Figure 19-6

Your RSS feed will take readers to a page that looks like this.

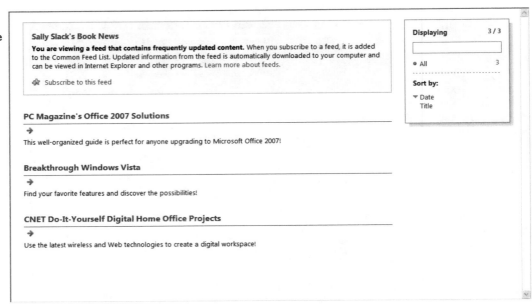

Here's how a feed looks once it's been placed into Internet Explorer 7 feeds:

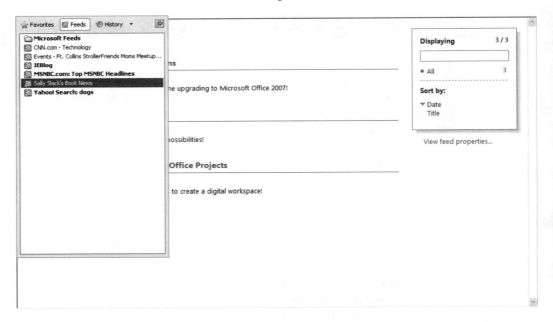

So, there you have it. You have created an RSS feed for your web site, and you can update it as much or as little as you like. For maximum effectiveness, of course, you should update it on a routine basis—readers enjoy seeing new information and will return regularly to your web site if they find that information compelling enough. There's one more option to consider for RSS feeds, however. Many blogs offer RSS feed options, so we'll take a quick look at that before we leave this topic.

Other Considerations: Blogging and RSS Feeds

You've probably heard about blogging by now, and the chances are good that you've read many blogs recently, perhaps without even knowing it. That's because blogs—or weblogs as they are officially known—are just web sites that are ridiculously simple to create and update, even by those with very minimal technical knowledge. There is no code involved, and the content is entered directly onto a web-based application that updates your blog instantly.

In some ways, blogs are really just online journals—the author writes about whatever he or she wants with no editing involved, can add hyperlinks within the blog, and can accept comments from readers about the content provided. A URL is given to every blog, so it's easy to link to your blogs through your web site. Blogs typically change often, but the changes are at the author's whim. A sample blog is shown in Figure 19-7. If you like to write, you might really enjoy the freedom that a blog gives—as well as its ability to reach thousands and ultimately drive those readers to your web site.

Figure 19-7

A sample blog

Because blog content changes so often, it's a good partner for an RSS feed since people subscribe to feeds for access to routinely updated information. And the beauty of a blog is that most of the major blogging sites offer an automatic service to help you turn your blog into a syndicated feed. Newsreaders or aggregators—just specialized software on the Internet—scan the feeds that contain the blogs, and update information often.

The entire process involves the site feed settings on your blog. On Blogger, for example, some simple changes in the site feed settings will place all or just part of your blog content into a site feed, as shown next. Search engines like Google index blogs by their site feeds, which are checked frequently for new content.

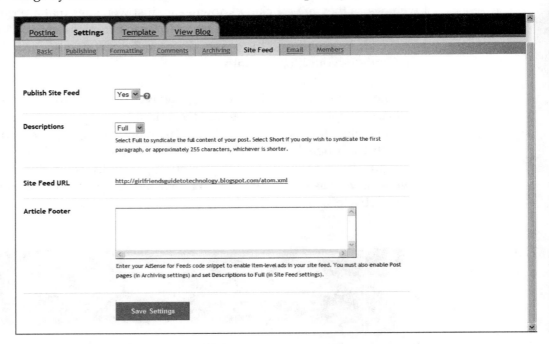

You can always add your blog to your own web site's RSS feed. Just add the blog as a new item in your Notepad RSS file, like this:

```
<item>
    <title>Girlfriend's Guide to Technology</title>
    <description>Technology tips, tricks and totally awesome features!
</description>
    <link>http://girlfriendsguidetotechnology.blogspot.com/</link>
</item>
```

As you can see, the URL used here is the one that links directly to my blog, not my web site. That's okay—because of the coding at the front and end of the RSS file, the feed knows that the new item belongs with the rest of my feed. In Figure 19-8, you can see how the blog shows up just like all the other items in my RSS feed.

There are lots of blogging sites available if you're interested in starting one. Most of them are incredibly simple to create and use, so don't be afraid to give one a try. While there is blog software available, it's worth taking a look at all the free blogging options before you spend a dime. Here's a look at five blogging options:

- **Blogger (www.blogger.com)**   Basic services are free; this one is owned by Google.

- **Blog.com (www.blog.com)**   Basic services are free.

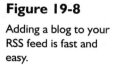

Figure 19-8

Adding a blog to your RSS feed is fast and easy.

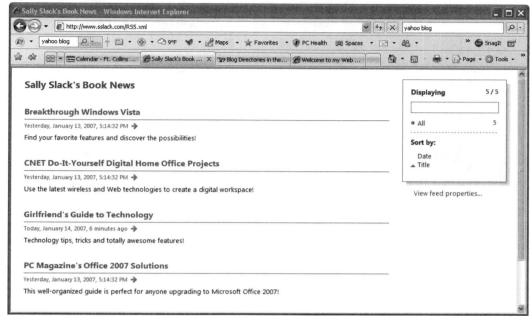

- **TypePad (www.typepad.com)**   A free trial is offered, and basic services start at $4.95/month.

- **Blogstream (www.blogstream.com)**   Basic services are free.

- **Squarespace (www.squarespace.com)**   Basic services start at $7/month.

You can submit your blog to various catalogs (try www.blogcatalog.com or www.bloghop.com) and indexes, too, for maximum reach.

tip   *At Blogger, your site feed settings can also include your AdSense code. You need to get AdSense for Feeds, and then you can enter the code to place your ads in your blog's feed.*

If you're still a bit doubtful about the coding involved, remember this: You are an intelligent, competent business person. There's no reason you can't copy some code from this book, add in your own details, and create an RSS feed for your web site. It's a great marketing tool that keeps your web site in front of your audience, and takes very little time to set up. After that, it's just a matter of adding content to keep the RSS feed updated regularly. Give it a try!

Part V

Work Securely from Home

Turn an Old PC into a Network Server

What You'll Need:

- **Operating system: Windows XP, Windows Vista**
- **Software: None**
- **Hardware: Unused personal computer with hard drive**
- **Cost: $0**
- **Difficulty: Challenging**

If there is one computer law to remember, it is to never discard a PC when you upgrade to the latest and greatest version. Another is that, eventually, you'll have a hard drive that crashes. It's a fact of life for anyone who owns a computer. Hard drives don't die gracefully, either—they die without warning and usually just when you have a major project due.

Backing up files regularly is the only way to be certain you won't be caught with your pants down at a critical moment—but if you own more than one computer, don't just back up your files anywhere. Have a plan that includes a central file server so that when a hard drive fails you, you won't fail your clients or company. You can easily do this with a network file server, which can very easily be set up using an old PC.

Another reason to set up a network server? Space. While newer computers have lots of storage space, newer computer programs take up more space as well—Windows Vista and all its media applications, for example, sucks up hard drive space quickly. Keep that space open on your primary computer so you'll have a system that is more responsive to your business needs, and use network server space to store the monster files you won't erase for years.

There are two more reasons to set up a network server: collaboration and convenience. A networked server lets you share and access files and printers on a computer on your network if you wish. And, even though you work from home, this feature comes in handy if you have, say, a personal computer that's separate from your work computer. If you have to watch a sick child in another room beside your office and still get work done, why not use the family computer in the playroom to access files on your home office computer down the hall? You can even print to a printer attached to the server without dragging files from one place to another. You can do all this with a networked server.

note *Projects 23 and 24 in this book show you how to set up and secure a wireless network.*

Before you get all worked up and begin thinking that creating this network server is beyond your capabilities, consider this: you wouldn't have a home office if you weren't extremely capable of tackling challenges on your own. Creating a network server from an old PC is just another one of those challenges. It may sound scary, but ultimately it's just a logical process.

note *This project can be done with a Mac, a Windows PC, or a Linux PC. While the basic pieces of the project will be similar, there may be some difference in network setup, so just check your operating system for specific details. For this project, the assumption is made that your old computer is not running Windows Vista, but that your new computer might be.*

Step 1: Check Out Your Personal Computer

Take a look at that old PC before you get started with this project. If the concept here is to ensure that you have a reliable backup system with plenty of space, you'll want to verify a few things on the old system:

1. Hard drive size is the most critical piece of this project. You don't need a lot of memory or a hypersonic processor, but you do need a hard drive that can store all your files. A sample hard drive is shown in Figure 20-1. You can buy a new hard drive with 320 GB of storage capacity for about $90 online. This amount of space is worth the price—you won't need to upgrade for a long time. But as long as you have a hard drive with 100GB of storage capacity, you should be able to do anything you need to.

2. Hard drive warranty is the next thing to consider. How old is the hard drive you plan to use? If it has passed its warranty period, you're taking a calculated risk as to how long it will last. There is no hard and fast rule on this; just take the hard drive's age into consideration. The hard drive is where your information is stored, so you want to feel confident that your hard drive is going to serve you well.

note *A warranty doesn't guarantee a hard drive will never fail, only that it can be repaired or replaced when it fails. No warranty covers the data loss, either.*

3. Motherboards and other hardware should be similarly inspected for age and condition. While you're unlikely to lose any information if a motherboard goes belly up, it can cause a delay in your backups.

Figure 20-1

Hard drive size is the most important aspect of this project.

4. A monitor is a "nice to have" item on this project, but really, you can use a monitor from another system on the network to check information on this used PC. If you do decide to use a monitor with this network server, check to be sure it's working well enough for you to see windows and dialog boxes on the screen.

> **note** *Systems with Windows XP and above can be accessed remotely from another machine that has Windows 98 and above; see Project 10 for more details.*

5. A network connection is the final key component. Your connection can be wireless or wired to a router—just be sure it's working before you start the project!

> **note** *If you don't want to use an old PC (or don't have one to use), you can purchase a network-attached storage (NAS) drive. These drives can be attached and accessed from anywhere on your network and are easily configured. This option is more expensive than using an old PC, however—NAS drives average about $200 or more, while using your old PC should cost you nothing.*

Step 2: Create the Folder

Configuring a desktop computer as a network server sounds daunting, but in reality, this configuration consists of creating a new folder on your old computer, sharing it with other computers, and giving users access to the folder and any files within it.

That doesn't sound too hard, does it? It's not—it will take a little bit of time, however, so grab some chips and caffeine before you get started.

1. Start your old computer.

2. Click Start | My Computer. This is where you can see all the drives on the computer. Decide which drive to put the network folder on. If you have more than one drive or partition on a drive, look for the drive with the most free space.

 To find the free space available on a hard drive, right-click the name of the hard drive. Click Properties. Used and free space will be shown under the General tab.

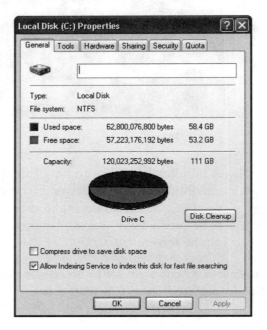

3. Double-click the hard drive you want to use.

4. Click File | New. Select Folder.

5. Give the folder a meaningful name but keep it concise so it's easy to remember.

That's it! Now you're ready to share the folder.

tip *When naming a folder, you can use up to 256 characters. Spaces can be included in the name but underscores are easier to use when trying to map from a desktop. Keep the name under eight characters if you, or anyone in your workgroup, are using Windows 95 or earlier or MS-DOS. Those operating systems cannot connect to a share that has a filename greater than eight characters or has spaces in the share name.*

Step 3: Share the Folder

Now that the folder has been created, you can use it to share files. You must have a network installed before you can share folders. Got to Project 23 for information on setting up a network.

note *See "Step 5: Give Access to Other Users" if you need more information on the permissions that can be provided to users.*

Here's how to set up sharing functions for the folder:

1. Right-click the folder you just created.

2. Click Sharing And Security. This action launches the Properties dialog box for the folder.

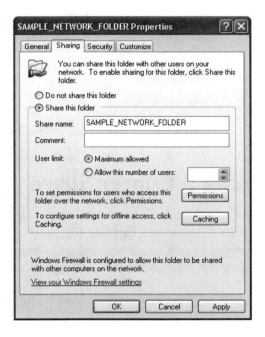

3. Click the Sharing tab.

4. Select Share This Folder.

5. In the Share Name field, type the name you want to call the share. Windows normally shows a suggested name and you can use that if you wish.

6. Click Permissions. In the Group Or User Names list, select those users that you will ultimately allow to access this network server.

7. In the Permissions box, select the permissions for each of those users you want to have access to the shared folder. These are the sharing permissions for the folder that will allow designated users to map to the shared drive; you will set up actual access for these users in the next section.

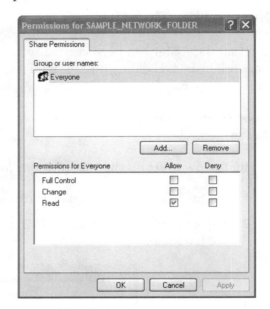

8. Click Apply.

9. Click OK.

10. In the folder's Properties dialog box, click OK.

Step 4: Create a Printer Share

When you work off a network, it's helpful if a printer is shared so that every computer on the network can use the printer. If one isn't shared, you'll spend precious time opening and accessing files from other computers just to print out a page or two. Creating a printer share on a network is really simple—just follow these steps:

1. On the computer you have designated for the network server, click Start.

2. Go to the Control Panel and double-click Printers And Faxes.

3. Right-click the name of the printer you want to share and click Sharing.

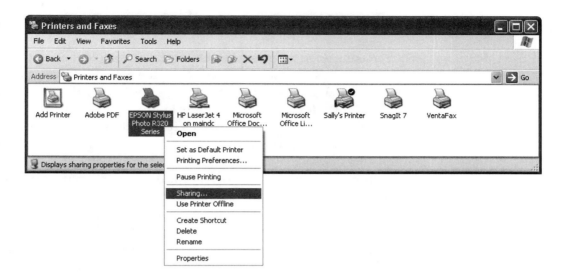

4. In the printer's Properties dialog box, click the Sharing tab.

5. Click Share This Printer.

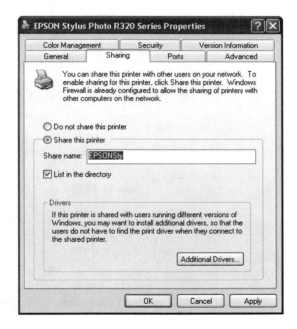

6. Click OK.

Repeat this process for every printer you want to share.

note *This section assumes you have all the proper printer drivers installed for all computers accessing the printer.*

Step 5: Give Access to Other Users

You're making good progress! You have created the folder and printer shares, and applied permissions so that others can access the network server. Next, you need to set up access so that others can use the folders, files, and printer on the network server. This is done by adding individual users or groups.

Giving access to users through the group method is the easiest approach because it lets you manage everyone from a single viewpoint. If you have lots of users and multiple directories to maintain, it's a particularly helpful approach. However, most home office users don't have extensive user lists; you may only want to give access to individual users.

Before we begin, take some time to review the varying permissions so you clearly understand the access you are providing to others. Permissions may seem harmless but accidental deletion of a file or folder can have dire consequences even if you have a great backup system in place. Table 20-1 lists and describes permissions that can be applied to files and folders, and Table 20-2 lists and describes permissions that can be applied to printers.

Full Control	User can make changes to, copy, delete, change permissions on, and do pretty much anything else to a file or folder. Only administrators or managers should have this access and only if they understand the consequences of what their actions can do.
Modify	Users can make changes to a file or folder, but cannot delete or move a file or folder.
Read and Execute	Users can start a program within a folder and read files. They cannot make changes to, delete, or even rename a file.
List Folder Contents	Users can see what is in the folder but cannot open or modify a file.
Read	Users can only read or open a file; they cannot run programs or make changes and save them to a file. (This is good for templates that you've created and do not want changed and for sensitive files.) When a user modifies a file and tries to save it, they will be prompted for a new filename or location.
Write	Users can write information to a file or create folders in the directory. Write permission is not normally used alone but it can be if you want to keep changes to a certain document in a separate location. Users can write to that directory but will be unable to modify or even read or see a file.
Special	Special is beyond the scope of this book.

Table 20-1   Permissions that Can Be Applied to Files and Folders

 If you grant the Read permission and don't grant List Folder Contents permission, users won't be able to browse for the file. They will have to know the exact path and name to get to the file.

Print	Users can print to the printer.
Manage Printers	Users can mange printer setting and control configurations on the printer as well as pause, move, remove, or delete print jobs.
Manage Documents	Users can pause, move, remove, or delete print jobs.
Special	Special is beyond the scope of this book.

Table 20-2   Permissions that Can Be Applied to Printers.

Create a User

To create a group, follow these steps:

1. Click Start.

2. Right-click My Computer and click Manage.

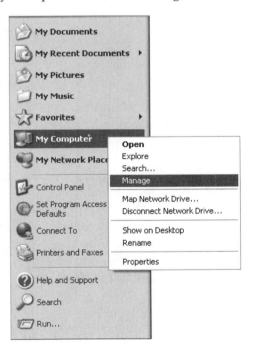

3. In the left navigation pane of the Computer Management window, expand Local Users And Groups by clicking the + next to it.

4. Click Users. The names of all users currently residing on your network will appear in the right pane.

5. Choose Action | New User.

6. In the New User dialog box, enter a name for the user in the User Name field. Add the full name and a description if you wish. If you want a password used for access, enter and confirm the password. Select password instructions by checking the appropriate check box.

tip *Be judicious when asking users to change their password at the next logon. If you do, when the user attempts to map a drive, it will fail with either an Access Denied message or no message at all, and this can be confusing for a user.*

7. Click Create. Continue adding names as needed.

8. Click Close when you have finished adding names. The names of the new users should now appear in the right pane of the Computer Management window.

Create a Group

Before you can create a group permission, you need to create a group. This group will consist of anyone you want to have access to the network files and folders; you have already set up the permissions to access the actual network. There are a lot of steps in this part of the process but don't let that intimidate you.

To create a group, follow these steps:

1. Click Start.

2. Right-click My Computer and click Manage. The Computer Management windows should appear.

3. In the left navigation pane, expand Local Users And Groups by clicking the + next to it.

4. Click Groups. All the groups currently residing on your network will appear in the right pane.

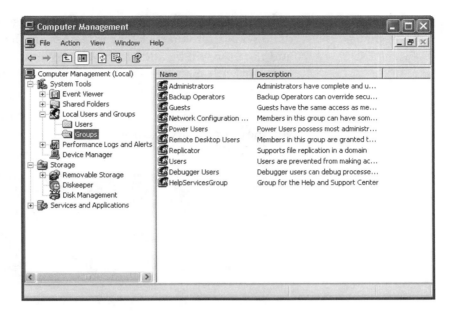

5. Choose Action | New Group.

6. In the New Group dialog box, enter a name for the group in the Group Name field. Add a description if you wish.

note *You might eventually need to use this security group for more than access to just one file or folder share, so do not give your group the same name as your network or printer share.*

7. Click Add. This launches the Select Users, Computers, or Groups dialog box.

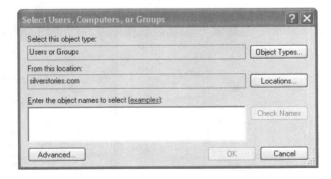

8. Under Enter The Object Names To Select (Examples), add the usernames you are approving for access.

9. Click Check Names. The user's name and identifying information will appear unless one of the following occurs:

   ● Multiple instances of a name launches the Multiple Names Found window; select the name you want and click OK.

- If the username is underlined in the Select Users, Computers, or Groups dialog box after you click Check Names and have added a user, click OK and the user will be added. If the username is *not* underlined, there is a problem with that user. Either the name is incorrect or that user doesn't exist on your network.

- If a name is not found, the Name Not Found dialog box appears to give you the opportunity to correct username details or remove that user from your selection.

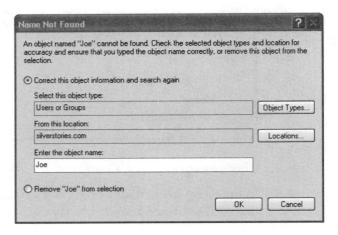

10. Click OK to return to the New Group dialog box.

11. Click Create.

12. Click Close. Your new user group should now appear in the right pane of the Computer Management window.

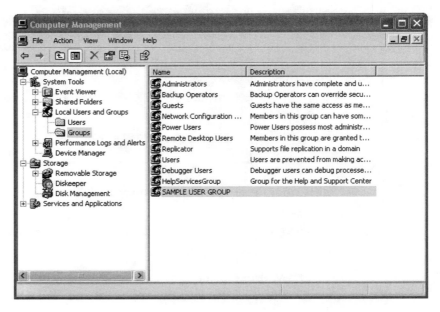

Give the Group or Individual User Permissions to Access the Shared Folder

At this point, you have created the folder and printer shares, applied permissions so that others can access the network server, and set up management access so that individuals or groups can use the folders, files, and printer on the network server. Now you need to go back to the shared folder that you created in Step 2 to add individual user and group access to that folder. Don't get confused, here—you're very close to completing this project. In the preceding steps, you created the users and groups and applied permission rules to them; this step takes those users and groups and actually provides them with specific access to the network folder.

To give the individuals or groups actual permission to access the shared network folder, follow these steps:

1. Click Start.

2. Click My Computer.

3. Open the hard drive where the network folder is located.

4. Click the network folder you created in Step 2.

5. Choose File | Properties. The folder's Properties dialog box will open.

6. Click the Security tab.

7. Below Group Or User Names, click Add. The Select Users or Groups dialog box will appear.

8. Under Enter The Object Names To Select (Examples), enter a group or individual name.

9. Click Check Names. The name of your user or group should change to underlined; if not, you will be prompted to make corrections or cancel the request.

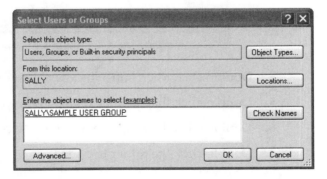

10. Click OK. The Properties dialog box for your folder will still be open.

11. In the Properties dialog box, take a look at the permissions assigned to the group. Double-check them and change them as needed.

12. When satisfied that the group has the correct permissions, click OK.

If you have trouble finding a group or user you created, double-check the location in the Select Users or Groups dialog box.

Step 6: Access the Network Server from Other Computers

Now that you have set up the network folder and established the users and appropriate permissions for access, it's time to test your work. For this step, you need to go to another computer on your network.

To Open the Network Server from a Windows XP Computer

1. Click Start.
2. Select My Network Places or My Network Neighborhood.
3. Double-click Entire Network.

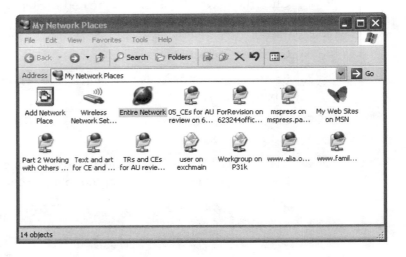

4. Double-click Microsoft Windows Network.
5. Double-click the network name where your folder is located.
6. Double-click the computer on the network where the folder is shared.
7. Double-click the folder to open it.

To Open the Network Server from a Windows Vista Computer

1. Click Start.
2. Click Network.

3. Double-click the computer where the network folder is located.

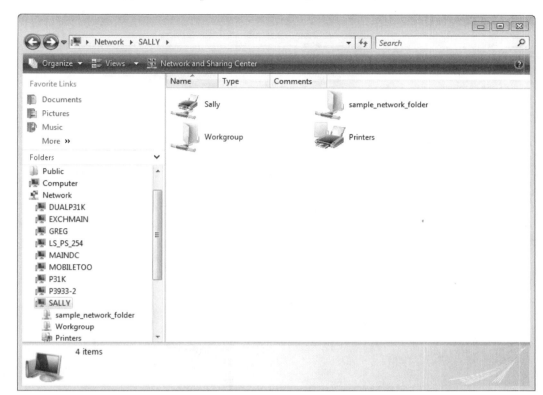

4. Double-click the folder to open it.

tip   *To avoid searching for the folder all the time, right-click the folder instead of opening it and click Map Network Drive. Either accept the default drive letter or choose one you want to use, then place a check mark in Reconnect At Logon, and click Finish. Each time you start the computer you are using, it will remap the network drive automatically and make the folder easier for you to find and use. You need to map a network drive on every computer in the network that you want to have access to the shared folder.*

Can you believe it? Now you have set up a network file server and can access those files from any computer on your network, plus you can print them from any file on the network, too. This project was a bit tougher than others in this book, but it's really just a series of logical steps.

Project 21
Automate Your File Backups

What You'll Need:

- **Operating system: Windows XP, Windows Vista**
- **Software: None**
- **Hardware: At least two hard drives, an external drive, or a network connection to another computer**
- **Cost: $0**
- **Difficulty: Challenging**

"Save early, save often!" That should be the battle cry for anyone who uses a computer. You just never know when a hard drive will fail, or a power failure will reduce your hard work on a business document to a pile of electronic ashes. Think about it: What would you really do if you lost your entire e-mail contacts list? Or all of your work documents?

After a data disaster is not the best time to think about backing up your data regularly. Sure, there are data recovery services that can scrape the tiniest bits of information off of a failed hard disk but it can cost tens of thousands of dollars to enlist aid from such services. The far easier method—and therefore my chosen method—is to back up files regularly using an operating system application that lets you schedule the timing and documents involved in the backup.

Windows XP Professional and Vista make the entire process simple and painless by including basic backup programs that allow you to automate the backup process. You can schedule backups to run daily, weekly, monthly, or at other times. Plus, there is software on the market that you can purchase or even download free if you prefer. This particular project is a must for anyone with a home office—your system isn't necessarily protected by corporate safety devices and IT support isn't always handy. With automated backups, you can rest a little easier at night knowing that your hard work isn't disappearing down an electronic black hole.

This project focuses on setting up automated backups for your computer through the basic programs provided by Windows XP Professional and Windows Vista. We'll also take a brief look at how to restore a file.

You need to have at least two hard drives on your computer or a network connection to another computer with enough space to hold all your backed up files. The whole point of backing up your files in case of hard drive failure is moot if you use the same hard drive to both create and back up your files! Easy-to-install external hard drives are sold at local computer stores if you need to add a hard drive to your computer; some even provide their own backup software.

note Windows XP Home Edition requires the manual installation of the Backup program separately.

Step 1: Get Your Files Organized

If you're the type of person who places files all over the place with no real rhyme or reason to structure, you've got a lot of work to do before you can get started with the automated file backup process. The idea is to be sure your files are all stored in a single, easy-to-find spot. For example, on my hard drive, I have "Sally's Documents" as a main documents folder, and all other documents are located in subfolders. When it's time to back up files, my computer just looks for Sally's Documents instead of trying to find every possible document in every possible folder.

If you don't have a similarly simple setup, take the time right now to create one. The hour or two you spend now will be well worth it in the long run. Windows XP and Vista help with this task by allowing you to set up individual profiles for every user. Each profile holds a set of subfolders under Documents And Settings, and includes the My Documents folder. Probably the easiest way to get organized is to place all documents in the My Documents folder; you can set up as many separate subfolders as you wish under that folder.

You have lots of options when you automate a backup, and one of those is to select individual files and folders to back up. While this may seem like a great option, it's a little dangerous. That's because it's easy to miss a file or folder as you schedule the backup, and everyone knows that if you forget to include a file or folder in your backup, that's the item that will fail. Play it safe and keep all your documents in a central location (okay, maybe two) that is easy for you to remember and locate.

tip AutoSave and AutoRecover are features in Microsoft Office products that automatically save and recover your work when most catastrophes strike. Check Help for the program you're using to learn how to turn one or both of these features on.

Step 2: Configure Your Backup Settings with Windows XP

Configuring backup settings might sound difficult, but it's really just a matter of telling your computer how and when to perform the backup. 'When you're ready to start automating your file backups with Windows XP, follow the steps on the next page:

1. Click Start | All Programs | Accessories | System Tools | Backup.

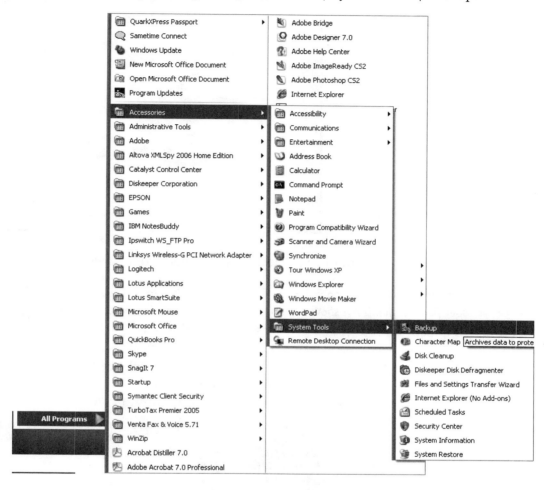

note *On the first page of the Backup and Restore Wizard, keep the check mark under Always Start In Wizard Mode for future forays you may make into this area of your computer.*

2. When the Backup or Restore Wizard launches, click Next. Under Backup Or Restore, select Back Up Files And Settings.

3. Click Next. Under What To Back Up, select My Documents And Settings unless you have other users you are concerned with. In that case, select Everyone's Documents And Settings.

note *Selecting All Information On This Computer backs up every single item on your computer and can take a lot of time, not to mention suck up space on the destination drive. Selecting Let Me Choose What To Back Up requires you to specifically select individual files for backup, which can take a lot of time and can result in missed files.*

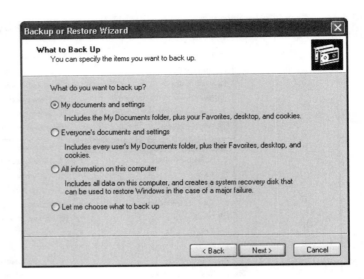

4. Click Next. Select the location for your backup and give it a name.

tip *Click Browse next to Choose A Place To Save Your Backup to bring up the Save As window if your specified location is not shown. From there you can select any location on your computer or network. Click Save when done with the Save As window.*

5. Click Next. You have the option of finishing the process now but the backup will not be automated to run later or at a specific time. Click Advanced to move to the automated portion of this process.

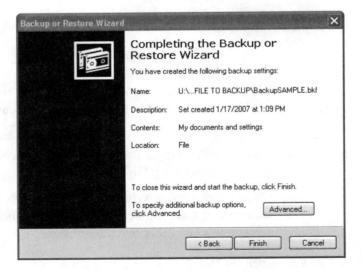

6. Select the type of backup you want performed. There are five options (Normal, Copy, Incremental, Differential, and Daily); use the drop-down menu to see the differences between each type. This project uses the Normal type.

7. Click Next. Select Verify Data After Backup. Leave Disable Volume Shadow Copy blank.

> **tip**
> *The Disable Shadow Volume Copy option disables the ability of Windows XP to back up file that reopen. If should be used only if you discover corruption in the backed up data and need to perform troubleshooting activities.*

8. Click Next. Select Replace The Existing Backups. If you are backing up sensitive data, consider placing a check mark in Allow Only The Owner And The Administrator Access To The Backup Data And To Any Backups Appended To This Medium. It is not required, but it is a good security measure.

9. Click Next. Select Later under When To Back Up. Under Schedule Entry, give the backup a Job Name.

10. Click Set Schedule. The Schedule Job window appears.

11. On the Schedule tab, select how often you want to run the backup and a start time. For most people, the best time to run a backup is during the middle of the night. Remember, though, your computer must be on to take advantage of the automated backup process!

12. On the Settings tab, select how long you are willing to let the backup run. This is useful if the backup gets hung up; there is no set amount of time that you should or should not allow. You can also select whether to start or stop the backup after a certain amount of idle time and choose Power Management options (these are used for laptops). Click OK.

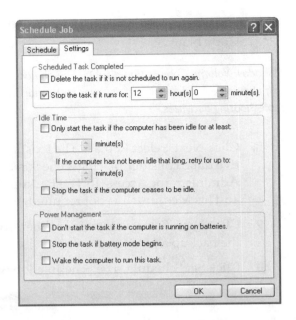

13. In the Set Account Information window, enter a username that has read/write access to all the documents and settings you are backing up. Enter and confirm a password as well.

14. Click OK.

15. Click Next.

16. Click Finish.

That's it—your automated backup is now scheduled. To check up on your automated backups, choose Start, | Administrative Tools | Event Viewer. Look for an NTBACKUP event in the application log and double-click it to see details. Caution! This will only appear after a backup has run.

Configure Your Backup Settings with Windows Vista

When you're ready to start automating your file backups with Windows Vista, follow these steps:

1. Chose Start | Control Panel. This launches the Backup And Restore Center window.

2. Under System And Maintenance, click Back Up Your Computer.

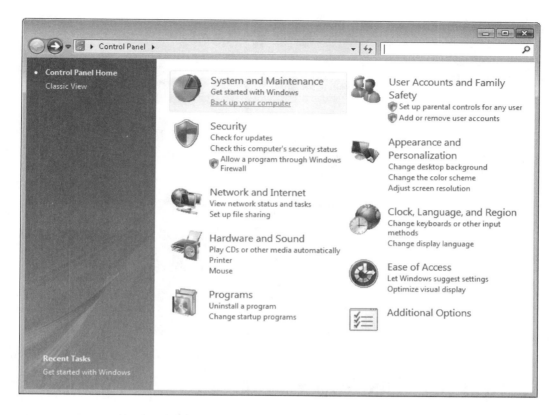

3. Under Back Up Files Or Your Entire Computer, click Back Up Files.

4. Choose a network or hard disk location to back up your files to. Click Next.

5. Choose the file types you want backed up. Click Next.

6. Select the timing for your scheduled backup. Click Save Settings And Start Backup. The first time you do this, a full backup will start immediately and then begin the scheduled backups.

That's it—you're done! In the Backup And Restore Center main page, the Change Settings option allows you to change settings and see the automated backup status at any time. Click this now to see the Backup Status and Configuration window, shown in Figure 21-1.

tip *Appending data means that the file or tape you are writing to will keep growing every time a file is changed. This is a good choice if you need to recover previous versions of a file, but it takes up a lot of space, so most people replace existing backups instead. If you are concerned about version control or need access to early versions of a document, consider saving the new versions of the document with new version numbers (i.e., "v 3" or "v 4") to help you track documents as well as keep your backup drive space contained.*

Figure 21-1

A single click in Windows Vista Backup And Restore Center will show you details about your automatic file backup.

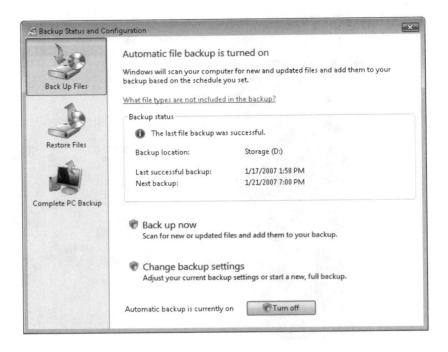

Restore Files with Windows XP

Backing up files won't help you if your system crashes before a backup has occurred. If you need to restore a file, you can do that through the Backup or Restore Wizard by following the steps here. This process is a bit more advanced than automating backups, but you've come this far, so why not go the distance?

1. Choose Start | All Programs | Accessories | System Tools | Backup. This launches the Backup or Restore Wizard.

2. Click Advanced Mode. This launches the Backup Utility.

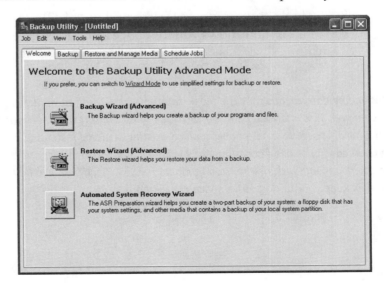

3. Click the Restore And Manage Media tab. To restore from a backup file, expand File in the left pane. To restore from a tape backup, expand the tape device you want and then expand the item you want.

4. At the bottom left of the Backup Utility, use the drop-down menu in Restore Files To for location selections. To select Original location if you want the file placed back to its original location; select Alternate Location to move the file somewhere else, or select Single Folder to place the file in a separate location from all other files.

tip *Choosing Alternate Location prevents the restoration from overwriting existing files.*

5. Choose Tools | Options.

6. On the Restore tab, select the method you want used when Backup restores a file already on the computer. Click OK.

7. Click Start Restore.

8. Click OK when the Confirm Restore prompt appears. The Restore Progress dialog box will launch when the restoration begins.

9. Click Close when the restoration is completed. If prompted to restart your computer, click Yes. Be sure all other applications are closed!

Restore Files with Windows Vista

Windows Vista makes it incredibly easy to restore files. Here's how to do it:

1. Click Start and click Control Panel. This launches the Backup And Restore Center window.

2. Under System And Maintenance, click Back Up Your Computer. This opens the Backup And Restore Center.

3. Under Restore Files Or Your Entire Computer, click Restore Files.

4. Select the type of files you want to restore. Click Next.

5. To select the actual files you want to restore, click Add Files or Add Folders or conduct a search. Click Add until the proper file is selected; Vista will return you to the Restore Files window when the file is properly added.

6. Click Next. Choose a location to save the restored files to. If an error window occurs because there is already a file with the same name in that location, click the file you want to keep. The restoration process will commence.

7. Click Finish.

Other Considerations

If you don't have Windows XP or Vista, run a search on your operating system for Backups to see if your system has the proper software. You can also check on Microsoft's web site (www.microsoft.com) for add-on programs that perform this task.

Freeware and shareware is available that can help you back up your files, too. Always exercise caution when downloading anything off the Internet. Here is a sample of automatic file backup freeware found online through the Free Downloads Center at www.freedownloadscenter.com:

- **SimpleBackup**   Uses drag-and-drop features to back up groups of files and folders; can be used to back up files on a hard disk, over a network, or via FTP servers.

- **AKG Backup**   A multiplatform-compatible backup program that offers compression options, and can be used on any media.

- **Adept for Oracle**   Backs up most Oracle databases to local storage but must be used on a Windows-based PC. The data can be hosted on any server.

It's smart to take advantage of the automated file backup process. It lets you do what you do best and leaves the annoying computer details to the computer. After all, weren't personal computers supposed to make our lives easier? This is one simple way your computer can help you out, so take a few minutes to set this up. The next time your system crashes, your heart won't.

Teach Your PC to Recognize Your Voice

What You'll Need:

- Operating system: Windows XP, Windows Vista
- Software: Yes, depends upon solution chosen
- Hardware: Headphones
- Cost: $0–$199

D o you type on your keyboard using just index fingers? Perhaps you type beautifully but the thought of sitting in front of the computer for hours at a time to get things done makes you stir crazy. You're not alone. An entire industry is coming to life to specifically address your needs: the speech recognition industry.

Speech recognition—or voice recognition as it is sometimes called—allows you to use your own voice to input text and commands on the computer. The patterns of your speech are remembered by the computer with a bit of training, plus the grammatical context and frequency of the words you use are placed into memory and retrieved as you begin speaking, which means that before you even speak the next word, your computer is anticipating what that word will be.

A decade ago, speech recognition was a great idea but it didn't consistently deliver on its promises to understand your voice easily and help create documents more quickly. Today, advances in technology have created products that are actually worth using on a regular basis. Accuracy has improved, and the software involved typically offers easy-to-follow tutorials. Since most software also works with Bluetooth wireless technology, you don't need to be tethered to your computer to use these programs, either. Run on the treadmill, cook dinner, chase your child—all while working. Sure, background noise is still somewhat of an issue, but the latest microphones offer noise reduction features that improve on this problem.

It may sound like a commercial in some respects, but as you read through the options outlined in this project, you should find that the hype is finally worth listening to with speech recognition products. You can spend a lot of money on these programs, but this project will also cover the speech recognition program most people don't realize they already have. If you like to gab instead of type, then this is the project for you.

 Did you know that some speech recognition programs can recognize, translate, and type the spoken word at up to 160 words per minute? Most typists can enter just 40–60 words per minute.

Step 1: Review Your Options

You probably already know that you can buy speech recognition software at the local computer store, but I bet you didn't know that you could add speech recognition to your Windows XP operating system for about $30 or possibly even free, or that Office 2003 and Windows Vista have speech recognition built in. Most people don't know about the last three options, so you're not alone.

These Microsoft programs are incredibly simple to use, and the newest (Windows Vista Speech Recognition) is as robust as some of the more expensive software from other vendors. Since these programs are primarily free and just languishing on your computer, it's worth giving them a try before you go spending a lot of money. You'll get used to how speech recognition works and can begin to identify whether or not you need a more complex solution.

Beyond Microsoft, here are two programs to consider:

- **Dragon NaturallySpeaking 9 (www.nuance.com/naturallyspeaking)** Comes in a variety of versions and claims to be up to 99 percent accurate. Compatible with almost all Windows applications.

- **ViaVoice (www.nuance.com/viavoice)** Offers versions for Windows and Mac; ViaVoice Standard v10 works well with older computers. Although ViaVoice is not as accurate as Dragon NaturallySpeaking 9, it is much less expensive.

Other solutions do exist, but many are built upon Dragon's technology or are designed for large enterprise use. Still others were created for niche use—mathematics, for example, or call centers.

 Dragon NaturallySpeaking 9 is almost universally rated as the best voice recognition package on the market today.

A Few Words about Training Your Speech Recognition Program

Training your speech recognition program to recognize your voice and speech patterns is critical to obtaining accuracy. Most programs recognize about 85–90 percent of the words you dictate; accuracy improves every time you use speech recognition because the program has more time to learn how you speak. Additional training usually helps to improve recognition and accuracy in any program.

Speech recognition programs don't understand what the words mean when you say them; your computer can't use common sense the way you do. To compensate, the program tracks how frequently words occur by themselves and in the context of other words. When it hears you speak, it chooses the most likely word or phrase from several possibilities.

If you have ever been fortunate enough to have a secretary who took dictation, you know that you need to help fill in the blanks with punctuation (although you won't need to do this during actual training sessions). Your computer won't know when you expect a sentence to stop, for example, or when you want to add a dash or colon to your sentence. As you speak, think of the way newscasters speak, too. They enunciate well, and speak clearly so that you can understand every word that is said. That's exactly how you should speak into your microphone—you don't need to speak extra slowly, just clearly.

Training typically works by showing you text on a screen and requiring you to read the text into your microphone. As the program hears you speak the words it already knows, it applies your speech and recognition patterns to the words spoken, as well as to other words in the program's vocabulary.

tip *Think logically as you use a speech recognition program. For example, if you want to close a program in Office, you might normally use your mouse to click the Close button. But speech recognition typically understands menu and navigation commands, so instead say "file" and, when the File menu opens, say "exit."*

Step 2: Activate Speech Recognition Through Office 2003

When you activate the speech recognition features in Office 2003, you actually accomplish it in Word 2003. Once you've completed the activation steps in Word 2003, speech recognition becomes available on the Tools menu in all Office 2003 programs.

note *If you will be using Windows XP or Vista or a third-party program for speech recognition, you can move to Step 3, 4, or 5 as applicable. In this project, the major steps do not need to be followed in order; each is a separate process dependent upon your needs.*

To complete the activation:

1. Open Word 2003.
2. Choose Tools | Speech.
3. Click Yes when asked if you want to install the feature.

You'll see a speech recognition Language bar appear at the top of your screen above your main toolbar, with options such as Microphone, Dictation, Voice Command, etc. The Welcome To Office Speech Recognition window will appear; go to Train Speech Recognition Through Word 2003 for further instructions. You won't be able to use the feature until you have completed at least the initial training.

Train Speech Recognition Through Word 2003

Once the speech recognition program is activated, you need to train the program to understand and recognize your voice. Without this step, you won't have high accuracy and reliability when speaking to your computer. The steps involved here are twofold: adjust your microphone for the best sound, and actually train Office 2003 for speech recognition. The process takes about 15 minutes and you must complete at least one training session before you can use the speech recognition function.

Before you begin, be sure you are in a quiet environment. Then follow the steps provided next. The tutorial is very simple and offers a lot of explanation about the speech recognition function.

note *If you have closed Word 2003 and are returning to complete the voice training, choose Tools | Training on the Language bar. If you don't see the Language bar, choose Tools | Speech on the standard toolbar.*

1. In the Welcome To Office Speech Recognition window, click Next to open the Microphone Wizard. After reading the Welcome screen, click Next.

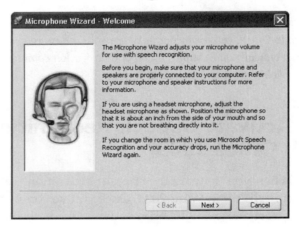

2. When the Voice Training window opens, follow the wizard instructions.

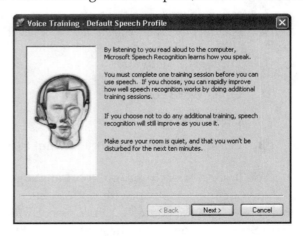

3. Click Finish when the training is complete.

For additional training, choose Tools | Training on the Language bar. Select a passage to be read aloud and click Next each time you complete a passage until that training is complete.

> **tip**   *If your microphone and headset do not appear to be working, you may need to reinstall the drivers on your computer.*

Use Speech Recognition Through Word 2003

To use speech recognition in Word 2003 and other Office 2003 programs, go to the Language bar and click Dictation or say "dictation." Use your mouse to place the cursor wherever you want the text to begin on the page and begin speaking slowly and clearly. As you use the function more, you'll find you can speed up your rate of speech. The trick is to not get discouraged in the beginning if the program doesn't understand you. Either you aren't giving the correct command (I ran into that a lot in the beginning) or you might be in the wrong mode (I would use voice commands while in the dictation mode, for example). Patience is key to making this work for you.

If you make a mistake or want to change something, click Voice Command on the Language bar or say "voice command." Voice commands allow you to control the computer and program you're in by opening dialog boxes and other commands. For example, if you were to say "format," Word 2003 would open the Format menu. Say "font" and the Font dialog box opens. To change the font, say the name of the new font you want, such as "Arial." To change font style, say "italic," for example, and to change font size, say the new size you want, such as "ten." As the program moves through the commands, it highlights the new item you want just as it highlighted text during the training session.

You can navigate through mouse and keyboard commands with your voice, too—for example, "backspace" can help you correct minor mistakes, "right-click" will open a context menu, "up" or "down" will move the cursor up or down a line, and "delete" plus the word to delete will delete any word in your text.

There are dozens of commands; you need to take some time to experiment and use the Help feature to learn them all.

Step 3: Activate Speech Recognition Through Windows XP

Setting up speech recognition with Windows XP requires a bit more technical skill. You need the following items:

- Windows XP Service Pack 1 (or higher)

- Microsoft Speech Recognition Engine (SRE) v5.0

- Windows XP Office applications and other applications that accept speech (Word 2002, Excel 2002, Outlook Express, Notepad)

tip   *Speech recognition in Windows XP will work with Office 2007 applications.*

To determine the Service Pack and SRE that you have:

1. Right-click My Computer.

2. Click Properties.

The information you need is shown in the Properties dialog box. Service Packs are downloaded from Microsoft.com. If you don't have the Microsoft SRE, you may need to download and install it, too. However, it is usually available with Office XP applications. If you need to install the SRE component, find your Office XP CD-ROM and place it into the CD-ROM drive and follow these instructions:

1. Click Start.

2. Click Control Panel.

3. Click Add/Remove Programs and select Microsoft Office XP.

4. Click the Change button.

5. Click Add Or Remove Features.

6. Click Next. The Installation Options dialog box appears.

7. Expand Alternative User Input and click Speech.

8. Click Update.

tip   *Another option to installing the SRE is to purchase the Windows XP Plus! Pack available online from Microsoft.*

Next, you need to enable speech recognition. You do this through Microsoft Word. Open Word 2002 and choose Tools | Speech. You might be prompted for the Office XP CD-ROM to finish loading the SRE. If so, Word will handle the rest of the installation for you. Once the installation is complete, reboot your computer.

Train the Speech Recognition Engine

Once the speech recognition engine is installed, you need to train the program to understand your voice. The process takes about 15 minutes and you must complete at least one training session before you can use the speech recognition function.

1. Click Start.

2. Click Control Panel.

3. Click Sound, Speech And Audio Devices, and the click the Speech icon. This opens the Speech Properties dialog box.

4. Click Configure Microphone and follow the steps to ensure that your microphone is working properly.

5. Click Train Profile to open the Speech Recognition Training Wizard.

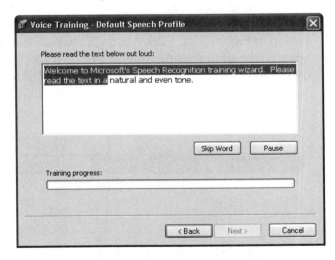

6. Click Next when the wizard opens, and follow the wizard's instructions.

Check Settings in Windows XP

You're almost ready to begin using speech recognition in Windows XP applications, but there are a couple more things to do first:

1. Open the Control Panel.

2. Click Regional And Language Options. Click the Languages tab.

3. Click Details.

4. In the Text Services and Input Languages dialog box, click the Advanced tab.

5. Select the Extend Support Of Advanced Text Services To All Programs check box. This option allows Windows XP to accept dictation anywhere there is a box that can be filled in with text, including Notepad, Internet Explorer's Address bar, and Outlook Express.

note   *You can't use speech recognition for operating system commands in Windows XP. The operating system itself does not respond to Voice Command mode, although the individual applications within it do. The only exception is in the Tablet PC Edition of Windows XP.*

Use Speech Recognition in Windows XP

Speech recognition is ready for you to use Windows XP. When you open any program using Windows XP that accepts speech recognition, you'll see the Language bar as shown in Figure 22-1. Click Microphone and then say "dictate" or "voice command." Speech recognition commands in Windows XP work almost identically to the ones in Office 2003 programs; see "Use Speech Recognition Commands in Office 2003" for more details about voice and dictation commands.

To close the Language bar, right-click Microphone and click Close Language bar.

Figure 22-1

The Windows XP
Language bar

Step 3: Enable Speech Recognition in Windows Vista

This section is the shortest of all due to the complete simplicity of the Windows Vista Speech Recognition program. The tutorial is breathtakingly easy and the commands ("go to," "open Excel," "close that," "show desktop") are easy to remember.

To open speech recognition in Windows Vista, click the Start button and enter "speech" in the Start Search box. Windows Speech Recognition appears under the Programs section of the results.

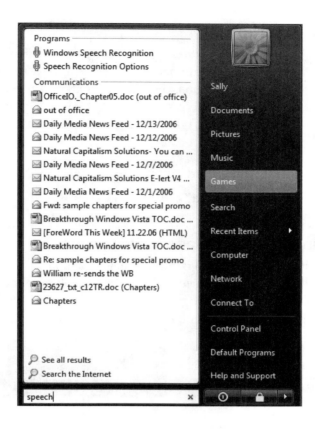

1. Open the program. The Welcome to Speech Recognition window appears.

2. Click Next. Select the type of microphone you want to use.

3. Click Next. Follow the instructions for setting up the microphone, clicking Next as prompted.

4. When the Improve Speech Recognition Accuracy window appears, select Enable Document Review. This allows Windows Vista to check through your documents and e-mail to learn how you write. Click Next.

note *By reviewing the e-mails you've sent and documents you've created, a speech recognition program gains a good understanding of your writing style and uses that along with your speech patterns to translate your spoken words into written ones.*

5. Print out the commands sheet. Click Next.

6. Select Run Speech Recognition At Startup. Click Next.

You can now control the computer by voice, but taking the tutorial is highly recommended.

Run the Tutorial

The Windows Vista tutorial is completely different from all the other speech recognition tutorials mentioned in this project; it walks you through the actual opening and closing of programs, dictation of text, and use of various commands. As you work in the tutorial, the program uses the words you say to build its profile for you. It's a nice way to learn how the program works as you teach the program your speech patterns.

1. Click Start Tutorial.

2. Say "next" as you work your way through each tutorial screen.

Use Windows Vista Speech Recognition

When the tutorial is complete, you will know a variety of simple commands and can begin dictating to your computer. It took me about 15 minutes total to get started with this particular program. Say "start listening" to turn on the microphone and "stop listening" when you need to take a break.

You can use both dictation and voice commands in the same mode; the program knows the difference based on the words you use. In Windows Vista, say "What can I say?" when you've forgotten a command. A Speech Reference card window with commands will appear as shown in Figure 22-2.

You can start and use both computer applications (Control Panel, for example) and Office applications (Word, Excel, etc.) with the same basic commands. When I tried out the Windows Vista Speech Recognition program, it easily moved between programs and was very fast at understanding my voice and patterns, so I didn't have to correct very often. For overall ease of use and very simple training, this program is very effective.

A nice feature with Windows Vista Speech Recognition is the option to "show numbers" for the commands on the screen. This is helpful because sometimes you don't always know what a particular command is called—when you tell the computer to show you the numbers, it numbers every single command on the screen. You choose the number that corresponds to the command you want, and say "okay."

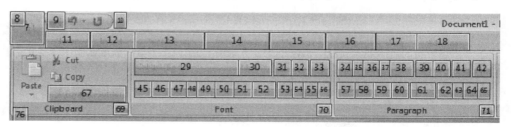

Figure 22-2

The Speech Reference card is activated with a simple voice command.

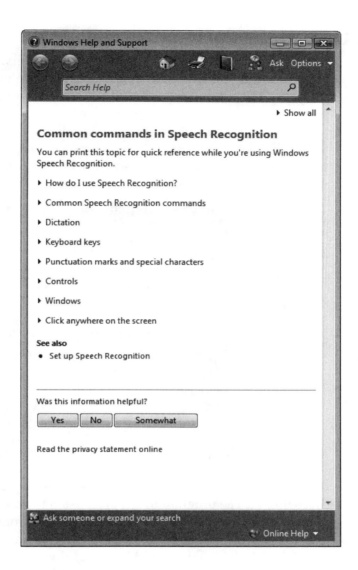

> **tip**   *Always use your natural inflections when speaking. The computer has been trained to listen to your speech patterns; using a monotone voice won't improve recognizability for the program.*

Step 5: Use a Third-Party Speech Recognition Program

As explained earlier, there are dozens of speech recognition software providers. Each one touts its ability to do more, and understand more, than any other program. Most, however, are not designed for the average home office user. Dragon NaturallySpeaking 9 is an exception. It comes in many different versions, so you can find one to meet your needs and your budget. For this example, I'll show you how to use Dragon NaturallySpeaking 9 Professional.

If you have this program, follow the instructions to install the program. You will also be asked to activate the program the first time you use it.

New User Training

The New User training is self-explanatory and very simple to use. It launches automatically and you'll be asked to create a user profile. Then, a wizard will launch to help you with a few simple tests to be certain your microphone and sound are working correctly.

After that, you will begin speaking directly to your computer so that Dragon NaturallySpeaking 9 can learn your speech patterns and voice characteristics. The voice training is similar to the way Microsoft speech recognition works, except that it doesn't highlight the words you speak as you train; it grays out the words.

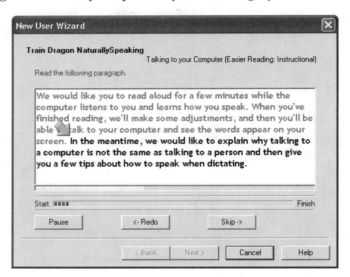

One part of Dragon's process, however, is very similar to Windows Vista Speech Recognition. The program doesn't just listen to how you speak, it also analyzes how you write. It does this by accessing your e-mail program, plus Microsoft Word, Corel WordPerfect, Text, and Rich Text files, as shown in Figure 22-3.

All other programs should be closed during this step, which can take as long as 30 minutes, depending upon the amount of documents and e-mails on your computer. When this step is complete, you're ready to begin dictation but you also have the option of taking a tutorial. It's worth taking the time to complete the tutorial.

tip   *NaturallySpeaking has an autopunctuation tool. When turned on, it automatically inserts periods and commas as it detects the need for them.*

Using Dragon NaturallySpeaking 9

This program places a toolbar (called a DragonBar) at the top of your desktop when the program is open. When you're ready to begin dictating, choose NaturallySpeaking | Turn Microphone On on the DragonBar. You can't turn the microphone on by voice, but you can turn it off by saying "microphone off."

Figure 22-3

Dragon Naturally-
Speaking 9 analyzes
your written docu-
ments as well as your
spoken words.

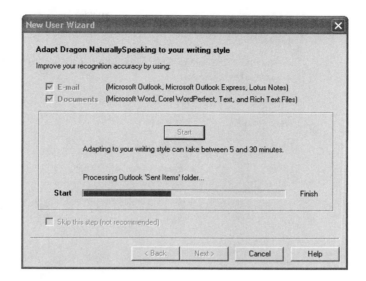

As you dictate, you'll find that NaturallySpeaking offers many more commands than other programs. They are typically in "natural" language, such as "scratch that" (which removes the last word) and "cut this paragraph." The text displays in a small yellow window as you speak, just before the text is inserted into the document you're working on.

Another helpful feature in this program is its ability to correct recognition errors. When you see that the program has incorrectly entered a word for you—noon instead of one, for example—you say "select noon" and a correction menu will appear with logical correction choices.

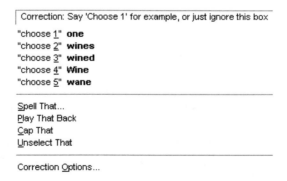

Instead of continuing to say the word and having the program ignore you or continue to incorrectly interpret your words, the correction menu gives you several numbered choices to select from. You select the numbered choice you want, and the program inserts it for you. If the correct word is not on the correction menu, you can elect to spell out the word with a simple "spell that" command.

Another nice bonus with NaturallySpeaking is that you do not have to switch between dictation and voice command modes. The program recognizes a voice command as you dictate, which reduces the amount of time needed to format or make corrections. Figure 22-4 shows how a dictated letter looks.

Figure 22-4

An example of
a dictated letter with
Dragon Naturally-
Speaking 9.

August 5, 2007

Dear Mr. Jones,

I will be in town the last three days of this month and would like to meet with you. If you are available,
let's plan to get together.

My itinerary is as follows:

Wednesday   available for dinner

Thursday   available from 9 a.m. to noon

Friday   available from noon to 3 p.m.

Thank you for your time.

Sincerely,

Sally

tip   *If you find that you are frequently correcting small common words, try correcting the entire
phrase containing the small word. For example, if the program doesn't understand "on" in the
phrase "going on a journey," use the correction features of your program and say "going on"
instead of yelling at the computer or talking slowly.*

Other Considerations

Patience is really critical if you decide to use these speech recognition programs. The
initial documents you work on might seem a little painful and discourage you from
continuing to use speech recognition. Don't let it stop you—the programs quickly
learn your style and patterns, and you will learn the commands and corrections needed to make the program more responsive and intuitive.

I did find that only Windows Vista Speech Recognition and Dragon Naturally-
Speaking 9 seemed to move quickly or understand commands well when jumping
from one program to another. It's probably a good idea to stay within one program
when initially using a speech recognition program unless you have a lot of patience
to help the program follow you around the computer.

My recommendation is to use these programs in short bursts the first several
times you try them out. This will help train the program and give you time to get used
to how it works, as well as help you avoid frustration. But overall, if you don't enjoy
typing and/or like to stand and move while you work, you should try one of these
options to see if it's the right solution for your home office.

Set Up a Wireless Network

What You'll Need:

- Operating system: Windows XP, Windows Vista
- Internet access: Yes
- Software: None
- Hardware: Wireless access point with built-in router, network interface card, RJ45 cable
- Cost: $150
- Difficulty: Advanced

When even McDonald's offers wireless access at more than 7000 locations worldwide, you know that the wireless revolution has taken hold and isn't going anywhere. That revolution can work to your advantage, you know. It allows you to take your laptop and work from all over town—or all over the world, really.

It also means that wireless networks have evolved to the point that even non-geeks can set one up without a lot of hassle. The primary reasons to set up your own wireless network in your home office are productivity and mobility.

With a traditional wired network, you're pretty much stuck at your desk in your office. If something is happening elsewhere in your home, you must leave your desk and your work to handle the situation. With a wireless network, you can head to the other part of the house and tote your laptop with you so that you can continue to work.

For example, my toddler is rarely content to sit and play in my office. She's very good about playing by herself, but that doesn't mean she will play for hours beside my desk. Instead, she wants to explore and play with things all over the house or even outside. With my wireless network, I can follow her with my laptop—to the backyard, upstairs to her room, over to the family room. She's happy, we're both mobile, and I stay productive because my work goes with me wherever I wander.

Other benefits include cost and ease of installation—wireless networks are increasingly cost-effective over traditional wired networks, and they are relatively effortless to install. Finally, scalability is excellent with a wireless network. By *scalability*, I mean the ability of the system to expand as your needs expand.

This project explains wireless network basics and shows you how to set one up in your home.

Step 1: Learn about Wireless Technology

Wireless networks work the same way wired network do, just without any wires. Instead of using cables to send out information, radio signals are transmitted between computers. Access points connect the computers to the network.

There are a variety of wireless network technology standards and terms that you should be familiar with before you begin your setup.

Wireless Standards

Wireless technology standards have been established to ensure that the various manufacturers of wireless products meet certain guidelines, including minimum speeds and signal rates. Here is a look at the standards:

- **802.11** This is the original standard that wireless networks used. Connections occur at just 2 megabits per second (Mbps), which isn't really very fast. This standard is rarely used.

- **802.11a** This standard offers increased connection speed over the original standard (54 Mbps) and operates at a high 5 gigahertz (GHz) frequency. This frequency is a regulated frequency so it offers less interference from other devices as you work with your wireless network. At the same time, the higher frequency causes trouble as the signals attempt to go through objects (like walls). These problems tend to limit the distance of your wireless network— you might not be able to go outside, for example, and work.

note Frequencies are the radio signals that the wireless network uses to transmit information. A frequency is the number of times that an electrical signal repeats itself in a specific amount of time. It is usually expressed in cycles per second, or hertz (Hz), with one hertz representing one cycle per second.

- **802.11b** This is the first wireless standard that was widely adopted by the general users. It offers connection speeds of 11 Mbps at a frequency of 2.4 GHz. While relatively slow compared to the wired networks of the time, it still handles basic web browsing and e-mail without any problems. The frequency is at just the right rate to allow signals to pass through walls and other objects easily. However, it doesn't handle high-bandwidth items such as streamed video very well and there is a minor chance of interference from other frequencies, such as the next-door neighbor's wireless telephone.

- **802.11g** This is the most commonly used standard today. It operates at 54 Mbps, which is a very fast connection speed, and 2.4 GHz, so signals travel well. It's fast enough to stream music and video, so you can do pretty much anything you need to with this standard.

- **802.11n** This standard is not yet approved at this writing but is expected to replace both 802.11g and 802.11b networks and be available sometime in 2008. It will operate at 600 Mbps by using multiple-input multiple-output (MIMO) technology to allow the increased speed. Signals will travel at 2.4 GHz. This standard will support any existing wireless connections and should offer better range and performance than the 802.11g standard. Be careful! Some manufacturers are already selling wireless equipment based on the draft for this standard. If you purchase 802.11n standard equipment before it has been fully approved, your network might not work with the approved standard when it becomes available. Instead, go with 802.11g or 802.11b—the new standard will be "backward compatible" with both, meaning that you will be able to easily upgrade to 802.11n in the future.

Some manufacturers offer custom wireless equipment that exceeds the defined connection speeds. On closer look, these custom devices aren't necessarily as fabulous as the manufacturers might have you believe. For example, some claim connection speeds of more than 100 Mbps. Although that may show as the connected speed in your taskbar, it's accomplished simply by compressing the information so that it takes less time to send the information. It's not the actual connection speed—that comes in slightly better than that of the 802.11g standard.

Another drawback? These custom devices are almost always proprietary, too. That means that any device connecting to your custom access point must be of the same brand—you can't mix and match brands. This typically leads to higher costs.

note *Wireless standards are approved by the Institute of Electrical and Electronics Engineers, Inc. Check its web site (www.ieee.org) for information on the 802.11n standard and to learn when the standard has been approved.*

Wireless Products

There are dozens, if not hundreds, of wireless products on the market. This is actually good for you because increased competition means lower prices. On the other hand, it can make finding the wireless product you need a bit of a challenge since there are so many to choose from. Here's a look at the basic wireless components most people work with:

- **Access points**   Access points connect wireless communication devices together to form a wireless network. These usually connect to a wired network and relay data between wired and wireless devices. Some access points have routing capabilities.

- **Client devices**   Client adapters and other items are used to connect your desktop and mobile computing devices (laptop, PDA, etc.) to the wireless network.

- **Network controllers/integrated switches and routers**   These items integrate into existing enterprise networks for advanced management capabilities and increased performance. They communicate with access points. These are not typically needed in a home office environment but are mentioned here in case you hear them discussed at a store.

- **Network management tools**   These tools help with wireless network planning, configuration, and management. These are not typically needed in a home office environment.

- **Mobility tools**   These tools help add support for things like wireless Voice over IP (VoIP), network security, and other technologies useful for mobile workers.

Encryption Methods

You should know the basics of encryption before you set up your wireless network. Encryption is a security method that keeps others from snooping around to find and use the information exchanged by your wireless system.

One popular method is Wired Equivalent Privacy (WEP). It is the standard security protocol for wireless networks. Even though it's the standard, it's not very secure and the key to unlocking it can be found pretty easily by anyone who knows what they are doing.

A second method is Wi-Fi Protected Access (WPA). This security protocol is more difficult to break than WEP but it can be done if someone has lots of time and a desire to find your security key. Ultimately, however, this method is far more secure than WEP.

A third method, Temporal Key Integrity Protocol (TKIP), works in conjunction with WEP and offers stronger security than just WEP alone. TKIP uses new encryption algorithms that constantly change the encryption keys so hackers have a tough time cracking them. Even if a hacker cracks an encryption key, by the time he does, it will have changed on your computer and the hacker will have to start all over again.

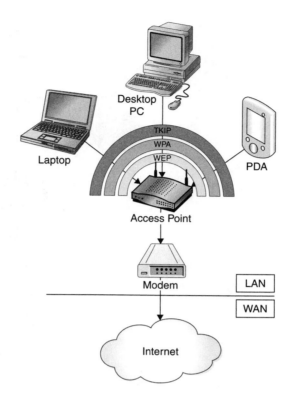

Step 2: Set Up the Wireless Access Point

Access points are required to actually form a wireless network. Without them, signals can't be sent and received between various computers and a wired network. For this project, you need a wireless access point (WAP) with a built-in router. If you don't have a built-in router, you're just making extra work for yourself. The end result—a wireless network as shown in Figure 23-1—is the same with both kinds of routers, however.

The following are some examples of brands that offer access point products that work well in home office environments:

- Cisco
- D-Link
- Linksys
- Hawking

Figure 23-1

The setup of a basic wireless network looks like this.

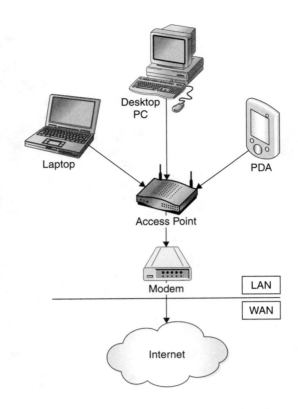

As an example, Figure 23-2 shows a Linksys broadband router access point.

When you are ready to begin setting up your WAP, remember that different brands may have slightly different instructions. These instructions are for attaching the WAP to your desktop computer:

1. Take the WAP from the box and check the instructions to be sure you have all the required parts. If an antenna is included, attach it to the WAP now.

2. Plug power into the WAP.

3. Plug the RJ45 cable into an open port on the WAP and to your computer. You'll recognize this Ethernet cable by its similarity to an oversized phone jack plug-in.

4. Turn on the power for your computer.

5. If a CD-ROM was included with your WAP, insert and run the CD-ROM. Follow the instructions on your screen. You don't need to follow the remaining steps here, but it might be helpful to read through them to understand why you are entering certain information with your CD-ROM. If you did not receive a CD-ROM with your product, go to Step 6.

6. Open your web browser on your desktop computer. It should go straight to the configuration page for your access point product. If it does not, refer to your instructions in the box.

Figure 23-2

Wireless access points come in a variety of brands.

7. Select and set your Service Set Identifier (SSID). This is the name you will give your wireless network—you will use this name to connect to your wireless network. You can call it anything you like; just keep it short, simple, and easy to remember and don't use punctuation marks or spaces.

tip   *Don't use the default name or your own name for your wireless access point. If you and your neighbor both use the default name for the same brand of wireless access point, for example, you will have trouble connecting. Also, hackers can get into your wireless network easily if a certain brand has security holes—they just look for the default name to find the available networks to break into. Finally, using your last name lets everyone know who the wireless network belongs to; use something different to maintain your privacy.*

8. Set the SSID to hidden or not broadcast. Not all WAPs have this feature but if yours does, it makes it much more difficult to detect and use your network because outsiders can't see it.

9. Set up your security for WPA-PSK and TKIP (if it's available). Enter and confirm your key. Make it at least eight characters and remember what it is or write it down (this will be discussed more in Project 24.)

10. Select the channel you want to use. This step may take some time and depends upon the WAP product you have. Some products support six channels, some support more. Most wireless networks use channel 6 by default, but this is a little dangerous since many of your neighbors will likely be using that channel as well. Try other channels until you find one that works well for you.

tip   *If you start noticing lost connections or that it takes longer than usual to access the Internet, the chances are that your selected channel is receiving interference from other sources. For example, my WAP was set to channel 4 and worked great...until the phone rang and all my wireless connections stopped for a few minutes. I changed the channel, restarted my system, and everything works fine now—even when the phone rings.*

11. Plug your WAP into your DSL router.

12. Restart your WAP.

Now you're ready to move on to setting up your computer.

Step 3: Set Up Your Computer for Wireless Access

Now that you have the WAP all set up, it's time to set up your computer so that you can use the wireless network. For this project, we'll use a laptop computer. However, you can set up any or all computers in your home on the wireless network. This is a great bonus because you can put your desktop computer wherever you want without worrying about Internet access, for instance.

The first thing you need to do is install a network interface card if you don't have one installed yet. These are sometimes referred to as NIC cards or wireless Ethernet adapter cards. Newer laptops come with built-in wireless cards, but older ones will require the installation of the card before you can take advantage of your wireless network. Some examples of companies that sell network interface cards are listed here but any card should work:

- D-Link
- Intel
- Linksys
- Smart Link
- 3Com
- USRobotics

Once you have a network interface card, you can move through this section pretty easily.

Install a Network Interface Card

This process involves inserting the network interface card into your computer and installing related drivers and a client utility program, although the client utility program won't be needed for what we are doing.

You need to follow your manufacturer's instructions to install these items on your laptop. If you have a Windows operating system, it should recognize that you've inserted your card and launch a Setup Wizard to help guide you through the installation process. After that is completed, you can just take the card in and out of your computer when you need it, as shown in Figure 23-3; you won't need to do anything else. Once the card is installed, move to the next section.

Figure 23-3

Network interface cards are necessary to help your laptop communicate with your wireless access point and are easy to use.

> **tip**   *You can link several wireless access points together to form a larger network. This kind of larger network is called a "roaming" network; it's sort of like roaming cell phone coverage that allows you to use your cell phone in a variety of areas far from your original location.*

Configure Your Laptop Computer with Windows XP

As you move through this part of the process, be sure to carefully enter information. If you make a mistake, your wireless access won't work and you'll have to go through the process again. When you're ready, follow these steps:

1. On your laptop, choose Start | Control Panel.

2. Double-click Network Connections.

3. In the Network Connections window, right-click Wireless Network Connection and click View Available Wireless Networks.

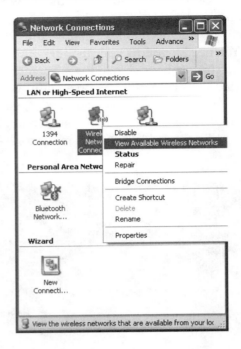

4. This launches the Wireless Network Connection window. Don't be surprised if you see neighborhood networks on the list in the right pane.

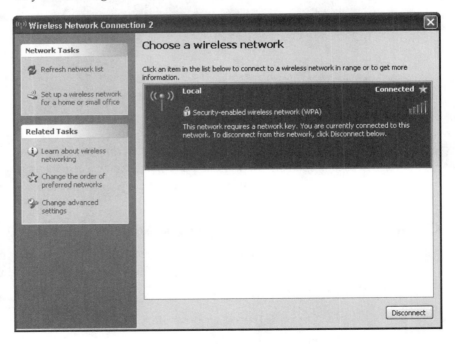

5. In the left pane, click Change The Order Of Preferred Networks. This launches the Wireless Network Connection Properties dialog box.

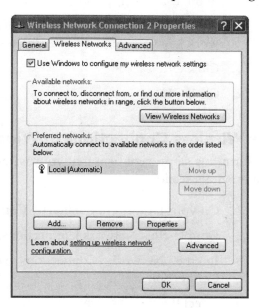

6. Under Preferred Networks, click Add. A second Properties dialog box will launch called Wireless Network Properties.

7. In the Network Name (SSID) field, enter the SSID for your wireless network.

8. In the Network Authentication drop-down list box, select WPA-PSK.

9. In the Data Encryption drop-down list box, select TKIP.

10. In both the Network Key and Confirm Network Key fields, enter the network key you created earlier in Steps 2–9.

11. Click OK.

12. Click OK.

Verify Your Wireless Connections in Windows XP

Perform this step to confirm that your wireless connections were set up properly in the previous section:

1. On your laptop, choose Start | Control Panel.

2. Double-click Network Connections.

3. In the Network Connections window, right-click Wireless Network Connection.

4. Select the Wireless Networks tab.

5. Click View Available Wireless Networks. This launches the Wireless Network Connection window, where your wireless network should now be listed (along with your neighbors' wireless networks).

That's it—if your wireless network appears on the list, you're ready to connect and begin working. If it doesn't, you need to go back through the configuration steps of the previous section and reenter the information.

Configure Your Laptop Computer with Windows Vista

Windows Vista makes it incredibly easy to configure your computer for wireless access. When you're ready, follow these steps:

1. On your laptop computer, choose Start | Connect To. This launches the Connect to a Network window.

2. Enter the name or your wireless network (SSID).

3. Click Connect.

4. Enter the network security key. Click OK. You will see a confirmation message that you have connected to the network.

Verify Your Wireless Connections in Windows Vista

Perform this step to confirm that your wireless connections were set up properly in the previous section:

1. On your laptop, choose Start | Network.

2. Look for your wireless network; you should see it in the list in the right pane.

With either operating system, if you see your wireless network in the list, you have set things up correctly. If you don't, double-check your steps.

Other Considerations

If you have to balance corporate network considerations with your home office wireless network, it's a very simple process to switch between the two networks. If you need to configure settings for the corporate wireless network for the first time, just follow the same instructions outlined for your home office wireless network.

After that, you will be able to just open the Network Connections folder, as shown earlier in this project, and select the network you need to use.

The wireless connection will launch automatically on your laptop every time you start it. You will need to give your computer a couple of minutes to get started and find the wireless network, so exercise a little patience when starting up your computer.

I can't recommend wireless networks highly enough for home offices. Part of the beauty of working from home is flexibility, and that includes the flexibility to move around. Listen to a conference call and keep your instant messaging program open and accessible on your laptop as you fix breakfast. Or get some sun in the backyard while you work on a client's proposal. The possibilities are endless when you install a wireless network in your office! Be sure to complete Project 24 so that your wireless network is well secured.

Secure Your Wireless Network and Computers

What You'll Need:

- Operating system: Windows XP, Windows Vista
- Software: None
- Hardware: None
- Cost: $0
- Difficulty: Challenging

Have you heard those horror stories about how personal computers have been used for evil reasons, such as launching worldwide cyber-attacks? Or for the storage of illegal files, like child pornography? Innocent people have found themselves staring at federal agents on the doorstep as investigations lead officials to suburban homes where wireless networks are in use. These people quickly learned that wireless network security is nothing to take lightly.

One study showed that as many as 70 percent of wireless networks were not secured properly, leaving owners wide open to attacks and hijackings. I understand why—there is probably little else in this world as boring as network security. Most people feel the same way, and rush through the process as quickly as possible. In fact, most people would finish Project 23 from this book and then unfortunately consider themselves well armed against attack. That's a risky approach to take, especially when you have sensitive business documents on your network.

The basic setup of a wireless network is fraught with security pitfalls that are well known to hackers. You are at risk, even if you live in a gated community with security guards. That's because hackers take every shape and form, and come in all ages and from all locations. All you need is one bored teenager looking for something to do, and you've got a potential security issue.

In this project, you'll learn as many tips and tricks as I can share with you about securing your wireless network, plus I'll toss in a few more computer security details, too. Each security detail in and of itself might not be powerful, but the combination of security approaches can be an effective deterrent to malicious attacks.

Step 1: Change Administrator Passwords

Passwords are strings of characters that are used to log onto a computer and access its contents. The entire point of a password is to ensure that unauthorized people do not access the computer. Passwords should never be given to other people; once a password is out of your hands, so is your computer!

Let me also make this clear: never, ever use a default password or identification provided by a manufacturer. Any given piece of equipment is already known to hackers, and so are the associated default passwords and IDs. If you need to use a default password to set up a piece of equipment or installed software, go back and immediately change it as soon as the equipment or software has been installed.

There are two schools of thought on this topic of administrator passwords. The first is to use a password so complicated that the average hacker (which is what most hackers are—average) will lose interest in trying to crack it. This isn't a bad idea as long as you can remember the password!

The second is to regularly change your administrator passwords. This isn't a bad idea, either. It just requires that you set up a routine for yourself that reminds you to regularly change the password.

Either way, a strong password includes the following:

- It should be at least six characters long.

- Those characters should consist of at least three of these categories: uppercase characters, lowercase characters, numbers, and symbols (such as &, #, and !).

- It should never contain all or even part of your account name or personal name.

tip *Passwords are typically not maintained by the network administrator, nor can the administrator retrieve your password if you forget it. If you forget your password, the administrator will reset your password to something and then, when you log on with the new password, you'll most likely be required to change it again. This prevents the administrator from using your account without your knowledge.*

Change Your Password in Windows XP

This process may seem a little lengthy but it will go quickly:

1. Choose Start | Control Panel.

2. Click User Accounts.

3. In the User Accounts dialog box, select an account to change. You may need to place a check mark in the Users Must Enter A User Name And Password To Use This Computer check box before you can select an account.

4. Click Reset Password.

5. Enter the new password you want to use. Re-enter it to confirm it.

6. Click OK.

7. Click OK.

note *A different process is used in Windows XP if your computer is on a domain. Go to Windows XP Help and Support for further instructions.*

Next, you'll need to determine whether you are in a domain or a workgroup. Follow the steps for either Windows Vista or XP depending upon the operating system you have.

To Find Out Whether You Are in a Domain or a Workgroup in Windows Vista

1. Click Start.

2. Right-click Computer.

3. Click Properties.

4. Click Advanced System Settings.

5. Click the Computer Name tab in the System Properties dialog box.

6. Look for "domain" or "workgroup" to determine which one you are in, as shown in Figure 24-1.

Figure 24-1

Domains and workgroups are clearly listed system properties for both Windows Vista and XP.

To Find Out Whether You Are in a Domain or a Workgroup in Windows XP

1. On your desktop, right-click My Computer.

2. Click Properties.

3. Click the Computer Name tab in the System Properties dialog box.

4. Look for "domain" or "workgroup" under Full Computer Name to determine which one you are in.

Change Your Password in Windows Vista

Administrators can create a password for any account in Windows Vista. To change your password in Windows Vista, follow these steps:

1. Press CTRL-ALT-DEL.

2. Click Change A Password.

3. Enter your old password.

4. Type in your new password. You need to type it in again to confirm it.

5. Press ENTER.

If you change a password for another user in Windows XP or Windows Vista, encrypted files and e-mail messages for that account will no longer be accessible to that user.

Step 2: Turn On Encryption for Your Wireless Devices

If you set up your wireless network using this book's Project 23, you turned on WPA/WEP encryption and can skip this particular step. If you already have a wireless network set up, you need to be sure that you have encryption technology enabled. This technology scrambles information so that it can't be easily read as it is sent over a wireless network.

Lower-end wireless access points limit security options to the WPA and WEP encryption methods discussed in Project 23. However, there are higher-end newer products that offer Temporal Key Integrity Protocol (TKIP). TKIP works in conjunction with WEP, offering stronger security than just WEP alone.

TKIP uses new encryption algorithms that constantly change the encryption keys so that hackers have a tough time cracking them. Even if a hacker cracks an encryption key, by the time he does, it will have changed on your computer and the hacker will have to start all over again.

It's important to choose the strongest form of encryption you possibly can for your wireless network. Keep in mind, however, that all the wireless devices on your network must have the same encryption settings. If just one device won't accept TKIP, then you can't use it on any of them.

To turn on encryption for a wireless access point, see Project 23.

Step 3: Enable MAC Address Filtering

In every network-accessible device, including wireless devices, there is a unique identifier called a MAC address. It is sometimes referred to as a physical address. Wireless access points and routers track all the MAC addresses that connect to them. One way to keep your wireless network secure is to manually enter these MAC addresses into your wireless access point or router instead of letting those devices accept all MAC addresses. This ensures that other mobile devices (neighbors or hackers) can't connect to your wireless access points or routers.

This feature is typically turned off by manufacturers to make the wireless device installation process easier for consumers. Once the feature is enabled, though, the wireless access point or router compares the MAC address of all access requests. If the MAC address doesn't match the one you have entered, access is denied.

Obtain the MAC Address of Your Computer

Follow these steps to enable the MAC address filtering feature.

In Windows XP:

1. Choose Start | Run to open the Run dialog box.

2. Type **cmd** in the Open box. Click OK.

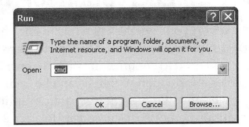

3. A command prompt window appears. At the end of the string of text, type **ipconfig/all** and press ENTER.

```
C:\WINDOWS\system32\cmd.exe

C:\Documents and Settings\Sally>ipconfig/all
```

4. The command prompt window shows you the details of all your computer's network adapters.

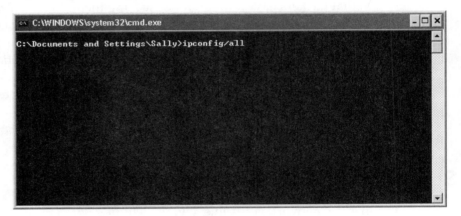

```
C:\WINDOWS\system32\cmd.exe

er with SpeedBooster
        Physical Address. . . . . . . . . : 00-0C-41-69-33-78
        Dhcp Enabled. . . . . . . . . . . : Yes
        Autoconfiguration Enabled . . . . : Yes
        IP Address. . . . . . . . . . . . : 10.0.0.58
        Subnet Mask . . . . . . . . . . . : 255.255.0.0
        Default Gateway . . . . . . . . . : 10.0.0.1
        DHCP Server . . . . . . . . . . . : 10.0.0.250
        DNS Servers . . . . . . . . . . . : 10.0.0.251
                                            10.0.0.250
        Primary WINS Server . . . . . . . : 10.0.0.250
        Secondary WINS Server . . . . . . : 10.0.0.251
        Lease Obtained. . . . . . . . . . : Friday, January 19, 2007 6:24:51 AM
        Lease Expires . . . . . . . . . . : Friday, January 26, 2007 6:24:51 AM

Ethernet adapter Bluetooth Network Connection:

        Media State . . . . . . . . . . . : Media disconnected
        Description . . . . . . . . . . . : Bluetooth Device (Personal Area Netw
ork)
        Physical Address. . . . . . . . . : 00-02-72-CD-C8-44

C:\Documents and Settings\Sally>
```

The Physical Address is your MAC address. Write it down; you need to enter it into your wireless access point next.

In Windows Vista:

1. Click Start and type **Run** in the Search box to open the Run dialog box.

2. Type **cmd** in the Open box. Click OK.

3. A command prompt window appears. At the end of the string of text, type **ipconfig/all** and press ENTER.

4. The command prompt window shows you the details of all your computer's network adapters.

The Physical Address is your MAC address. Write it down; you need to enter it into your wireless access point next.

Enter and Filter the MAC Address into Your Wireless Access Point

Every wireless access point brand will have slightly different instructions for entering the MAC address.

 Use a wired connection to perform this process. If anything is entered incorrectly and the settings are saved, you'll lose connectivity to your wireless access point and need to set it up again.

Here are the basic instructions:

1. Open your web browser.

2. Type in the IP address of *your* wireless router as shown here. Press ENTER.

http://10.0.0.4

3. Enter your username and password to log into your wireless access point. Click OK. This brings up your wireless access point management screen.

4. Locate the Wireless section of the screen. Click it.

5. Click Wireless MAC Filter.

6. Click Enable.

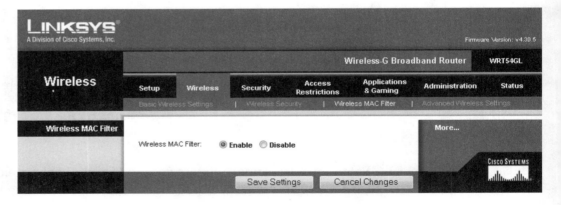

7. On some wireless access points, you have the ability to filter MAC addresses by either permitting or preventing wireless network card access. In this example, Permit Only PCs Listed To Access The Wireless Network was selected. This will only allow MAC addresses with MAC address recognized by your network to enter the wireless network.

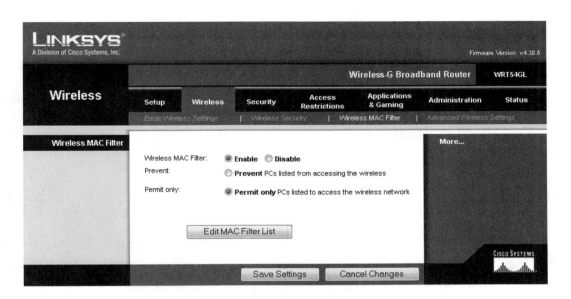

note *The Prevent PCs Listed From Accessing The Wireless Network option is typically used by larger corporations that have hundreds or thousands of users.*

8. Click Edit MAC Filter List to open the MAC Address Filter List.

9. Enter the MAC address you obtained in Step 3 (in the section "Obtain the MAC Address of Your Computer").

10. Click Save Settings.

Step 4: Turn Off SSID Broadcast

Remember the Service Set Identifier (SSID) you created in Project 23? It's the name of your wireless network, and by default wireless access points and routers broadcast the SSID over the air at regular intervals. The SSID isn't scrambled or otherwise protected. This is great if you own a mobile hotspot where people come and go constantly. In your home office, broadcasting the SSID just isn't necessary.

The regular broadcast is like a beacon to hackers—"Hello! Here I am!" which isn't great news for your home office wireless network. Luckily, this feature can be disabled. Here's how to do it:

1. Open your web browser.

2. Type in the IP address of your wireless router Press ENTER.

3. Enter your username and password to log into your wireless access point. Click OK. This brings up your wireless access point management screen.

4. Click the Wireless tab.

5. Select Disable.

6. Click Save Settings.

That's it—pretty quick, wasn't it?

Step 5: Stop Auto-Connect to Open Wireless Networks

When you go to a Starbucks for coffee and a bit of work, too, you can be exposing your computer to hackers. Most computers have a setting that allows these wireless hotspot connections to happen automatically, but the smart thing to do is turn off that setting. It will take you a little longer to connect if the setting is disabled, but the peace of mind you'll have knowing that you are foiling hackers should make up for that.

To turn off the Auto-Connect feature on your computer using Windows XP, follow these steps:

1. Choose Start | Control Panel.

2. Double-click Network Connections.

3. Right-click Wireless Network Connection.

4. Click Properties.

5. Go to the Wireless Networks tab and click Advanced.

6. Remove the check mark from Automatically Connect To Non-preferred Networks.

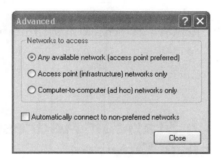

7. Click Close.

8. Click OK.

To turn off the Auto-Connect feature on your computer using Windows Vista, follow these steps:

1. Choose Start | Connect To.

2. Right-click the network name or icon.

3. Click Properties to open the Local Wireless Network Properties dialog box. Select the Connection tab.

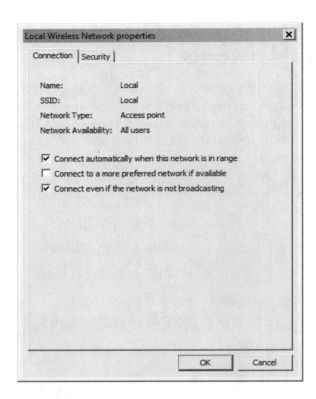

4. Remove the check mark from Connect To A More Preferred Network If Available.

5. Click OK.

Step 6: Assign Static IP Addresses to Your Wireless Devices

An Internet Protocol (IP) address uniquely identifies computers on a network. There are two kinds of IP addresses available: dynamic and static. Dynamic IP addressing allows you to move conveniently between different networks, which makes it easy to travel with your computer. Each dynamic IP address is assigned by wireless devices on the network on demand.

In contrast, static IP addressing uses a fixed IP address that is assigned to a computer by the system administrator. This makes it a bit more difficult to travel with your computer but static IP addressing does give better protection to your computer. Static IP addresses are also used as an alternative to dynamic DHCP when a network device does not support DHCP.

In the wireless network you set up using this book, you set up a DHCP server that used dynamic IP addresses. Using a static IP address on your wireless devices means that you will not connect directly to the Internet—and that computers outside your network can't connect directly to any of your wireless devices. That's because access to the IP address is hidden.

To use static IP addressing on your wireless network instead, you need to select one from within these approved private IP address ranges:

- 10.0.0.0 through 10.255.255.255

- 172.16.0.0 through 172.31.255.255

- 192.168.0.0 through 192.168.255.255

You may choose any address ranges you wish from within these approved ranges. However, avoid addresses that end with 0 or 255, and don't choose addresses that start a private IP address range, such as 192.168.0.0—these are the first addresses hackers will try when trying to break into your wireless network.

tip   *IP addresses are also known as network addresses.*

Find Your Network's IP Addresses

To find the IP addresses your computer is using in Windows XP, follow these steps:

1. Choose Start | Run to open the Run dialog box.

2. Type **cmd** in the Open box. Click OK.

3. A command prompt window appears. At the end of the string of text, type **ipconfig/all** and press ENTER.

4. The command prompt window shows you the details of all your computer's network adapters.

The IP Address shown is the one related to the computer you are on—it is the current IP address for that wireless device.

To find the IP addresses your computer is using in Windows Vista, follow these steps:

1. Click Start and type **Network** in the Start Search box.

2. Click Network And Sharing Center under Programs.

3. In the Network and Sharing Center, look for Connection. To the right of that, click View Status.

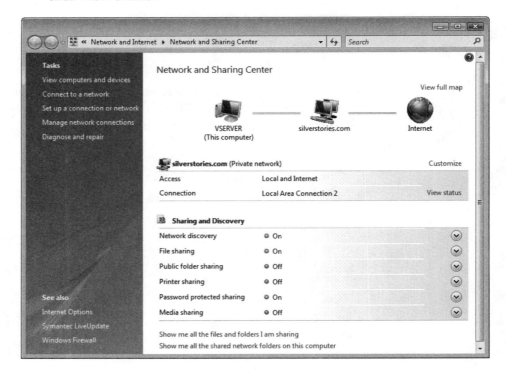

4. In the status dialog box that appears, click Details. The Network Connection Details dialog box will appear. Your computer's IP address appears in the Value column next to IPv4 IP Address.

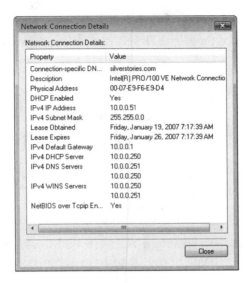

Change Your Network's IP Addresses

This is where you need the new static IP address you have chosen. To change the IP settings in Windows XP, do the following:

1. Choose Start | Control Panel.

2. Click Network Connections.

3. Right-click the device you want to configure and select Properties.

4. Under This Connection Uses The Following Items, select Internet Protocol (TCP/IP). Click Properties.

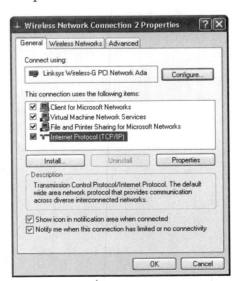

5. Select Use The Following IP Address. Enter the static IP address information.

6. Click OK.

7. Click Close.

To change the IP settings in Windows Vista, follow these steps:

1. Choose Start | Control Panel.

2. Click View Network Status And Tasks.

3. Click Manage Network Connections.

4. Right-click the connection you want to change. Click Properties. You may be prompted for an administrator password or confirmation. Note whether your computer is using Internet Protocol Version 4 or 6 (also shown as TCP/ IPv4 or TCP/IPv6).

5. Click the version that is selected. Click Properties.

6. To specify a TCP/IPv4 address setting, click Use The Following IP Address. Type in the IP address settings.

7. To specify a TCP/IPv6 address setting, click Use The Following IPv6 Address. Type in the IP address settings.

8. Click OK.

9. Click Close.

Step 7: Enable Firewalls

While most modern wireless access points and routers have built-in firewall capability, the option does exist to disable that capability. In addition, there is firewall software available for your computer. If you don't have firewalls on your computer, you're just asking for trouble.

To check your wireless devices for firewall settings, you need to refer to each product's manufacturer instructions. However, lots of inexpensive firewall products are available on the market, such as McAfee Personal Firewall Plus and Symantec Norton Personal Firewall 2006 for Windows. Windows XP (Service Pack 2) and Windows Vista even come with built-in firewalls.

To turn on the firewall in Windows XP, do the following:

1. Choose Start | Control Panel.

2. Double-click Network Connections.

3. Right-click Wireless Network Connections and click Properties.

4. Click the Advanced tab.

5. Under Windows Firewall, click Settings.

6. Select On (Recommended). Click OK.

7. Click OK.

To turn on the firewall in Windows Vista, follow these steps:

1. Click Start and type **Firewall** in the **Start Search box.**

2. Under Programs, click Windows Firewall.

3. Click Turn Windows Firewall On Or Off. You may be prompted for an administrator password or confirmation.

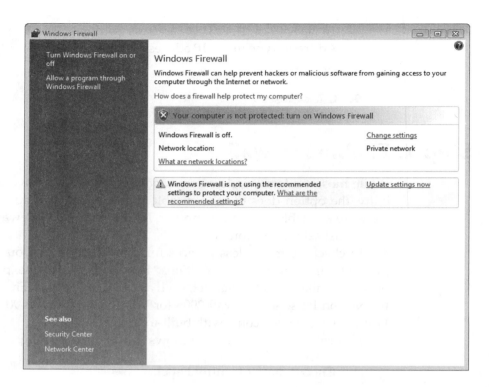

4. Select On (Recommended). Click OK.

tip *If you will be gone from your home office for an extended length of time (for a vacation or business trip, for example), power down your network before you leave.*

Step 8: Combat Signal Leakage

Every wireless network has a small amount of "leakage"—wireless signals that reach outside the home. This is okay; in fact, it's preferable if you want to work outside. However, the further the signal leaks, the more vulnerable you are to attack.

If you can, position the wireless access point or router near the center of your home. Locations far from windows do a better job of minimizing leakage.

tip *When you move your wireless access point or router, test it by going outside to the spot where you normally prefer to work. Turn on your computer and see whether or not you can access your network. Then, go down the street a block—if you can still access your wireless network, you still have a lot of leakage. Keep repositioning your wireless devices until you find the spot that lets you work outside but keeps predators at bay.*

Setting up a secure wireless network isn't as hard as it seems; it just takes time and diligence. It's worth it, however, because your office computer is filled with a lot of sensitive information that shouldn't fall into the wrong hands. That's it for this book; I hope you found these projects useful. Guess what? Those 24 cool things you didn't know you could do? You *can* do them, and have a little fun along the way.

Index